THE DIARY OF RICHARD WAGNER

THE BROWN BOOK

The Brown Book

The Diary of Richard Wagner 1865–1882

THE BROWN BOOK

presented and annotated
by
JOACHIM BERGFELD

Translated by
George Bird

CAMBRIDGE UNIVERSITY PRESS
London
Cambridge   New York   New Rochelle
Melbourne

First published in 1980

Published in the USA and Canada by the Press Syndicate
of the University of Cambridge
32 East 57th Street, New York, NY 10022, USA

Library of Congress Catalog Card number: 79-56128
ISBN 0 521 233119 hard covers

Printed in Great Britain at
The Camelot Press Ltd, Southampton

TRANSLATOR'S NOTE

I depart from the established practice of improving Wagner's style and ironing out ambiguities, whether contrived or accidental. The style is an aspect of the man. The ambiguities can be removed only by an act of faith, such as the reader ought, I believe, to be left to make for himself if he wishes. Words or phrases whose meaning, after research, is still uncertain or unknown are indicated by a note quoting the original German.

My work has been greatly and most generously assisted by Dr Joachim Bergfeld, Director of the Richard-Wagner-Gedenkstätte, Bayreuth, whom I thank wholeheartedly.

G. B.

BRITISH PUBLISHER'S NOTE

Throughout the main body of this book Dr Bergfeld's commentary and explanatory notes which appear interspersed with Wagner's writings, have been printed in italics. Wagner's writings, are printed in roman type, the words underlined in the text being those that he himself underlined. Wagner's own use of accents and his spelling of proper names have also been followed. The preliminary matter, Introduction and end matter are set in the usual publishing style.

CONTENTS

* indicates most important of first-published material.
Where two page numbers are given, the first refers to Dr Bergfeld's notes,
the second to Wagner's text.

Bibliography	9
Editor's Introduction	13
Entries addressed to Cosima, in part first publications	25/28–92
'Above the Abyss I Stand': poem	30
* Ill-feeling on account of Mathilde Maier	34/37
* Thoughts on future life and work	37/39
For the Birthday of King Ludwig II: poem	45
Parzival: first prose sketch	46
* Concerning the journey to funeral of Ludwig Schnorr von Carolsfeld	62
* Ill-feeling concerning Liszt	63/64
Concerning the blood-stained lance in *Parzival*	65
* Suffering, loving, dreaming	66
* Against Ludwig II's plan for a Munich Festival Theatre	68/71
Thoughts on German character ·	73
* Fatalistic mood	74
* Composure following Cosima's return	75
* Two lines of music	81
From Hohenschwangau: two poems	83
Search for new Asyl	85
'Roland's death': an allegory	85
* Annals for the years 1846 to April 1864	93
Annals for the years 1864 to 1867	118
Three sonnets to David Strauss	125
Foreword to 'German Art and German Politics'	127
Foreword to second edition of 'Opera and Drama'	128
* Order for Complete Edition of my Writings	131
'Recollections of Ludwig Schnorr von Carolsfeld'	134
'Romeo and Juliet': musical theme	146

Thoughts on Buddhism for The Victors 148

'Score of *Mastersingers* to the King': poem 150/151

Ideas for a Luther drama 153/154

* Two who are truly in love have only one religion 155

'Addendum to Dedication of *Mastersingers*': poem 156

* 'Comedy in 1 Act': sketch 157/158

Three sonnets to Heinrich Laube 161

Continuation of Annals for year 1868 164/166

New Year's Eve 68–69: music: 'Sleep, baby, sleep' 170

'Siegfried Act III to the King': poem 171

'Rhinegold', lines against Munich performance 172/173

'To the King (dernier effort!)': poem 174

* 'Beethoven and the German Nation': notes 176

'For the King's Birthday 1870': poem 178

* Journalism: one's own writings the cause 179

* 'The Capitulation': sketch for comedy 181/182

Poems to and for the German Army, January 1871 186/187

'*Twilight of the Gods* Act III to the King': poem 189/192

'Epitaph for Karl Tausig': poem 192/193

'To Georg Herwegh': lines 193/194

* Four bars of a musical motive 195

'Collected Writings, Vol. 9 to the King': poem 195

World history a disappointing document of human endeavour 197

* *Thoughts on regeneration of humanity and of culture* 198/199

War as negative selection 199

Possession is chance – intellectual and moral equality 199

Change of property relationships 200

Latin poetry – moral attempt at regeneration 200

Dilettantism as reaction to science – Concerning prayer, God, Jesus 200

Property and state theories – recognition of decay 201

Distortion of concept of property – circumvention of Ten
  Commandments points to their worldliness 202

Christ as poetic ideal – Male and Female in mixing of Races 202

End of civilization 202

Progress by virtue of the poet's morality 203

* 'On Male and Female in Culture and Art': essay fragment   203/204
   Notes   205
   Index   215

Facsimiles of original manuscript
Richard Wagner / The Brown Book   23
First entry: Hochkopf, 10 August 1865   27
Parzival: first prose sketch of poem   49
Spring sun / Day – Night   87
Thoughts on Buddhism   149
Music: Sleep, baby, sleep   171

BIBLIOGRAPHY

Bayreuther Blätter 1931/III: *Richard Wagner, Gedanken aus Tagebüchern* (Thoughts from Diaries).

Bayreuther Blätter 1936/I–1938/I: *Richard Wagner, Aussprüche aus Tagebüchern* (Remarks from Diaries), continued over eight numbers.

Du Moulin-Eckart, Richard, Count: *Cosima Wagner / Ein Lebens- und Charakterbild* (Her Life and Character), 2 vols, Munich 1929 and 1931.

Glasenapp, Carl Friedrich: *Das Leben Richard Wagners* (Life), 6 vols, Leipzig 1905–12.

Glasenapp, Carl Friedrich: *Gedichte von Richard Wagner* (Poems), Berlin 1905.

Millenkovich-Morold, Max: *Cosima Wagner / Ein Lebensbild* (A Life), Leipzig 1937.

Strobel, Otto: *König Ludwig II und Richard Wagner / Briefwechsel* (King Ludwig II and Richard Wagner, Correspondence), 5 vols, Karlsruhe 1936–9.

Strobel, Otto: *Richard Wagners 'Braunes Buch'* (His Brown Book), in: Bayreuther Festspielführer 1934, p. 113.

Strobel, Otto: *Über einen unbekannten Brief Richard Wagners an Mathilde Wesendonck und seine Geschichte* (Concerning an Unknown Letter of Richard Wagner's to Mathilde Wesendonck and its History), in: Bayreuther Festspielführer 1937, p. 152.

Strobel, Otto: *Richard Wagner: Gedanken zu einem 'Luther'-Drama* (Ideas for a Luther drama), in: Bayreuther Festspielführer 1937, p. 158.

Wagner, Richard: *Mein Leben* (My Life), Popular Edition, 2nd impression, Munich 1915, and Jubilee Edition, Munich 1963.

Wagner, Richard: *Sämtliche Schriften und Dichtungen* (Collected Prose and Poetry), Popular Edition, 2nd impression, Leipzig 1915, 16 vols.

Westernhagen, Curt von: *Wagner* (Biography), Zürich/Freiburg 1968.

Westernhagen, Curt von: *Vom Holländer zum Parsifal / Neue Wagner-Studien* (From *Dutchman* to *Parsifal* / New Wagner Studies), Freiburg/Zürich 1962.

Westernhagen, Curt von: *Richard Wagner, sein Werk, sein Wesen, seine Welt* (His Work, his Personality and his World), Zürich 1956.

Other bibliographical references will be found in the notes.

EDITOR'S INTRODUCTION

EDITOR'S INTRODUCTION

A PECULIARITY OF Wagner scholarship is that his diary for the years 1865–82, the *Brown Book* as he called it on account of its calf binding, should not so far have been published in its entirety. Only parts have been made available and these are preserved in a variety of publications either difficult of access or now out of print. Its early part excepted, this *Brown Book* cannot properly be termed a diary since it also contains sketches, essays and poems, as well as ideas for works. Nevertheless, it does constitute a whole, and for the reason that it was, albeit with considerable breaks,[1] used by Wagner over a seventeen-year period to within one year of his death. For Wagner there was something special about it, and it is this which imposes the obligation to present it in complete form, and particularly as almost half its contents are so far unpublished.

History of the Brown Book

The history of the *Brown Book* is linked with the developing intimacy between Wagner and Cosima von Bülow (v. note p. 25) after mid-1864 when Wagner settled in Munich. As circumstances constantly prevented their seeing or talking to each other, Cosima presented him with the *Brown Book* in which he was to enter all that he felt and thought about her, for her to read later. No date can be established for this, but it was presumably before their first separation on 8 August 1865 when Cosima was obliged to accompany her husband Hans to Hungary.

Wagner and Cosima's relationship was fraught with torment and suffering, and in 1865 there can have seemed no prospect of a legitimate union between them. Moreover, Wagner had for years been a friend of Hans von Bülow, and Cosima's father, Liszt, thought highly of Bülow and regarded him as his best pupil.

But Cosima and Wagner were bound by inescapable destiny. On 20 August 1870, five days before his marriage to Cosima, Wagner wrote to his Swiss friends Eliza and François Wille: 'You shall be the first to see us man and wife. To achieve this state has cost great patience, for what for years has been irremissible was not to resolve itself without suffering of every description. Since I last saw you in Munich' [at the première of *Mastersingers* on 21 June 1868], 'I have not left my Asyl' [Tribschen] 'whither she too has fled whose work has been to testify that I am to be helped, and that the axiom of so many of my friends to the contrary, is false. She knew that I could be helped, and has helped me, braving every insult and accepting every damnation. . . . Thus we have helped each other, and without "society", from which our withdrawal has been complete.'[2]

The Brown Book, the work of a master craftsman, measures 14 × 21·5 cm., and is bound in simply-tooled brown leather set with twelve gems of malachite. Originally it could be locked, but the lock is now missing. Two hundred and forty-one pages are in Wagner's hand; a further fourteen, of which more below, have not been preserved.

After Wagner's death the book was scrupulously guarded by Cosima on account of its often confidential contents. In her seventieth year she gave it into the care of her daughter Eva who in turn presented this valuable document, subject to certain safeguards, to the Town of Bayreuth for its Richard-Wagner-Gedenkstätte. The deed of gift states, in part:

> 'This "Brown Book with Jewels" I do present, this 14 May 1931, to the Town of Bayreuth with the wish that it be preserved in the "Richard-Wagner-Gedenkstätte".
>
> 'It contains, amongst other things, the prose sketch for "Parcival", and various poems and thoughts, all of which have already been published by Frau Cosima Wagner in the volume "Sketches, Thoughts, Fragments".[3]
>
> . . .
>
> 'This Book I received as a gift from my mother prior to my marriage,[4] together with the right to dispose of it.
>
> . . .
>
> 'I hereby direct that this Book be never removed from the rooms of the Gedenkstätte in which it is preserved. None but trustworthy persons shall be permitted to examine it.
>
> . . .
>
> 'Out of heartfelt gratitude for most manifold demonstrations of great and active devotion to the work of Richard Wagner and to his family on the part of the Town of Bayreuth, this, my gift, is made in this sacredly solemn Year of Remembrance.[5]
>
> 'Eva Chamberlain-Wagner
> Bayreuth, 14 May 1931.'

The *Brown Book* has remained in the Richard-Wagner-Gedenkstätte of the Town of Bayreuth ever since. In 1933 two copies were made by Frau Gertrud Strobel for Frau Winifred Wagner and the Wahnfried Archivist Dr Otto Strobel respectively.

14

Measures taken by Eva Wagner concerning the original manuscript

Once granted the right to dispose of the *Brown Book* Eva Wagner took various measures which must be mentioned in some detail. They involved the cutting out and destruction of seven pages (fourteen sides), the pasting over of five sides to render the contents illegible, and the inking over of pencil entries.[6] For the last of these no blame attaches to her. The work has been done with care and serves the better preservation and legibility of Wagner's notes. Not all pencil entries have been inked-in, e.g. the poem 'Above the abyss I stand' on pages 30–31 below. Here Eva has made her own copy in ink and pasted it into the original. She has also pasted in four scraps of paper, two containing lines of music by him, and two containing jottings, on pages 81/82 and 124 below. Still in pencil are, for example, the three sonnets to David Strauss. From page 73 onwards, Wagner has written mainly in ink.

When these regrettable moves were made it is not possible to determine, and it cannot be taken for granted that Cosima was aware of them. For Cosima herself can only be shown to have destroyed letters, in particular the following: from Wagner to Mathilde Wesendonck, following their appearance in print in 1904 and their return to the Wahnfried Archive by Mathilde's son Karl; from Nietzsche to Cosima, except for three which, together with seven of Nietzsche's to Wagner, have been preserved by Glasenapp in the Richard-Wagner-Gedenkstätte;[7] from Cornelius to Wagner;[8] and all her own letters to Wagner – this according to Eva who, writing to Max Millenkovich-Morold on 4 October 1935,[9] states that Cosima burnt them.

Nothing written by Wagner was destroyed by Cosima, apart from the letters to Mathilde. She expressed a wish that Wagner's letters to her should be destroyed too, but did not herself destroy them. Instead, she presented them to her daughter Eva – on 17 February 1905 according to the dedicatory note enclosed – remarking 'You can take a look at these and then destroy them'. The source for this is also Eva's letter of 4 October 1935 to Millenkovich-Morold just quoted. The truth of these statements by Eva is hard to doubt because she concludes this letter with 'I am prepared at any time to swear to these facts before God'. Eva complied with her mother's wish, and later burned Wagner's letters to Cosima, or rather had them burnt. Dora Zahneisen, a former employee of the Chamberlain household, swore an affidavit on 6 June 1949 to the effect that, at Eva's instigation, she 'at some time' burned a packet of letters written by Richard Wagner to Cosima Wagner, or *vice versa*. The original of this is amongst Eva Wagner-Chamberlain's papers in the Richard-Wagner-Gedenkstätte. This 'at some time', according to a note of Eva's to Villa Wahnfried, was in 1930. This reads:

'I hereby confirm having, shortly after the decease of my brother (1930), destroyed by fire a collection of letters from my father, Richard Wagner, to my mother, Cosima Wagner.

'This was done at the express wish of my mother and my brother.

'Eva Chamberlain

Bayreuth 5 November 1934.'

Eva did not, however, destroy all Wagner's letters to Cosima, but merely those which, narrow-mindedly, she may have thought compromising. Thus twenty-four of these letters from the years 1859–72 have been preserved and subsequently presented by her to the Richard-Wagner-Gedenkstätte, where they now are. There is some confirmation of selectivity on Eva's part. Dora Zahneisen, in the affidavit of 6 June 1949 quoted above, writes that she did the burning 'after she [Eva] had previously spent some time going through the letters with her sister, Daniela Thode'. Cosima herself, be it noted, destroyed nothing written by Wagner, apart from the letters to Mathilde Wesendonck.

Of the pasted-over pages all five have been recovered by the Stuttgart curator and restorer, Hans Heiland, who, on 13 November 1974, removed the end-paper pasted in by Eva, leaving the pages undamaged and Wagner's entries perfectly preserved. The pages in question are those numbered 14, 17, 61, 67, and 72 by Eva in the original, and numbered 37, 64, 71 and 74–75 below.

On pasted-over page 14, Eva had pasted three autograph scraps by Wagner which now were placed on blank page 84 of the original (pages 81–82 below). On page 17 between pages 14 and 18 Eva had pasted, also numbering the pages, her three-page copy of the poem 'Above the abyss I stand'. This copy, as also a sheet of the end-paper she used for pasting over, has been placed at the end of the Brown Book. As a result, page numbers 16 and 17 are missing in the original, since unpasted page 17 was numbered 15 to follow uncovered page 14. Accordingly, page 15 follows immediately after page 18 in the original.

Detailed consideration will be given later to the content of the recovered pages, but here let it be said that it is hard to see why Eva thought it necessary to paste over. Certainly Wagner's tone when expressing irritation concerning Cosima and Liszt is sharper, but not essentially different from that of other entries in the Brown Book. Some remarks at the expense of Gottfried Semper and King Ludwig II are also so harmless as to offer no grounds for eradication. The only explanation that remains is that Eva was too petty to endure harsh words concerning her mother and grandfather.

What prompted Cosima to give the Brown Book, her own diaries and Wagner's letters into the care of her daughter Eva requires some clarification. Eva, as we have said, enjoyed her mother's complete confidence, but that is not in itself sufficient to account for the hand-over and its timing. What caused Cosima to take measures to protect from possible abuse those three items which were her especial concern, was her own grave illness, and the proper course seemed to lie in transferring ownership and right of disposal to one who best knew her thoughts and intentions. The dedicatory note mentioned in Eva's letter of 4 October 1935 to Millenkovich-Morold,[10] which lay in the box containing Wagner's letters reads 'To my angel' and is dated 17 February 1905, Eva's birthday. They were thus a birthday present for Eva. The wording testifies to Cosima's special confidence in and gratitude to her daughter. For some years Cosima had been obliged to dictate most of her letters on account of eye-trouble. At first Daniela had written them for her, but following Daniela's marriage on 3 July 1886, Eva took over and saw to her mother's needs in every other way too,[11] so that by 1905 her devotion had stood the test for almost two decades.

Cosima, now sixty-seven, was in real need of her daughter's care. Siegfried Wagner, in his memoirs (Stuttgart 1923, p. 142), records: 'My mother entrusted more and more to me. . . . In 1904 she left the scenic production of Tannhäuser to me completely. She herself worked mainly with the soloists.' He then speaks of Cosima's frequent over-exertion and the many emotional upsets this involved, from which 1904 and 1905 may be seen as years offering serious cause for concern about Cosima's health.

A consequence of Cosima's impaired health was her complete collapse at the end of December 1906 and associated heart spasms of a severity occasioning concern for her life. A 'virtual withdrawal from the world' was called for. Dr Ernst Schweninger, Bismarck's physician, took over treatment or, as Eva puts it in a letter of January 1907 to Klindworth, 'attendance as brilliant as it was circumspect'. Above all he imposed a strict ban on the dictating of letters, and Cosima complied. There could no longer be any question of her writing letters herself, especially in view of worsening eye-trouble. The last letter, written by her a few weeks before her collapse at the end of 1906, was to her friend Countess Wolkenstein. In her letter to Klindworth, Eva writes: 'We must not conceal from ourselves that for a long time yet we shall need special care, rest, looking after, and moderation in every sphere before we shall be in a position to talk of recovery.'[12] This recovery did later come about, and Cosima's exceptional vitality, combined with constant special care, saw her into her ninety-third year. But in the early period of her illness, in 1907 and 1908 especially, she must herself have reckoned with the possibility of death, and this supplies a reason for gifting to her daughter, after the Wagner letters, her own diaries also, on 25 December 1908, and before this, the *Brown Book*. 'With you,' she had said, actually handing the diaries to Eva on 22 October 1911, 'I know them to be safe'.[13]

Publication of the Brown Book

The present edition reproduces without alteration the full text of Wagner's original manuscript, including errors and without correction of mistakes. Dr Bergfeld's notes are placed at the head of the relevant entries in order to clarify the contents for the reader in advance, and to limit the number of end-notes which are always an interruption to reading. To enable the reader unfamiliar with Wagner's biography to understand the *Brown Book* in the context of Wagner's later career, i.e. from 1864 on, the notes are, in some cases, detailed.

To date, something over half of the *Brown Book* has already been published. This is made up mainly as follows:

Published by Wagner himself in 1873 in Vols VIII and IX of *Collected Prose and Poetry:*
four poems
Recollections of Ludwig Schnorr von Carolsfeld
Foreword to second edition of *Opera and Drama*

By Glasenapp (Berlin 1905): Wagner's poems

By Wolzogen (Leipzig 1907) and in 1911 included in Vol XI of *Collected Prose and Poetry*:
Parzival, first prose sketch

In *Bayreuther Blätter*, 1931: some isolated reflections.

Then, in 1936, Otto Strobel, in his *King Ludwig II and Wagner – Correspondence*, included the Annals from 29 April 1864 to the end of 1868 and much else, although omitting anything having no bearing on the subject of the correspondence. Strobel quotes from the *Brown Book* in the Bayreuth Festival Guides of 1934 and 1937, and in some of the later Festival programmes and elsewhere, and his publications provide numerous explanations and footnotes which, for scholarly purposes, may supplement the present complete edition.

Of the various drafts entered in the *Brown Book* of, for example, poems and essays, almost all are original drafts, in part unpublished as yet in this form, and show discrepancies when compared with the final versions. Such discrepancies are not indicated here, but they can be determined from the appropriate publications, such as Glasenapp's edition of the poems.

The most important hitherto unpublished parts of the *Brown Book* are as follows:

Annals 1846 to April 1864 (p. 93)
Order for Complete Edition of Writings and Works, dated 1868 (p. 131)

Synopsis of 'Comedy in 1 Act' (p. 158)

'Beethoven and the German Nation', notes (p. 176)

Synopsis of 'The Capitulation' (p. 182)

'Thoughts on the Regeneration of Mankind and of Culture' (p. 199)

'On Male and Female in Culture and Art': essay fragment (p. 204)

'Thoughts from my sick bed concerning future life with the King, Bülow and Cosima' (p. 38)

Thoughts on the theme 'Two who are truly in love have only one religion' (p. 155)

Three musical motives, each of four bars (pp. 96, 97 and 195

The remaining briefer and to some extent even more important unpublished sections are from time to time mentioned in the notes and are specially indicated as described on p. 20.

The contents of the Brown Book

The *Brown Book* was originally intended for entries addressed to Cosima, but it was so used only up to 17 February 1868, Eva's first birthday (cf. note p. 91). After this Cosima was with Wagner almost constantly, and on 16 November 1868 joined him at Tribschen permanently. From then on[14] she kept her own diary which may, in a sense, be regarded as a continuation of Wagner's entries at the beginning of the *Brown Book*. Six months after the 1868 entry, while they were both together at Tribschen, Wagner did, however, again deal with matters affecting Cosima, and arising from differences of opinion concerning her divorce from Hans von Bülow and her change of religion (cf. notes on pp. 152–154). No other entry after 17 February 1868 concerns Cosima. Of the entries prior to that date there are a few that also do not concern her. These are three poems to the King, pp. 45 and 83; the *Parzival* prose sketch, p. 46, together with the supplement, p. 65; and 'Thoughts on German Character', p. 73.

If the entries at the beginning addressed directly to Cosima are disregarded, the *Brown Book*, viewed as a whole, seems at first to lack unity. But such entries form only a minor part of its contents. Wagner also made use of the *Brown Book* when not addressing Cosima, and did so almost to the end of his life. An examination of individual entries by content makes clear why. There is first a group of ten entries for King Ludwig II. These are poems for his birthday or other occasions, in each case first drafts which would be copied and sent to the King, the poems being too important to be committed solely to letters and so lost.

It also becomes apparent that Wagner had recourse to the *Brown Book* when deeply moved inwardly, when affected by grief, irritation or even anger, and desirous of dissipating the mood or letting off steam. Not always, of course, but

19

there is a sufficiency of examples. 'Recollections of Ludwig Schnorr von Carolsfeld' (p. 134) and his 'Epitaph for Karl Tausig' (p. 193) are products of grief. 'Comedy in 1 Act' (p. 158) has the postscript 'To counter grave depression'. In the poems 'To David Strauss' (p. 125), 'To Heinrich Laube' (p. 161), 'To Georg Herwegh' (p. 194) and in the lines anti the Munich première of *Rhinegold* (p. 173) he works off anger. Also in the *Brown Book* went anything he thought it essential to preserve, such as the Annals (pp. 93 and 166) and the Order for the Complete Edition of his Writings and Works (p. 131).

Wagner began his entries on 10 August 1865 at the age of fifty-two. By this time – except for *Parsifal* – his great works (*Mastersingers, The Ring / Siegfried*) had already been completed. What he wrote or intended to write further, and that includes essays and other writings, are – except where work such as the essays 'German Art and German Politics', 'Recollections of Rossini', 'On Conducting' and others, was done straight off – to be found in original version, outline or note form in the *Brown Book*. Such originals are:

the first sketch of *Parzival* of 27–30 August 1865[15]
Foreword to 'German Art and German Politics' (p. 127)
Foreword to second edition of 'Opera and Drama' (p. 128)
the poem 'To the German Army' (p. 187)
'Luther' (p. 154)
'Comedy in 1 Act' (p. 158)
'Beethoven and the German Nation' (p. 176)
the essay fragment 'On Male and Female in Culture and Art' (p. 204)
'Thoughts on Buddhism for "The Victors"' (p. 148)
'Thoughts on regeneration of humanity and of culture' (p. 199)
the musical theme 'Romeo and Juliet' (p. 146)

It was important to retain the above in a safe place, and the *Brown Book* provided one. The beginning of the 'Romeo and Juliet' theme, for example, was first written on 21 April 1868 on a loose sheet of music paper, but two weeks later, on 7 May, transferred to the *Brown Book* in more precise and extended form.[16]

Concerning the manner of presentation
Original text and Editor's notes are differentiated by the type employed. The hitherto-unpublished sections of the Wagner text are indicated by double square brackets. Words underlined by Wagner are also thinly underlined in the text. Editorial interpolation in Wagner's text is set in square brackets and italics.

*

For support and encouragement in the present work the Editor expresses his thanks to the Oberbürgermeister of the Town of Bayreuth, Herr Hans Walter Wild, to Frau Winifred Wagner, to Herr Wolfgang Wagner and to his successor in the Office of Director of the Richard-Wagner-Gedenkstätte, Dr Manfred Eger; for valuable advice and suggestions – to Wagner's biographer, Dr Curt von Westernhagen; for important information – to Frau Gertrud Strobel of the Wagner Archives; for active help – to his collaborators Frau Margarete Wiersbitzky and particularly Frau Anna Schuster who, while over eighty, has joined tirelessly in the labour of bringing this work to completion; for the accurate printing and attractive presentation of the book – to the Atlantis Musikbuch-Verlag and to the Publisher, Dr Daniel Bodmer.

Richard Wagner

Das braune Buch

From 9 to 21 August 1865 Wagner lived in complete seclusion, accompanied only by his manservant Franz Mrazeck and his dog, Pohl, in King Ludwig II's hunting lodge on the Hochkopf above the Walchensee. The reason for this withdrawal from the world was a deep depression resulting from his relationship with Cosima, which was a heavy burden to his mind and heart, and from the death of the tenor Ludwig Schnorr von Carolsfeld who, a short time previously, in the première of Tristan and Isolde *on 10 June, had lifted him to the height of his fame, and from whose sudden death he was hard put to recover. It was his realization of this last fact which prompted the King to offer Wagner his hunting lodge on the Hochkopf for 'refuge and recovery'.*[17]

The year 1863 had been one of the most troubled of Wagner's troubled life. He was oppressed not only by financial worries but even more by the uncertain circumstances of his private life. Following his final separation from his first wife Minna on 7 November 1862 at Dresden, and with his hopes for Vienna as a new place of residence ever receding, he saw himself homeless and abandoned. He travelled from one city to another earning his keep by conducting concerts in Prague, St Petersburg, Moscow, Budapest, Karlsruhe, Löwenberg and Breslau, during which time creative work had to be almost completely in abeyance. This uncertain state came to an end only on 3 May 1864 when King Ludwig II called Wagner to Munich.

On 28 November 1863, on one of his concert journeys, Wagner passed through Berlin and spent a day there with Hans and Cosima von Bülow. Cosima, who had long taken an ardent interest not only in Wagner's creative art, but still more in the unhappy circumstances of his life, was undergoing an emotional crisis similar to his own. With her the reason lay in the difficulties of her marriage to Hans von Bülow.[18] *The coming together of the two of them at this time made it likely that they would mutually confess their agony and distress. Wagner was in need of a companion who could offer him help and peace, and who believed in him and would provide the home he had been without all his life; Cosima needed the creative artist whom she unreservedly revered, and whom she could love, and who required her love and help and understood the nature and aspirations of her soul. Both knew that they alone could fulfil each other's human and emotional needs. They had sensed it since their time together in Zürich from 31 August to the end of September 1857, when Bülow and Cosima visited Wagner on their honeymoon. They had known it with certainty when, a year later, from mid-July to 16 August 1858, the Bülows joined in*

25

experiencing the tragic events surrounding Wagner's departure from his 'Asyl' at the Wesendoncks'.[19] In the subsequent years and in spite of long separation, their desire for each other had remained, partly subconsciously, since the realization of their union seemed impossible, but less so whenever they met, as at Biebrich in July 1862 to study Tristan with Schnorr von Carolsfeld and his wife, or whenever they corresponded. After Biebrich, on 21 September, Wagner wrote Cosima a letter in which for the first time he uses the intimate 'Du'-form of address and signs himself 'Richard', suggesting a new understanding between them of which we have no exact knowledge. This letter, addressed solely to Cosima and not to both of them, reads: 'My dear Cosima, . . . The other day, alighting from the station, I gazed at your[20] windows in real misery. Believe[20] me, I am as susceptible to love as a child! I no longer knew how to find my way, knowing you[20] not to be up there any more . . . Adieu! Adieu! Dear Cosima! Love me, and keep loving me!'[21]

Some eighteen months later, on 28 November 1863, came the crucial meeting in Berlin. That evening Bülow conducted a concert which Wagner attended. In My Life (1963 edition, p. 844) he records: 'Bülow having preparations to make for his concert, I drove with Cosima alone once again in a fine carriage to The Promenade. This time merriment failed us and we fell silent: we gazed mutely into each other's eyes and a violent desire for truth avowed overwhelmed us to the extent of an acknowledgment, requiring no words, of an immense unhappiness weighing upon us. Amidst tears and sobs we sealed the acknowledgment of belonging mutually solely to each other.'[22]

Six months of utterly uncertain existence followed for Wagner during which he reached the limits of despair. While fleeing his Vienna creditors, he wrote from Mariafeld in Switzerland on 8 April 1864 to his friend Peter Cornelius in Vienna: 'A good, truly helpful miracle is needed now, otherwise I'm done for!' A few weeks later that miracle came about. On 3 May 1864 King Ludwig II called Wagner to Munich and brought his anxieties to an end. Wagner moved into a house by the Starnberger See, but lacked the feminine hand to run it. However, as Wagner had induced Ludwig II to invite Hans von Bülow to Munich to play Wagner's works to him, Bülow, on 29 June 1864, dispatched Cosima to Starnberg to keep house for Wagner, and himself followed on 7 July 1864. It was now that Cosima and Wagner's Berlin vow of 28 November 1863 to 'belong mutually solely to each other' became a reality.[23] But again almost three months elapsed, from 3 September 1864, before Hans von Bülow and Cosima finally moved from Berlin to Munich on 20 November 1864.

Life together naturally created an agonizing situation for all three, and for Wagner especially it meant a grievous strain. But Bülow too had at least an inkling of what was going on, even though then unaware that Isolde, born 1865,

26

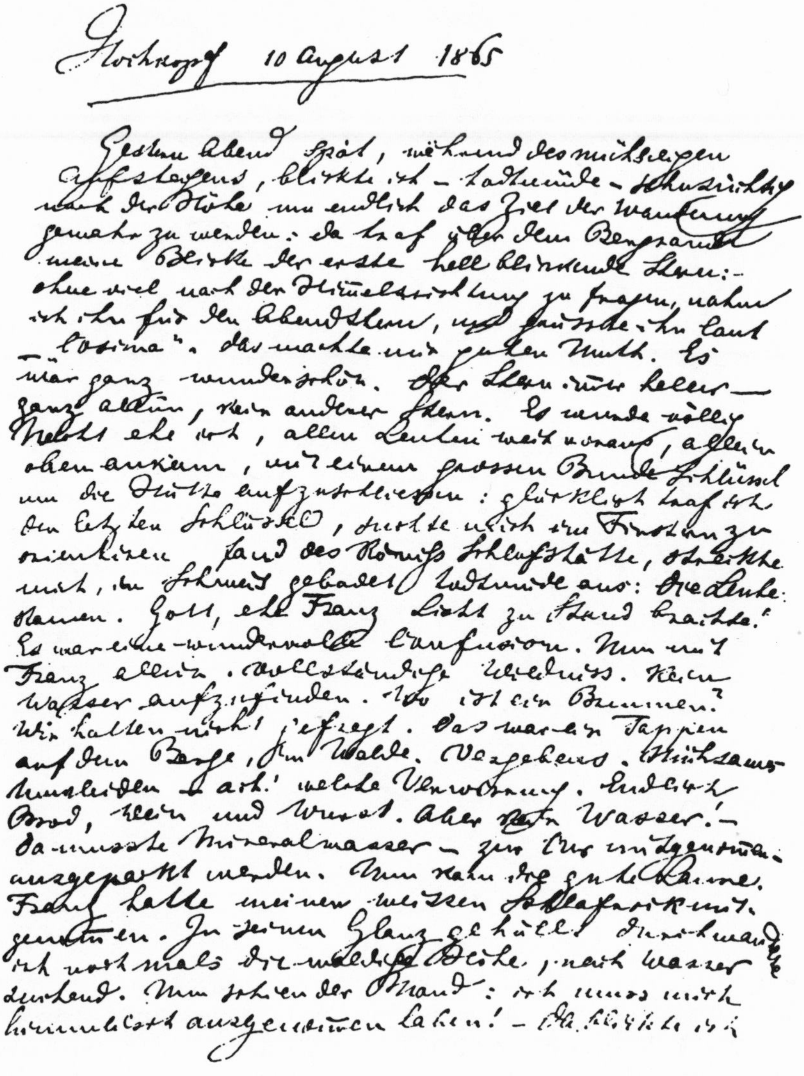
Hochkopf 10 August 1865

Gestern Abend spät, während des mühsamen Aufsteigens, blickte ich – suchend – sehnsüchtig nach der Höhe um endlich das Ziel der Wanderung gewahr zu werden: da traf über dem Bergrande meine Blicke der erste hell blinkende Stern: ohne viel nach der Himmelsrichtung zu fragen, nahm ich ihn für den Abendstern, und grüsste ihn laut „Cosima". das machte mir guten Muth. Es war ganz wunderschön. Der Stern war heller – ganz allein, kein anderer Stern. Es wurde völlig Nacht ehe ich, allen Leuten weit voraus, allein oben ankam, um einen grossen Bund Schlüssel um die Hütte aufzuschliessen: glücklich traf ich den letzten Schlüssel, suchte mich im Finstern zu orientiren, fand des Königs Schlafstätte, schmückte mich, im Schweiss gebadet, suchend aus: die Leute staunen. Gott, als Franz Licht zu Stand brachte. Es war eine wundervolle Confusion. Nun mit Franz allein. Vollständige Wildniss. Kein Wasser aufzufinden. Wo ist ein Brunnen? Wir hatten nicht gefragt. Das war ein Tappen auf dem Berge, im Walde. Vergebens. Mühsam umsuchten – ach! welche Verwirrung. Endlich Brod, Wein und Wurst. Aber kein Wasser! – Da musste Mineralwasser – zur Cur mitgenommen – ausgepackt werden. Nun kam die gute Dame. Franz hatte meinen weissen Schlafrock mitgenommen. In seinem Glanz gehüllt durchwandr ich nochmals die waldige Höhe, nach Wasser suchend. Nun schien der Mond: ich muss mich himmlisch ausgenommen haben! – Als blickte ich

was not his daughter but Wagner's. On 8 August he travelled to Budapest with Cosima to meet Liszt who was giving the première of his St Elisabeth *there. The journey had, from the first, been planned to take some weeks, and was, as Millenkovich-Morold in his biography of Cosima (1937, p. 160) aptly observes, supposed to divert her mind from Wagner and 'on to other thoughts'. After all that had occurred, such a course could not succeed, but Wagner who, following Bülow and Cosima's departure, sought refuge in the Hochkopf hunting lodge, suffered from the separation greatly. How greatly, is testified by the entries which follow. To some extent they are the replies to Cosima's letters which he could not himself make by letter and therefore wrote in the* Brown Book *for her to read later.*

Hochkopf 10 August 1865

Late yesterday evening during the wearisome ascent, I was gazing – dog-tired – longingly upwards to discern at last the goal of our march, when, above the edge of the mountain, I caught sight of the first brightly twinkling star. Not bothering much about the direction, I took it for the evening star, and hailed it loudly –

'Cosima'. That gave me heart. It was quite wonderful. The star ever brighter – quite alone, no other star. It was completely dark by the time I got up there far ahead of all the men, with a big bunch of keys to open up the lodge. Luckily I got the last one to fit, tried to find my way about in the dark, found the King's sleeping place, and stretched out bathed in sweat, dog-tired. The men arrived. God, before Franz[24] produced a light! There was marvellous confusion. Now alone with Franz. Completely in the wilds. No water to be found. Where is there a spring? We hadn't asked. Much groping about mountain and forest. In vain. Laborious changing of clothes – ah, what a muddle. Finally, bread, wine, sausage. But no water. So mineral water – brought for the cure – had to be unpacked. Arrival of good mood. Franz had brought my white dressing-gown. Enveloped in its splendour I again traversed the wooded eminence seeking water. Now the moon was shining. I must have cut a celestial figure! – Then I gazed again towards 'Cosima'. Now I could see that it was not the evening star but Jupiter. Shining splendidly. – Everything up here is beautiful beyond description. The sleep of dog-tiredness worked. In the morning, fresh unspeakable confusion. Once Franz interrupted smiling 'But your Excellency, it's beautiful outside'. – Glorious morning loveliest weather. Tour of the height. All expectations exceeded. Quite incomparable. My true 'Asyl' for the future is discovered. [[There stands the couch on which I can picture you lying. – Many thanks for the greeting! Certainly! Certainly! – I love you with an ultimate love. – Recovery is what I hope for too. Forgetting and remembering! –]]

> (Strange about the star! But in the end whether it's Cosima or Jupiter is all the same thing. –)

Wagner had sent a copy of the poem 'Above the abyss I stand' to King Ludwig who expressed his thanks to Wagner in a letter dated 14 August 1865. This is an interesting document revealing the highly responsive and effusive manner of the King's reaction. He writes: 'Reason of my existence, delight of life, ardently loved friend, at last I am able to write; above all I express to the Dear One my warmest most ardent thanks for two such loving, inspiring letters and for the gift dear to me above all![25] – Rest softly Brünnhilde, watched over by Loge's fiery blaze. The blissful awakener "Siegfried", the most blessed hero approaches! Jupiter's heavenly light that illumined your nocturnal walk, shall shine upon the lofty mountain dwelling promising you peace and happiness. Insidious day let conceal for ever his scorching fire! . . . How I love you with constantly growing ardour! Eternally, into the beyond, your faithful Ludwig.'

Am Abgrund steh' ich; Grausen hemmt
die Schritte;
der mich geführt, verloren ist der Pfad:
ob ich nun kühn auf Flügelrossen ritte,
ob mich entschwänge auf des Glückes Rad,
von seines steilen Rückens schmaler Mitte
entführte aufwärts keines mich dem Grath;
die mir selbst abwärts birgt wo ich gekommen,
die Wolke zeigt, die Höhe sei erklommen. –

Was mich dem steilen Gipfel
zugetrieben,
hält jetzt gebannt mich an des Abgrunds Rand:
verlassen musst' ich, die zurück mir blieben,
dem Druck entglitt wohl manche
Freundeshand;
wo einst ich mich gesehnt nach letztem Lieben,
der Nebel deckt mir manches Heimatland.
Und darf ich zögernd nicht mehr rückwarts
schauen,
wie späht' ich in den Abgrund nun mit Grauen?

Wie schreckte mich, nun ich zu ihm
gedrungen,
das raumlos nächt'ge Weltennebelmeer?
Ist's nicht, die ich so sehnsucht-kühn besungen,
die Nacht der Wunder, heilig still und hehr?
Dahin sich Tristan traut vor mir
geschwungen,
wie dünkte mich der nächt'ge Abgrund leer?
Den Weg, den ich so lockend ihm gepriesen,
nun hat er lächelnd mir ihn selbst gewiesen.

Was steh' ich jetzt, und zögr' ihm
nachzusinken?
Wie bangte mir vor der Erlösungsnacht?
Ist es, weil dort den Stern ich seh' erblinken,
des' Leuchten meinem Schicksal hold gelacht?
Wie strahlt er jetzt, als ob mit mächt'gem
Winken
dahin er deute, wo ein Glück mir wacht?
Ist's Tristan, der mir seinen Gruss ensendet?
Sieglinde, die des Bruders Blicke wendet?

Das Eine Aug', ich muss es jetzt
erkennen,
das unverwandt nach jenem Felsen schaut:
mag weit und breit man Jupiter dich nennen,
mir strahlest du als Wotan deutsch und
traut:

Above the abyss I stand; horror checks
my step;
the path that guided me is lost:
if boldly now I rode on winged steeds,
if now I swung myself on fortune's wheel,
from the knife-edge of its narrow ridge
neither would lead me away and up;
the cloud that hides even from where I've come,
shows that the eminence has been ascended.

That which has driven me to the steep
summit,
now holds me spellbound at the abyss's edge:
those who remained behind I had to leave,
many a friendly hand slipped from my
grasp;
where once for love ultimate I yearned,
mist covers many a homeland from my sight.
And if I may no more look hesitantly
back,
how now to peer with horror into the abyss?

How should dismay me, I who now have
reached it,
the spacelessly nocturnal world's mist sea?
Is it not what I so yearning bold have sung,
the night of wonders solemn, high and still?
Whither Tristan his dear person swung before
me,
how should the night abyss to me seem void?
The way I praised enticingly to him,
he smilingly has now shown me himself.

Why stand I now and hesitate to
follow?
How should I fear deliverance's night?
Is it because I see shine there that star
whose light has sweetly laughed upon my fate?
How shines it now? As if with mighty
beckoning
it pointed where good fortune watched for me?
Tristan is it, sending me his greeting?
Sieglinde, who turns her brother's gaze?

I recognize it now, that single
eye
which gazes fixedly toward that rock:
Jupiter men may call you far and wide,
you shine for me as Wotan, German and
belov'd:

den Fels auch kenn' ich; seh' ich hell doch brennen
das Feuer dort zum Schutz der hohen Braut:
die einst in stolzem Schmerz du von dir banntest,
den Wecker ihr, du Banger, noch nicht sandtest.

that rock I also know: see blazing bright
the fire there to protect the exalted bride:
whom in proud agony once you banned from you,
and, fearful, have not yet sent her awakener.

Brünnhilde schläft, ermisst im Traum die Welten,
in denen Tristan heimisch nun verweilt:
bleibt er uns stumm, sie kann die Kunde melden,
die ihr der Liebende dort mitgetheilt;
doch Einem nur, dem furchtlos kühnsten Helden,
der jauchzend mit ihr hin zum Abgrund eilt:
nur Er, den Drachen nicht, noch Feuer schrecken,
gewinnt die Kunde, darf die Braut erwecken.

Brünnhilde sleeps, in dreams considers worlds
in which Tristan tarries now at home:
if he is mute to us, she can the tidings tell
which the Loving One has told her there;
but tell to One alone, bold hero without fear,
who hastes with her exultant to the abyss:
only he whom dragon frightens not, or fire,
will gain those tidings, may awake the bride.

Und Er erwuchs in holder Jugend Prangen,
als Brünnhild schlief, und Tristan liebend starb.
Er naht, von dem der Wurm den Tod empfangen,
der neid'scher Zwerge tück'sches Spiel verdarb:
durch Ihn soll Kunde nun zur Welt gelangen,
wie sie Brünnhilde traumend sich erwarb.
Von Siegfrieds That, zum Schrecken aller Bösen –
es winkt der Stern, – das Räthsel will ich lösen.

And he has grown in splendour of sweet youth
while Brünnhild slept and Tristan, loving, died.
He draws near who dealt the dragon death,
who spoilt the treacherous game of envious dwarfs:
tidings shall through Him now reach the world
such as Brünnhilde, dreaming, has acquired.
Of Siegfried's deed, to all evil ones' dismay –
the star is beckoning – I shall solve the riddle.

Hochkopf   12 August *[1865]*

---

13 Aug. *[1865]*

Sick and wretched. Bad cold: fever! Lonely here – Can't so much as move. Franz lamenting. You know how quick I am to take the extreme view! –

But I wanted to write at least one line in the book. It ought to help, complaining to you. Let's see. Hope so. – Ah, how wretched man is! – Even the sky is bleak. –

14 Aug. *[1865]*

A good night of beautiful easy slumber. Stretched full length as in a coffin and without turning, I lay and bathed in wholesome sweat. Now it's passing, and the

31

supposed 'major' illness has not appeared. I'm weary but clear headed and feel better. – We must not part again, do you hear? – That's one thing, and if we stay together for ever we'll see what happens about the rest. –

[[You have, it's true, got your beautiful letter writing only from our being so much apart! –

But at the present moment I would like to talk to you.

Ah, dear wife!]] How dreadful the world is! – In my fever I've just been reading those dreadful things by Hugo:[26] – once again I've been lucky as I was that time with the underground passages in Rudolstadt![27] – Enormous talent! – couldn't help exclaiming as much out loud a few times. But why hang about for ever with this awful stuff into old age, as Hugo does? That ought to be left to the police, chambers of deputies, councils and councillors, etc. Plain statistical reports say it all better. A writer is only he who knows of all that, only without ever even having observed it, and, because it is so clearly and obviously comprehensible just wastes not one word more over it but simply and solely devises and offers deliverance from evil. True, even here at times sublimity is allowed: e.g., the former Jean-Valjean's struggles of heart and mind before he denounces himself are masterly. – [[Ah, what dreadful stuff! A lovely world! –

I have read your letter once more, and then my poem. I didn't know what to say about it, I was quite stupid, with regard to my poem, that is. –]]

15 Aug [1865]

Dragging myself to the Brown Book. Iller again. – So poorly that letters from you which arrived together today I had to leave unread for several hours, although opened. I saw at a glance that I would not be able to bear them. See, that is how things are with me! – [[Is that unfeelingness? – Oh, if I were only vain – how much reason I would have through you to feel only proud whenever you are suffering. But it's not like that. I feel everything as well – and can't any more, – I can't any more – the suffering is getting too much for me! –]] At last I have read them. And now – I am silent! I stare dully in front of me and think that I'm once again going to give up talking completely. Ah, what madness! What madness! And that fool Hans who wouldn't let you go to Penzing[28] and showed you the shops of Vienna instead! Can one believe it? Can one believe it? And this, if you please, is my one friend! – Ah, foolish hearts! Blind eyes! – [[But how beautiful, how beautiful you are, my wife! – Yes, you are mine, and]] only you have any right to me. No one else has any knowledge of me. –

Oh heavens, how long shall we have to go on tormenting ourselves in this existence? And yet – what am I saying? Was it not in this existence that we found each other? –

*

Why is this page blank – ?[29]

[15 August 1865]

And so today everyone's kept in by rain. If I could only work I wouldn't mind. But if I could walk right out of the world and be alone with you, I should like that best of all. Oh, to find a refuge like that! My abominable fame gives me no proper peace even up here. Yesterday was Sunday. Franz had a job being polite to the sundry tourists etc., who 'happened' to get lost in this direction. –

The announcement of poor Zahlberg's[30] death has reached me here. What a fate that is! Can you understand it? This is all so frantically quick – everyone slipping quietly away. Ah, only Peter[31] left! The ridiculous side has ever to be present. Horrible! –

And I worry about you in Pest! – Am just going to pick up a book again. Ramayana![32] – Adieu! –

16 Aug. *[1865]*

[[Good morning, dear wife. Again somewhat better. I am going to take care of myself now so as not to get a fresh relapse. – During the night I stayed awake for hours with the light burning. All sorts of things went through my memory and several times I couldn't help laughing out loud so that Franz, who sleeps close by, woke up. God, the things I thought about! Can't now remember anything at all of it any more, whereas of a dream earlier I have a clearer recollection. What is waking, what is dreaming? –

Now let's see how it goes today. –]]

*

Oh how grand the Rama poem becomes, and ever finer! – Really, merely to secure for oneself the right mood for such a thing one must be able to withdraw from all the vulgarity of the present. That costs total effort, and at the beginning one thinks it won't work at all: the incomprehensible excesses of the introduction, for example, one feels like yawning and jeering at. But just go on: at last it dawns on you! What sort of a world that is, and how it is built up and executed! A work of art to marvel at – against which a modern novel seems like a newspaper article: I am into the second volume. It is all alive, sounding and moving around me. –

33

Oh, Rama is divine! How grand, how vast everything becomes for me at having to deal with such people! – A glorious drama stands there before me, different from all others! But who is to make it?

Rama with Sita and Lakshmana marching into the jungle – who would not like to be Rama, who not Sita or Lakshmana. –

It is almost the finest thing I know! – Divine Land of the Ganges! –

*

[[Rama: the 'dancing' Queen Mother ! ! –
– Lakshmana: – Fate
– Rama: Lamentation
    the 'licked at' crown.[33, 34]]]

17 Aug. *[1865]*

Good morning! Slept beautifully. – Today there shall at last be a return to the Siegfried score.[35] Maybe I shall have a letter too? –

Rama accompanies me. I was reading the Farewell, his final departure from the city. At this point everyone gives way to tears, sighs, cries, sobs, weeping, howling and wailing – it beats one how the houses stay standing – and I sought the authoress of this misery wondering how she begins to endure such success for her not ardently malicious but merely ambitious undertaking? Then I saw hunch-backed Marantha who had given the counsel, and imagined her gazing down on all the monstrous misery and saying to herself coldly: 'Well, it will all pass, and soon at that. Then it will be as if it never was, and we shall be lords!'

Ah, the malicious ones! They know more than the good-natured, only not everything: only the saints know that! –

Here's a letter coming –

*

That was a sad letter! A real separation letter. To know now that you will meantime be in quite a different mood, and to have, through the letter, to see you like this today – those are the confusions of separation. This mix up of time and space is very harrowing – Yes, separation! –

Against that I have been doing a neat job on Siegfried: the spell is broken! –
[[Good night, dear wife!]]

The entry for 18 August 1865 which follows, had originally been pasted over by Eva. The reason for this obviously lay in Wagner's mention of Cosima's jealousy

34

of Mathdile Maier (M.M.). This jealousy was then understandable but, in August 1865, no longer justified.

Wagner had met Mathilde Maier who was twenty years his junior in 1862 at Schott's house in Mainz. Their acquaintance soon developed into a more intimate relationship. A year later, when considering settling permanently in Vienna, or rather in Penzing, he begged Mathilde, on 4 January 1863, to set bourgeois prejudice aside and come and keep house for him, but she refused. He would doubtless have been glad to have Mathilde as 'mistress of the house', holding out the prospect of marriage in the eventuality of the death of his wife Minna, ill with heart disease, as he did a year later, on 14 May 1864, on settling by the Starnberger See.[36] Nevertheless his deep attachment to Cosima and their Berlin[37] vow of fidelity remained unaffected.

In June 1864 it was impossible to conceive any circumstances under which he and Cosima might live together permanently. But a woman's hand was needed to run his large establishment, and he was not to know that on 29 June Cosima was going to come to him at the Starnberger See without her husband and alone. Had he known, or had merely a presentiment, he would not on 22 June have written to Mathilde Maier telling her to come and look after his house, or, on 25 June, gone so far as to say 'I have never had anyone else in mind to fill your place for me'. But Mathilde again declined, and this time to Wagner's relief since Cosima had arrived, and not just to manage his house. That same day he wrote to Mathilde Maier: 'Of any change in our mutual status there can for the present be no *question,' and a letter of 19 July states that any accession to his wish 'would now at once find me in a frame of mind where I would* not *be able to accept any sacrifice that might be offered. . . . Your coming to me in the* now *only possible circumstances would have completely the opposite result from that which I desired: it would be a source of nameless, now totally insupportable torments for my heart.' Mathilde, being unaware of the state of matters between Wagner and Cosima, can hardly have understood this change of heart.*

It is remarkable that, even after the vow of fidelity with Cosima, Wagner's letters continue to assure Mathilde Maier of his love. On 3 December 1863 he writes: 'My dearest love, . . . go on loving me.' On 7 January 1864 he concludes: 'With heartfelt kisses from your R. W.' On 23 January he writes 'go on loving me immutably', and on 18 May 1864: 'Heartfelt kisses from your R.W.' This explains why both Cosima's biographer, Max Millenkovich-Morold, and Wagner's, Curt von Westernhagen, doubt the accuracy of the My Life *dating of the vow of fidelity as 28 November 1863. Millenkovich is of the view (p. 139) that the sentence, 'Amidst tears and sobs we sealed the acknowledgment of belonging [mutually] solely to each other' (*My Life, *1936 edition, p. 844), may have been suggested to Wagner by subsequent feelings, and Westernhagen*

(Wagner, *1968, p. 312*) writes: '*One can understand Wagner's feeling the need in his autobiography which, of course, ends with his being called to Munich, to raise yet another monument to Cosima by this antedating.*' *The accuracy of these suppositions cannot be determined.*

Deserving of attention, however, is that in the hitherto unpublished Annals for the years 1846 to May 1864 there is the entry (p. 117 below): 'Night journey via Frankfurt to Berlin [27/28 November 1863]: 'Bülows at station. Stay one day. Concert. . . . (<u>28 Nov:</u>*) – .' Here, departing from custom, and for the only time in the Annals, Wagner underlines a date, and without apparent reason. Wagner knew the reason and so do we: this was the day of his and Cosima's vow 'to belong mutually solely to each other'. Wagner wrote the Annals in February 1868 having, in the dictation of his autobiography, reached no further than 1846. He completed the dictation in 1880, and as* My Life *ends at 3 May 1864, five months after the Berlin vow, Wagner did not make use of the Annals note above until eleven to twelve years later. A material point also is Wagner's having made the entry at a time of separation from Cosima when he could not have been influenced by her. On 5 April 1867 Hans von Bülow was appointed Royal Bavarian Court Kapellmeister in Ordinary, and on 16 September Cosima moved back to her husband's house in Munich with her daughters (except for Eva). It was not until 22 July 1868, following renewed denunciations in Munich, that she again joined Wagner at Tribschen.*

Wagner's close relationship with Mathilde Maier was formed between 1862 and 1864 and terminated by Cosima's joining him at the Villa Pellet on 29 June 1864. Why, as late as 1865, and evidently on other occasions, Cosima should hark back to Mathilde Maier requires explanation. Wagner had no grounds or justification for breaking off the affair with Mathilde Maier abruptly. He wished and had to deal gently with a lady of whom he was fond and to whom, a short while before, he had held out the prospect of marriage. So he continued correspondence with her, and Cosima knew this and also the harmless nature of the letters. Nevertheless she was jealous at Wagner's addressing 'loving' words to Mathilde, and who shall blame her? But this jealousy was as harmless as its cause. And in the letter which prompted Wagner's entry below, it was completely unfounded. Obviously Cosima was merely trying to pay him back in his own coin for being jealous of Liszt for 'abducting' her from him for weeks on end. Clearly Wagner's depressed state on the Hochkopf prevented him from appreciating Cosima's intention. Other entries supply evidence of injustice on Wagner's part, and especially towards Liszt, but this, since it is a product of his depression, must be viewed with leniency.

Wagner's attitude in his letters to Mathilde Maier is touching and considerate and a reproof to those who like to regard him as a callous egoist. The best

36

illustration is provided by a letter of 12 July 1865 following the première of Tristan *at which she had been present, a letter which, though there were many others,[38] may be described as one of farewell. 'You, my dear,' it reads, 'can only be to me what it has been permitted and possible for you to be: if this has become greatly restricted, just as much has still remained as I have left you – in those very letters – so gladly and appreciatively. I have rejected or retracted nothing: merely acknowledged what, without desire, is left of our relationship . . . You will always remain for me what you are, and judge from that what you have been. From all my heart, your R.W.'*

[[18 Aug. *[1865]*

Good morning, naughty child!

What a nasty letter you wrote me yesterday! I am discovering more and more how naughty it is. What you are saying to me in it is really the same as that you have been wrong to love me so much, and, against that, to treat your father who alone loved you, badly. That's nice! And this you find goes quite easily, especially when you are away from me and with your father! And now poor M.M. has to come in for it again: God, the things I'm not going to get up to with her – yes! How I'm supposed to be keeping company with her – what loving speeches I lavish! etc. That's very nice, that is, and looks exactly as if you're aiming for a 'break' with me. Well, just you get on with it! Well, I never! –

And all this in the lap of joy and bliss while I, sick and sad, am wasting away here in clouds of mist! – Very nice! – That shall be a lesson to me, – and 'you will have the surprise of your life!'

Hope there'll very soon be a sensible letter, otherwise it's all over! –

For all that, dear wife, I've slept well! God, how much sleep I would need to rid myself of the fatigues of my long waking! – Must inquire closely one day of some clever doctor what I have to do to preserve myself in a state to finish all that I have to do in this world. –]]

For the whole of his stay in the Hochkopf, from 9 to 21 August 1865, Wagner was ill almost constantly. Of this he complains repeatedly in earlier entries, speaks also of fever, and on the eve of his return to Munich, 20 August 1865, writes: 'I have become iller'. There is therefore some justification for regarding the following, hitherto unpublished entries of 18 August 1865 as fever fantasies. Nothing else could account for such sentences as: 'I shall set up full court . . . Once weekly court shall be held in my presence: I shall then receive the report of

my general and his adjutants . . . then things shall proceed as at Versailles under
Louis XIV . . .' Or: 'Then I shall come to you both in your tiny parlour . . . I shall
then be quite poor . . . I shall keep only my sick bed: and with that I shall come to
you both, Hans will be receiving a better salary, and I shall live on you both just
like a beggar.'

[*18. August 1865*]

[[I can only live reasonably if I acknowledge reality and come to terms with it, i.e.
put myself completely out of rapport with it. I can and must live only in a kind of
cloud. Just as I am solely an artistic being, I can too lead only an artistic
existence. Part of which is: hardly having anything to do with people any more;
hardly talking at all any more, or merely in jest, never seriously, for that always
straightaway becomes painful and useless. If the King assents to my proposals,
and as a result I see my life made pleasantly secure unto death, and freed from all
care, my thoughts will be only of creating and not any more of working. Then I
shall set up full court. Hans will have to take over all 'working': school,
performances, etc. I shall go on dealing with the world only via him and really
only jestingly at that. I shall no longer concern myself with anything direct. Once
weekly, court shall be held in my presence: I shall then receive the report of my
general and his adjutants: what is accomplished will please me, what is not, will
not trouble me, for I shall not have expected it for myself. So that will be the way
of it. But with the doctor I shall have agreed a proper diet: I shall then so arrange
my day as to derive the greatest possible advantage for my work. That will have
to be organized wholly artistically, and then things will proceed as at Versailles
under Louis XIV, with most rigid etiquette, as if worked by strings. Ill health
must no longer trouble me. Cosima will have always to be near me – ever
present: there can be no other way. But we shall never speak, and especially
never seriously. Then, I believe, I shall still achieve the full seriousness of my
artistic works: but there alone must be the place for seriousness, all else must be
light and cheerful. But Cosima will secretly be serious with me too: that goes
without saying! –

But she'll show no sign of it. Only Brünnhilde, and all these characters
whatever their names are, shall show signs of how seriously it's all intended. Shall
they not? – That's how it is to be! –

If the King is <u>not</u> able to! Then everything the other way round: then it will be
just 'working' – and no creating at all. Then I shall come to you both in your tiny
parlour: all day long, commissions, doing things, dealing with people, teaching,
giving instructions, talking, and God knows what. But all cheerful, without

anger: for I shall then be quite poor, possessing nothing but your letters and Parzival's,[39] and not even my manuscripts any more: I shall have given everything, everything away. I shall keep only my sick bed: and with that I shall come to you both, Hans will be receiving a better salary, and I shall live on you both just like a beggar. Then it will be all right too: then I shall be able to work a lot, found a school, and all in good spirits. Then – that shall be, and not the other. – Also good! And you will be ever present and allowed to talk much!]]

[18. August 1865]

O Cosima! You are the soul of my life! Completely and utterly! – I gazed into the flat country; looked for 'home' – imagined Munich without you. All a grave! – Nothing, nothing more without you! You are the soul of all that lives within me. –

*

Good night! – Parzival has written nicely! – Also done some work! – Good night, Cos! –

19 Aug *[1865]*

[[Good morning, my soul! –]] Weather grey – rainy! cold! – So one must keep oneself bright and warm within. –

Rhinegold has also arrived. Now I'm going to repack it and send it to the King at Hohenschwangau for his birthday.[40] The letter post is terrible: my letter of 10th was received by the King on 14th; his of 14th I received on 18th. He will be pleased to see me at Hohenschw. on 25th; but – I shall not go. It really is too strenuous for me. Such is my condition that only with the greatest care and quiet shall I elude the illness that's threatening. I shall write to him today and send the score. You've taken care, have you, to see that the cushion[41] goes off in time? Hope so.

What useless chatter all that is; as if you could answer!

[[My life plan, it seems, is to incline towards the Versailles arrangement, i.e., refined peace, pleasant withdrawal, unlimited work. At least I gather from Parzival's letters that he considers possible all that I desire. – Strange! How shall I feel when I again sit, whole and solitary, at this miraculous loom. It is the only thing that befits me. The world I cannot shape, I must merely forget: this is the only relationship I can stand in towards it. Wholly artificially, like a tropical plant in the winter garden, I must shut myself off against the atmosphere of reality, there is no other way. All else is abuse, extirpation – a squandering of my life forces. –

Now, soul, create sun and warmth for me! <u>You</u> shall be my climate, my atmosphere!

One thing is bad! –]] A certain aversion to existence is engendered from the fact that one's conception is at length filled with the essential image of the world, and no longer can much about it be changed or much new added either. I can think what I will, always in the end I turn away with a certain disgust, because I feel I have thought it all once already. In everything I light upon ideas which I've had already: the incentive of discovery has wholly disappeared. Thus nothing arresting any longer remains other than the execution of form, the pure artistic joy of perfecting performance. In this I hope again to find great satisfaction. Certainly that constant, unconscious sidelong look for the desired reality of performance from the common run of performers will have a disturbing effect. Even now – after my 'tasting blood' with Tristan and suddenly seeing everything melted into common water – the death of Schnorr represents a still immeasurably significant epoch in my life. What <u>that</u> was meant to mean – that is something before which I stand dulled and astounded, incapable of thought, indeed, even of feeling. I cannot yet grasp, let alone explain it. A big, big change will and must come over me: thus far my steps were headed towards a possibility: – now this has petered out – and no possibility makes sense for me any more. –

[[I can only cocoon myself, weave for you and Parzival: otherwise all has no longer any sense! Can you think of anything else? – Impossible! –]]

*

[[This attempt too then has, it seems, to be abandoned. Retreat from wooded summit decided upon. Weather intolerable; air chill, damp and impeding my recovery. Feel ill constantly. There is no forcing anything. Men ordered for six on Monday: down! –

Worked with difficulty! – No inclination for anything! Mist and cold in my very vitals. God, how hard for <u>me</u> it is all becoming! Always only to be battling with life's cruellest elements –

News today of another death: my dear brother-in-law, Fr. Brockhaus,[42] has died! Everyone's dying! Getting time to include oneself! –

No news of you for two days. – What a sad existence! Oh, to be united in a better climate! By the Ganges! – Good night, dear Soul! Good night! –]]

20 Aug *[1865]*

[[My soul, good morning! –

It really is a dreadful time hearing nothing at all from you any more. To end this bad state of things too, I've decided to proceed to the valley again tomorrow. – I really am ill. Nothing will help me but – – God knows? Since the proper thing is always not supposed to be uttered. But let's – for the time being – call it 'work' still! My ideal is still, under Parzival's protection, in the constant proximity of your eloquent silence, to complete my works, there at the loom! – It remains to strive solely for this still. I am writing to the King today to hand everything else over to Hans. Will there be a letter from you today? ?]]

*

It's evening. All packed. I've kept the Brown Book back to write something more in before going to bed. Here I sit: What shall I write? –

Your letter has come. Shall I answer it here? It contained news – of Pest,[43] of Father, of Elisabeth, of rehearsals and much else. To me it has said that you still love me. That's what I've liked best. – [[Why will I simply not take heart any more? Shall – now I have abandoned hope – only love still remain to me, and even faith, faith in myself, vanish? You love me, so I still believe. But am I not flattering myself? I have no longer any joy. Maybe I never did have. I feel as if all that I have known is ecstasy, powerful, violent – but fleeting. Why does all that is pleasant desert me so swiftly?]] How sadly, sadly I gaze today at these beautiful mountains which ten days ago, when I arrived, were laughing so profoundly refreshingly at me? I can explain all to myself. I have become iller: ? but why can I suddenly laugh again, feel full of spirits, like a lion? [[And then grief, again and again grief, revulsion, dejection lasting a long, long time. Even the weather, the rent sky is no longer so beautiful as when I came. All that is an explanation. Except I can see that it is always like that in life: if I am to keep courage and faith, then everything that can be like this today, and tomorrow different, must to me be a matter of indifference. I say to myself: It's work, that's what you lack! Certainly, if I am working then I am independent of weather and sun: that has always been a help to me. Then the past, despite the desolation of my house, seems more cheerful to me. But I must be working, you see, just working. What keeps me from it eternally? To know that I cannot stick at it.]] Yes, the daemon is awake. Even here I got everything ready for myself – gathered myself deep down. For three days I composed myself. Attended only to what had to be attended to. 'Tomorrow,' I told myself, 'tomorrow at last you will again take up your music-pen.' Then I become ill, feeble and fit for nothing. O fate! – [[Now I am glad merely to have got to the point of being able to escape from here and return. The rain is beating against the wooden walls: I could laugh out loud – How is that to be?

But all this, certainly, can finally be overcome. By undertaking nothing any more, nothing any more. That's one way.]] – And by having deep inside no

41

longer any joy in my own work! How can I think of the one joy I ever had from one of my works, how can I think of – Tristan without renouncing all joy for ever. When I think of Tristan I am seized with terror! And was that the only time, the only time that I was glad? – Where does delight come from, where does faith? –

[[From love? – Yes, my soul, from love of <u>you</u>, my wife! Certainly that will work: I know.]] You still entice my work from my soul. But oh! Give me the peace for it! Stay with me, don't go again. Tell poor Hans openly that without you I cannot manage any longer. Oh heavens, if only you could be my wife to the world! This constant coming and going, coming back, having to go again, letting you be at the disposal of others, – it's dreadful! Peace, peace! You, my poorest, are being destroyed by it for me too. Instead of just smiles and happy waves, now always these convulsions, dreams horrors, ghosts! – Oh heavens! Who knows the person at his side? What do our dearest friends know of us? If it does not come to them, as to Parzival, from the stars, no one discovers from within himself who the other is. Thus I fear that we *shall* perish: we're wearing each other out. Against that, is one now to break? Break with – ? What would that mean? Madness! Could peace, beautiful cheerful smiles ever favour us? – Oh, then, it will be sighs! May God illumine the blind! – I'm going to bed! Good night! <u>You are my wife!</u> –

21 Aug *[1865]*

Now one last good-morning from the forest hut! – It's grey. All packed. But not yet the book. – I'm coming nearer to you. Tomorrow I shall be able to telegraph to you. – Here you have ten days out of my life. As these have been, so are all. A flickering into flame – delight – good spirits – wonderful pleasure. – Then long agony; everything seeming in vain. Soon a state so unbearable that one had to force oneself to think about changing it. But the fact that once again I learn to realize this clearly is the good thing about such experiments. Remote from you, I have come closer and closer. That is what I feel! You are my one and all. If only you will come again, then all will be well! –

Adieu, mountain forest summit! – Lonely but firm! Step out, step out! That's what's needed! – Farewell, Jupiter! Farewell! I salute you.

5 a.m.

<u>Munich</u>. 22 <u>Aug</u>. *[1865]*

Crossing the Walchensee yesterday in the boat, I saw something beautiful.

The shallows: how clear, how light everything on the bottom; the water was

42

merely glass: a beautiful white sandy bottom, each individual stone, there, there, here a plant, there a tree-trunk – all plain. Then came the deep abyss: the water dark, dark, all clarity gone, all hidden; but then, suddenly, the sky, the sun, the mountains – all tangibly bright and clear upon the mirror – – Shallow souls, deep souls! I have gazed to the bottom of many shallow souls: how few deep souls has the world reflected for me! –

En route I picked up your letter: it was the poem.[44] That was beautiful! –

In the evening I found everything nice at home. I can't help laughing at my smartened rooms: <u>that</u> lasts, or <u>can</u> at least be made to last. Beautiful weather, and whatever else swiftly and powerfully delights me, vanishes so swiftly, leaving such long bleak days behind. Strange how one helps oneself – or how the daemon helps us – to endure it. – Today your fat letter! – I can see it really will be a wonder if you return! –

23 Aug. *[1865]*

[[Good morning, my dear? – Yesterday I visited the children. But merely saw Boni[45] and Isolde. Isolde was asleep, but woke up at once and had a mind to cry: I stopped her, then she gave me a laugh. Strange to say she reminds me of a sister, i.e., an ideal sister for which the possibility has always existed without so far being realized. The purely-sisterly, proto-mother-related! It may be that I, never having had any children, am able to recognize the related only under the concept of sisterhood. – Boni was very beautiful! She's going to be an unusual child. –

I didn't go into your rooms. But I could see your bed just as if you had just risen from it. –]]

How much longer are you going to stay away? A very, very long time, I suppose. –

The Gypsies[46] have not impressed me favourably. Artificially cultivated barbarians; not complete nature, not complete art. Their music, half arranged, with barbarously dilettante mutilation. Not all that we enthuse over, out of revulsion at German philistinism, is worth it. All that is good for a bout of intoxication, but we ought to be above being intoxicated. Your father as much as me. It's pretty, this éljen, Rákóczy etc., – but those are by-ways, reversions, foibles: I'm not insensitive to it but I avoid it. Tears and laughter! Good, on the mirror of the deep lake, as a delineated world: but the shallow lake bottom is soon surveyed: hiding oneself there is no escape. –

'On Sunday, on Sunday, at early morn,
my darling wrote me a letter forlorn.'

43

Where does a tender German folk song like that come from? – The Gypsy doesn't know what to do with it: heard from the depths of the lake, the world is mirrored in it! –

[[Oh, I'm so different from everyone! – From where now are my joys to flow? –]]

24 Aug. *[1865]*

I turn ever more sadly to the Brown Book. I feel as if I ought now to let myself be deprived even of being near to you! No letter for three days. – I can understand! ! – These pious wordlings are, and remain, incomprehensible to me! God knows how it is with their genuineness. To me most things about it are alien and unintelligible! – Good morning!

The following entry for 24 August 1865 refers to the tenor Ludwig Schnorr von Carolsfeld who sang Tristan. His sudden death on 21 July 1865 was a heavy blow for Wagner by which he was long affected. On 19 August 1865 he had written in the Brown Book*: 'What that [Schnorr's death] was meant to mean – that is something before which I stand dulled and astounded . . . I cannot yet grasp, let alone explain it.'*

My Tristan! My beloved! – I drove you to the abyss! I was used to standing there. I have a head for heights. But I cannot see anyone standing at the edge: I am seized with frenzied sympathy. I grab hold to pull back, and I push over, just as we kill the sleep-walker we shout at in alarm. – It was thus I pushed him over. And myself? – I have a head for heights – I can look down, – indeed, it pleases me to – But my friend? It is him I lose.

My Tristan! My Beloved!

*

[[This has been another day! – Nameless anxiety for my dear wife! She does not write: is something being concealed from me? – There is one comfort! Comfort? ? Were you to fall into the abyss, I would not stand any longer at the edge. At present I am still living – Where are you? –]]

25 Aug [1865]

Die Glocken hallen, die Kanonen dröhnen;
die Luft ist rein, der Himmel blau und klar:
will mich der Tag von Neuem sich gewöhnen?
soll mir vergehn, wie trüb die Nacht mir war?
Geboren ist ein Heiland Deutschland's Söhnen:
heut' feiert er sein zwanzigst Erdenjahr!
Kanonen, dröhnt! Hallt laut u. hell, ihr
    Glocken!
Mich will dem Gram der frohe Tag entlocken![47]

The bells resound, the cannons roar;
the air is pure, the sky is blue and clear:
will Day accustom me to Day anew?
Shall I forget how troubled was my night?
To the sons of Germany a Saviour's born
who celebrates today his twentieth year!
Roar cannons! Loud and clear resound, you
    bells!
The joyous day will entice me from affliction![47]

The lines that follow, also dated 25 August 1865, were written obliquely across the page by Wagner. They are addressed to Cosima who had informed him that, in Hungary, Liszt had been fêted enthusiastically, and that he – and with him Cosima – had been acclaimed by 'four thousand Magyars'.

Vom fernen Ost, vom Lande der Magyaren
kam morgens mir ein Traumbild bang und
    wüst:
dem Liebchen ist gross' Freude widerfahren,
mein Weib ward dort viertausendmal gegrüsst.
«Mein Weib?» Du Thor! Frag' erst bei
    kund'gen Leuten,
was solcher Freudentraum dir mag bedeuten!

From distant East, from land of Magyar
with morning came a vision, fearful,
    wild:
my dearest one befell a great delight,
four thousand-fold they greeted there my wife.
'My wife?' You fool! Ask first of those who
    know,
what so delightful a dream may mean to you!

26 Aug [1865]

How wonderful! – The King ardently desires to hear about Parzival.[48]

In a letter to Wagner at the Hochkopf dated 21 August 1865, King Ludwig had written: 'Dear One, Only One, fulfil a request! – I beseech you. – Impart to me something of your plans concerning "The Victors" and "Parcival". I am <u>parched</u> *with thirst for them. Slake my burning thirst.' Wagner did not receive this letter until 26 August 1865 after returning to Munich and writing the note above. The following day, 27 August, he began the prose sketch of Parzival which he completed in only four days, on 30 August 1865, an indication that he already had the whole plan in his head. A further indication is a sentence in Wagner's answer to the King of 26 August: 'Ah, it's becoming difficult, you know, to hold myself back and not immediately execute those subjects with which I am so intimate.' Wagner did not, as the King had also requested, proceed further with the 1865 sketch for the drama of Buddha, 'The Victors'. He did not decide in favour of the spelling 'Parsifal', as opposed to 'Parzival', until he began the first draft of the work in the middle of February 1877. He adopted Joseph Görres' 1813 derivation of the name as being from the Persian* fal parsi, *pure fool. The note 'Well, that was help in need!!' at the end of the sketch refers to the four days of relief from his anxieties concerning Cosima. On 31 August he notes: 'As long as I sat over Parzival, my imagination helped beautifully . . . Now the ideal tension is dispersed. – Reality, whole and naked, has again to be overcome!' On 31 August 1865 Wagner prepared for the King a copy of his sketch which reveals divergencies over numerous points of detail, and at once dispatched it to Hohenschwangau. On 5 September 1865 the King conveyed his thanks in an effusive letter stating, inter alia: . . . 'Oh how I love you, my adored, sacred friend!'*

27 Aug *[1865]*   <u>Parzival</u>

<u>Anfortas</u>, Keeper of the Grail, lies stricken of a spear-wound received in some mysterious love adventure, which will not heal. His father, <u>Titurel</u>, original Winner of the Grail, in advanced old age has entrusted his office to his son, as also dominion over Monsalvat, the Castle of the Grail. This office, despite his feeling of unworthiness in view of his error, he is obliged to discharge until one worthier shall appear to relieve him of it. Who will this be? Where will he come from? By what will he be recognized? –

The Grail is the crystal cup the Saviour once drank from at the Last Supper

46

and gave to his disciples to drink from: in it Joseph of Arimathea caught the blood shed from the spear-wound of the Saviour on the cross. Holiest of relics, it was for a long time mysteriously lost to the sinful world. When finally at a most harsh and hostile time, and in the face of opposition by unbelievers, the holy distress of Christianity was at its highest, heroes, inspired by God and imbued with holy charity, were moved by their fervour to go in quest of the vessel – that mysteriously consoling relic of which there was ancient report – wherein the Saviour's blood (Sang seale, whence San Gréal – Sanct Gral – the Holy Grail) had been preserved, living and divinely life-giving, for mankind in need of redemption. This relic has been miraculously disclosed to <u>Titurel</u> and his loyal followers, and given into their care. Titurel has gathered about him a body of holy knights to serve the Grail, and build, in wild, remote and inaccessible mountain forest, the Castle of Monsalvat, which none unworthy to care for the Grail may find. The relic has proclaimed its miraculous power chiefly by freeing its custodians from earthly care by supplying the community with food and drink; and by mysterious writing which, comprehensible only to the Keeper of the brotherhood of knights, appears upon the glowing surface of the crystal, making known the worst afflictions suffered by the innocent of the world, and issuing instructions to those of the knights who shall be sent forth for their protection. Those who are sent forth, it endows with Divine power, rendering them everywhere victorious. From its votaries it banishes death: he who sets eyes on that Divine vessel cannot die. But only he who preserves himself from the allurements of sensual pleasure retains the power of the Grail's blessing: only to the chaste is the blessed might of the relic revealed. –

Beyond the mountain height in whose hallowed, night-dark forest, at a place where charming valleys wind towards the south and its laughing lands and Monsalvat lies, accessible only to the votary, there lies another castle, as secret as it is sinister. It too can be reached only by magic paths. The Godly take care not to approach it. But whoever does approach cannot withstand the anxious longing that lures him towards the gleaming battlements towering from the never-before-seen splendour of a most wonderful forest of flowering trees, out of which magically sweet birdsong and intoxicating perfumes pour upon all around. – This is <u>Klingsor's</u> magic castle. Concerning this sorcerer dark things are said. No one has seen him: he is known only by his power. That power is magic. The castle is his work, raised miraculously in what was previously a desolate place with only a hermit's hut upon it. Where now, in a most luxuriant and heady fashion, all blooms and stirs as on an eternal early-summer evening, once, in bare wilderness, only the lonely hut was to be seen. Who is Klingsor? Vague, incomprehensible rumours. Nothing else is known of him. Maybe he is known to old Titurel? But nothing can be gathered from him: dulled by his great age, he is kept alive only by the wondrous power of the Grail. But there is Gurnemans, an old squire of Titurel's, still loyally serving Anfortas; he ought to know something of Klingsor: also he sometimes lets it be understood that he does; but not much can be got out of him: no sooner does he seem on the point of reporting something unbelievably strange, than he falls silent again, as if such things should not be spoken of. Perhaps Titurel has at some time forbidden him to speak. It is supposed that Klingsor is the same man who once so piously inhabited the place now so changed: – he is said to have mutilated himself in order to destroy that sensual longing which he never completely succeeded in overcoming through prayer and penance. Titurel refused to allow him to join the Knights of the Grail, and for the reason that renunciation and chastity, flowing from the innermost soul, do not require to be forced by mutilation. No one knows the precise facts. All that is certain is that it is since Anfortas' time that people have suddenly heard of the castle, also that the Knights of the Grail have often been warned against becoming ensnared in the toils cast from that place against their chastity. In fact, concealed in that castle are the most beautiful women in the world and of all times. They are held there under Klingsor's spell for the destruction of men, and of the Knights of the Grail especially, he having endowed them with all powers of seduction. Men say they are she-devils. Several Knights of the Grail have failed to return from their journeys; they are feared to have fallen into Klingsor's power. What, unfortunately, is certain is that Anfortas himself, going forth to combat the sorcery threatening his knights, has been trapped in these toils, lured aside by a strange, wondrously beautiful woman and treacherously set upon by armed men who were to bind and take him to Klingsor: with difficulty he fought back, and, turning to flee, received in his side the spear-thrust of which he now lies afflicted, and which nothing can heal.

The Knights, the whole Community of the Grail, are now most keenly concerned on their Keeper's behalf. Pilgrimages are made to all parts in quest of the right cure, of the mercy balm; from the furthest zones they return: whatever the remedies found, none will heal the wound. Daily it reopens. The agony of the wounded man is unspeakable. Nothing can assuage it. But it is not only the pain of the wound that benights Anfortas' soul: his suffering goes deeper. He is the Chosen One whose task is to care for the miraculous vessel. He, and he alone, has to work the sacred magic that refreshes, strengthens and directs the whole company of knights, whilst he alone has to suffer dreadful self-reproach at having betrayed his vow. He, the most unworthy of all, must daily – to his fearful punishment – touch the sacred vessel: at his prayer, must the Divine contents of the cup flow bright purple, at his intercession must nourishing grace be unfolded to the votive knights. Aye, suffering and beyond recovery, he is daily filled with warmth of new life by the wondrous power of the Grail: seeing death as his only

48

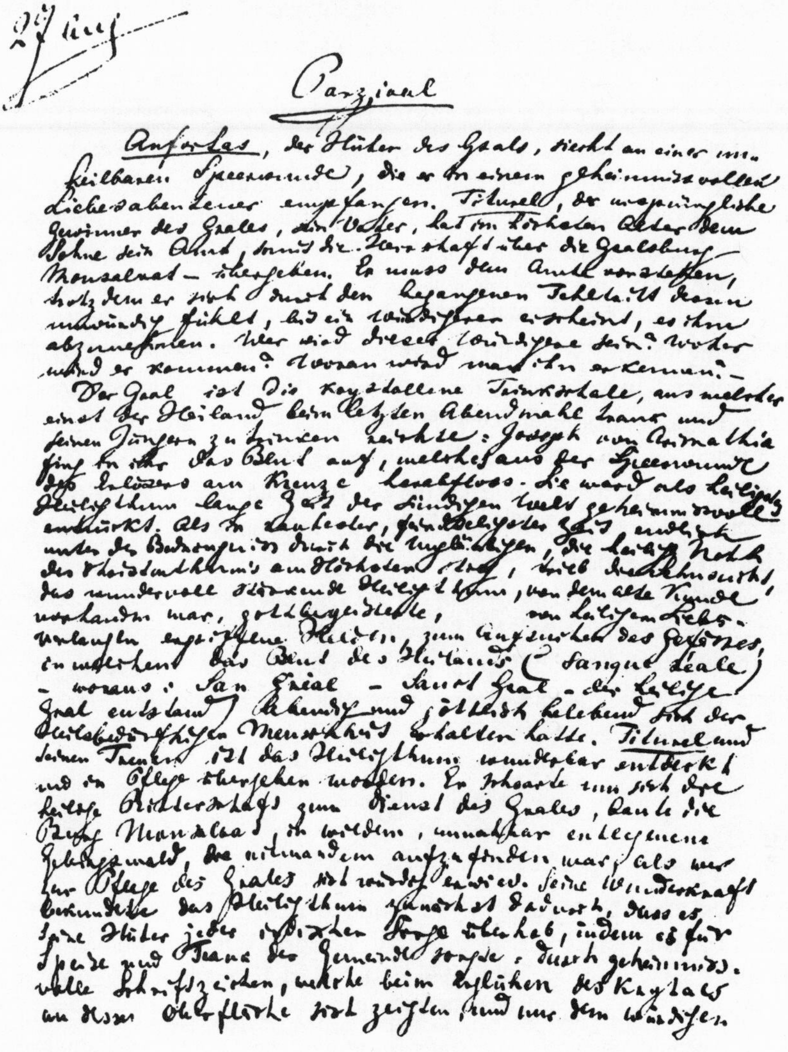
27 Aug.

Parzival

Anfortas, der Hüter des Grals, siecht an einer unheilbaren Speerwunde, die er in einem geheimnissvollen Liebesabenteuer empfangen. Titurel, der ursprüngliche Gewinner des Grales, sein Vater, hat im höheren Alter dem Sohne sein Amt, sowie die Herrschaft über die Gralsburg Monsalvat – übergeben. Er muss dem Amte vorstehen, trotzdem er sich durch den begangenen Fehltritt dessen unwürdig fühlt, bis ein Würdiger erscheint, es ihm abzunehmen. Wer wird dieser Würdige sein? Woher wird er kommen? Woran wird man ihn erkennen? –

Der Gral ist die krystallene Trinkschale, aus welcher einst der Heiland beim letzten Abendmahle trank und seinen Jüngern zu trinken reichte: Joseph von Arimathia fing in ihr das Blut auf, welches aus der Speerwunde des Erlösers am Kreuze herabfloss. Sie ward als heiligstes Heiligthum lange Zeit der sündigen Welt geheimnissvoll entrückt. Als in räuberischer, gottfeindlicher Zeit, endlich unter den Bedrängnissen durch die Ungläubigen, die heilige Noth des Christenthums am höchsten stieg, trieb die Sehnsucht das wundervolle stärkende Heiligthum, von dem alte Kunde vorhanden war, goldbegürtete, von heiligem Lebeverlangen ergriffene Helden, zum Aufsuchen des Gefässes, in welchem das Blut des Heilands (sangue reale – woraus: San Greal – Sanct Gral – der heilige Gral entstand) lebendig und göttlich belebend sich der heilsbedürftigen Menschheit erhalten hatte. Titurel und seinen Treuen ist das Heiligthum wunderbar entdeckt und in Pflege übergeben worden. Er schaarte um sich die heilige Ritterschaft zum Dienst des Grales, baute die Burg Monsalvat in wildem, unnahbar entlegenem Gebirgswald, der niemandem aufzufinden war, als wer zur Pflege des Grales sich würdig erwies. Seine Wunderkraft bewährte das Heiligthum zunächst dadurch, dass es seine Hüter jeder irdischen Sorge überhob, indem es für Speise und Trank der Gemeinde sorgte: durch geheimnissvolle Schriftzeichen, welche beim Erglühen des Krystalls an dessen Oberfläche sich zeigten, und nur dem würdigen

deliverance, he is now, by the grace of the Grail, condemned to eternal life! If, to secure death, he would, against his vow, fain forgo the delight of beholding the Grail, he is compelled by his soul's ardent yearning, to lose himself anew in the blessed sight of it, to see anew the golden purple shine bright, and let the glow of that Divine radiance penetrate again and again, blessing and bruising, into his innermost being. For as the heavenly blood of the Redeemer pours full of grace into his own heart, ah, how his own wicked blood is forced to flee the touch of the Divine! In timid desperation the sinful blood rushes from his heart, bursting the wound afresh and shedding itself in the world of sin, – and from a wound such as the Redeemer received on the cross and bled from, out of compassionate love for wretched, sinful humanity, he, sinful Keeper of the Divine Balm of Redemption, as an eternal reminder of his wickedness, bleeds hot, sinful blood that cannot be staunched! – The knights approach, the hour is striking, he must work the magic: they grieve and lament over his wound, seek most eagerly to help him, procuring remedies and balm, not suspecting where it is his wound is bleeding, and where it is he is beyond cure. So, finally, the wretched man prays fervently to the Grail for a sign, asking whether he may hope for deliverance, and who may be called upon to deliver him. The sign shines forth: he reads the enigmatic words. 'Aware, suffering in fellow-suffering, a fool will redeem thee!' – Who can it be who suffers only in fellow-suffering, and, without knowing, is wiser than others? – 'Oh, that longed-for one! If he lives, let him find the way to the sanctuary: an end to agony, a scar for the wound, peace for the heart; when will you bring them, aware fool suffering in fellow-suffering?'

His loyal followers do everything to assuage the agony of their beloved Master; in the morning they bear him on a litter down to the holy lake in the forest, there to bathe and drink at the noble spring. There, in the sweet coolness, he seems to revive a little: messengers arrive with new remedies found far away: alas, none will help.

<u>28 Aug [1865]</u>

The most indefatigable in quartering the world in quest of succour for Anfortas' wound is the High Messenger of the Grail, <u>Kundry</u>. Who this woman is and where she comes from, no one knows; she must be extremely old for she appeared here in the mountains in Titurel's day: although she is wild and dreadful to behold, one notices no real signs of age: she has a complexion which is pale one moment, sun-burnt the next; her black hair hangs down long and wild: sometimes she plaits it in strange plaits; she is only ever seen in her dark-red robe which she girds with a curious girdle of snake-skins: often her black eyes shoot from their sockets like burning coals; one moment her gaze is unsteady and wandering, the next – staring again and fixed. The brotherhood of knights treat her more as a strange, magical animal than a human being. Also she always lives apart, how she keeps herself is not known, nor where she seeks shelter: at times she vanishes completely; nothing is then seen or heard of her. Then one chances upon her in a cave, or in dense undergrowth, in a deathlike sleep, lifeless, numb, bloodless, with all limbs rigid. Gurnemans, the old squire, usually takes care of her then: he has known her for so long! – carries her to his home, warms, chafes her and restores her to life; on waking, she believes she has dropped off to sleep for a while, curses herself for letting sleep overcome her, gazes at the sun, heaves a dreadfully deep sigh, darts away, and begins her activity anew. If there is something difficult to be accomplished, something to be done far, far away, a message or order from the Grail for a Knight of the Grail contending in foreign zones, then suddenly one is aware of Kundry eagerly seizing the task which none can perform so speedily and reliably as she; one then sees her racing off in the storm on a tiny horse with a long mane and tail flowing down to the ground, and before one knows it, she is back. Never has one remarked the slightest disloyalty in her; her zeal, her care in the performance of her missions is boundless. Thus she is a true, indispensable servant to the company of knights: all her missions turn out well. Against which, she is greatly missed on the occasions of her mysterious disappearances: then some adversity, some mysterious danger usually befalls the knights, and there is alarm, and, often, the wish for Kundry to come. Because of that, many too are in doubt whether she should be considered good or evil: what is certain is that she must still be a heathen. Never is she seen at any religious act: nor elsewhere either, unless there is some uncommonly difficult service to be performed. Gurnemans, who at other times is not gentle in his behaviour towards the wild woman, takes her half grumpily, half humorously under his protection. One must look to her good works, he says, and be glad if she returns. He supposes her to be a woman accursed and having great sins to atone for in her present life. The services she performs are therefore as much to her credit as to the Knights', and one need not be afraid to accept them. – For the rest, she shows great indifference, indeed, scorn towards the knights, never accepting their thanks. Even Anfortas is not exempted. Now she is just returning on her panting horse from the wonderland of Arabia where she has found the most precious miracle balm. Hastily she hands it to Gurnemans, refuses thanks and without a word throws herself down in a corner of the forest, whilst Gurnemans hurries to the King and the knights by the holy lake, bearing the hoped-for succour. But even that balm brings no relief: Kundry smiles scornfully. 'You know who alone can help. Why drive me on the false track?' Nothing else is to be got out of her. She never gives advice or opinion: but simply shows the swiftest zeal in at once carrying out what is commanded or desired. She is therefore considered completely stupid and senseless, as well as animal. Yet she seems to attach great, indeed passionately great, importance to delivering Anfortas from his suffering: she betrays violent uneasiness over it. But then again she laughs scornfully: one should not wish the end of this distress; who knows whether the clever knights might not in future have to perform their own

51

missions; she too would like peace, etc. While the King is bathing in the sacred lake a wild swan circles above his head: suddenly it falls, wounded by an arrow; shouts from the lake: general indignation, who dares kill an animal in this sacred region? The swan flutters nearer and drops bleeding to the ground. <u>Parzival</u> emerges from the forest, bow in hand: Gurnemans stops him. The young man confesses to the deed. To the violent reproaches of the old man he has no reply. Gurnemans, reproaching him with the wickedness of his act, reminds him of the sanctity of the forest stirring so silently about him, asks whether he has not found all the creatures here tame, gentle and harmless. What had the swan seeking its mate done to him? Was he not sorry for the poor bird that now lay, with bloodstained feathers, dying before him? etc., – Parzival, who has stood riveted to the spot, bursts into tears and stammers, 'I didn't know!' – 'Where do you come from?' – 'I don't know!' – 'Who is your father?' – 'I don't know!' etc. Gurnemans' amazement at this stupidity which hitherto he has encountered only in Kundry, gives way to emotion as he prevails upon Parzival to keep him company for a little and tell him something about himself. All that Gurnemans can elicit from the shy Parzival is that he knows only his mother, Schmerzeleide [Painsorrow]; she has brought him up in great seclusion, and in such a way that he has never learnt anything of arms and knightliness. – 'Why?' As Parzival knows no reason, Kundry, recumbent in her corner, who all along has been staring hard at Parziv., quickly throws in 'His father was killed before his son was born: his mother wanted to protect her son from a similar violent death. – The fool!' She laughs. Parzival's memory and understanding of his past are thus awakened. Armed men had passed by their lonely farm: Parzival had followed but lost them. He has had many adventures: made himself the bow: with it, protected himself on his wild wanderings. – <u>Kundry</u> confirms that he has made himself feared through his heroic deeds and incredibly bold strength. 'Who fears me?' – 'The wicked.' – 'Were they who barred my way wicked?' – Gurnemans laughs. 'Who is good?' – Gurnem.: 'Your mother. You have run away from her; she will be grieving for you; there is no need to treat all straightaway with hostility.' – 'Am I hostile?' – 'Towards the swan you were, and towards your mother.' – 'My mother?' – Kundry: 'She is dead!' – Parzival: 'Dead? My mother? Who says so?' Kundry: 'I saw her die!' <u>Parziv.</u> leaping up seizes Kundry by the throat. Gurnemans holds him back. 'Will you again do wrong here? What has the woman done to you? She has surely spoken the truth, for Kundry never lies and knows much!' <u>Parzi.</u> stands dazed, as if paralysed. At length: 'I die of thirst.' He is on the verge of collapsing; Gurnemans holds him. Kundry goes swiftly to the spring and returns with a filled horn: she sprinkles Parz. with the water and gives him to drink. Gurnemans praises Kundry; so that was what was being done here, evil repaid by good. Kundry laughs: she never does good, but she wants peace. As Parz. recovers and is tended in fatherly fashion by Gurnemans, Kundry retires sadly, and as if in growing weariness, to her corner of the forest: 'Ah, I am weary. Where shall I find peace?'She drags herself off into the forest unnoticed. – Gurnemans sees that the King, together with his attendants, has long since set off back to the castle. The sun is at its highest; it is nearing the time to proceed to the sacred meal. Parz., supporting himself on the old man, asks where they are, for the forest seems steadily to be disappearing while they seem to be entering stone corridors. It looks as if they are on the right path, and the boy, he realizes, is still innocent, otherwise the way to the castle would not be opening to them both so easily. They climb stairs and again find themselves in vaulted corridors. Parzival, hardly feeling as if he is walking, follows in a daze. He hears wonderful sounds. Trumpet notes, long held and swelling, answered from the far distance by a gentle ringing as of crystal bells. At last they arrive in a mighty hall which, cathedral-like, loses itself in a lofty cupola. Light falls only from above: from the cupola – an increasing ringing of bells. Parzival stands enchanted. Gurnemans: 'Now hold up: a fool you are, now let me see if you are aware also.' Muted trumpet-calls draw near. Solemn chanting from bass male voices: tenor voices respond from half way to the roof; from the highest part of the cupola echoes the chanting of boys' voices. Then, at the rear, to left and right, two great folding doors open. From the right the Knights of the Grail enter in grave and solemn procession; they take their places at the laid tables stretching in three groups from front to rear. From the left come the master-workmen and servants of the King. Anfortas is borne in on a litter: in front of him a knight bears a shrine covered by a purple velvet cloth: (carried upright behind Anfortas is a lance with blood-stained tip).[49] At the rear, beneath a baldachin in the elevated centre, is the couch to which Anfortas is led: before it stands an altar-like table upon which the covered shrine is placed. When all are in their places the singing ceases. Gurnemans takes his seat at a table, staring the whole time at Parzival who stands motionless and speechless with amazement. From a vaulted niche far to the rear is heard the funereal voice of old <u>Titurel</u>: 'My son Anfortas, are you about your duty?' Silence – 'Must I die without welcoming the Saviour?' Anfortas breaks out in profound complaint: he cannot any longer discharge his duties. He describes his sufferings. The knights complain and mutter. Titurel's voice: 'Uncover the Grail!' The shrine is uncovered, the sacred crystal cup taken from within and solemnly set before Anfortas. – Anfortas covers his eyes. Titurel's voice: 'Speak the blessing!' Anfortas, gazing at last towards the vessel with increasing rapture, expresses his inspired and, at the same time, contrite emotions. The devotion of all is at its height. From the cupola a blinding shaft of light shines into the cup which begins to gleam fiery crimson. All sink to their knees: a ray of hope enters into Anfortas' soul also. Never, since

53

his fall, has the Grail gleamed with so pure a gleam as today: is it salvation, is the Redeemer here? With both hands he elevates the Grail, allowing it to shine in every direction. From Titurel – a sigh of well being. – From high up, voices sound. Titurel speaks the blessing: twilight descends on all the hall: only the Grail gleams bright. When it becomes light again, the tables are provided with wine and bread; the Grail no longer gleams and is returned to its shrine. During the singing, which celebrates holy brotherly love, the knights eat. Anfortas alone feels worse than before: he has again to be carried off in the litter; his wound has re-opened: the Redeemer has remained silent. The procession forms up in order of arrival. To sad, solemn music, all again depart: high up, the bells grow silent: the light grows fainter. – Parzival has stood motionless with amazement: but during Anfortas' complaint, has once put his hand hastily to his heart. As last to leave, Gurnemans ill-humouredly steps up to him and shakes him: 'Why are you still standing there? You are just a fool! Out you go, do your thinking there!' He pushes him out of a side gate and bangs it after him, muttering. –

29 Aug. *[1865]*

Kundry has again vanished, fallen into a sleep of death. Klingsor has again won power over her soul: he needs the help of this the most wondrous of womanly beings to deliver his main blow. At his castle, in an inaccessible dungeon, he sits in his magician's workshop: he is the daemon of hidden sin, the raging of impotence against sin. Using his magician's power, he conjures Kundry's soul to him; her spirit appears in the depths of a dark cave. From the conversation of the two the following relationship emerges. Kundry is living a never-ending life of constantly alternating re-births as the result of an ancient curse which, in a manner reminiscent of the Wandering Jew, condemns her, in new shapes, to bring to men the suffering of seduction; redemption, death, complete extinction is vouchsafed her only if her most powerful blandishments are withstood by the most chaste and virile of men. So far, they have not been. After each new and, in the end, profoundly hateful victory, after each new fall by man, she flies into a rage; she then flees into the wilderness and by the most severe atonements and chastisements is for some time able to escape the power of the curse upon her; yet it is denied to her to find salvation in this way. Within her again and again unconsciously arises the desire to be delivered by a man, this being the sole manner of deliverance indicated to her by the curse: thus does innermost necessity cause her constantly to fall victim anew to the power which drives her to be reborn as a seductive woman. The penitent then falls into a death-like sleep: it is the seductress who wakes, and who, after her mad frenzy, becomes again a

54

penitent. As no one but a man can deliver her, she has taken refuge as a penitent with the Knights of the Grail; here, amongst them, must the redeemer be found. She serves them with the most passionate self-sacrifice: never, when she is in this state, does she receive a loving look, being no more than a servant and scorned slave. Klingsor's magic has found her out; he knows the curse and the power through which she can be forced into his service. To avenge the dreadful disgrace he once suffered from Titurel, he traps and seduces the noblest Knights of the Grail into breaking their vow of chastity. What, however, gives him power over Kundry, this most exquisite instrument of seduction, is not solely the magic power through which he has mastery over the curse weighing upon Kundry, but the most powerful assistance he finds in Kundry's own soul. – Since only one man can redeem her, and she therefore feels given to him in complete submission, her experience of the weakness of these men cannot but fill her with strange bitterness: feeling that only that man can destroy and deliver her who withstands the full force of her feminine charms, she is again and again lured by something deep down in her soul to undertake the test anew: but mixed with this is her scorn, her despair at being subjugated to this feeble breed, and a fearful blazing hatred which disposes her for the destruction of men, but which at the same time repeatedly re-arouses her wild loving desire in a consuming, fearfully fiery manner to that fit of ecstasy by means of which she can work magic, at the same time, however, becoming the slave of it. Her latest task, under Klingsor's guidance, has been the seduction of Anfortas. The sorcerer's one wish was to have Anfortas in his power: he planned for him the same disgrace that, in raving blindness, he once inflicted on himself: he managed to lure the Keeper of the Grail himself into the arms of the wondrously seductive woman Kundry was recreated as, and while he was lost in her embrace, the knights now subservient to Klingsor fell upon him; they were not allowed to kill him; the vigilant Gurnemans, calling upon the aid of the Grail, was successful in freeing the already wounded Anfortas. Thus was Klingsor deprived of the prize of his venture: Kundry, to her distress, had fared better in proving her power anew! After violent ravings, she again awoke penitent. From one state to the next, she carries no real consciousness of what has passed: to her it is like a dream experienced in very deep sleep which, on waking, one has no recollection of, only a vague, impotent feeling prevailing deep down inside. Yet she gazes with both sadness and scorn at the wounded man, whom she, penitent now, again serves with most passionate devotion, but – without hope, without respect. Now it is necessary for Klingsor to have Parzival in his power. He knows the prophecies there are about this wonder-child. He fears that he may have been summoned to deliver Anfortas and take his place with a power that cannot be overcome. Against him it is that Kundry is now to exert all her power. Summoned by

55

Klingsor, Kundry's soul trembles. She resists. He threatens. She curses. Fearful secrets. Finally, discord in Kundry's soul: hope for deliverance through defeat: – but then an insane desire to enjoy love for a last time. Klingsor's laugh. – Sound of weapons. From outside, the threatening voice of Parzival. Kundry disappears. 'To work!' Klingsor springs on to the wall; he watches the fight between Parzival and the enchanted knights. Klingsor laughs at their loutish jealousy as they defend the way to the she-devils they love: he delights when they are overcome by Parzival and killed or put to flight. He grants it to all Knights of the Grail to kill each other in this fashion. His gaze follows Parzival now striding, childishly proud, through the open gate, now turning towards the garden. 'Ah, childish offspring! Be summoned for what you may: you are still too stupid, and you are forfeit to me. Here, eternal Lord of the Grail, you will come to a sweet end.' – He vanishes. –

  Parzival has entered Klingsor's wonderful magic garden: his astonishment at the unutterable charm is mingled with an uneasy feeling of alarm, hesitation and horror. But he is not to compose himself: from various directions, singly, beautiful women rush in, their hastily donned attire disordered, their hair dishevelled, etc. They have heard sounds of fighting: waking, they have found themselves abandoned by their lovers; some have run to the battlements, seen the fight, and report to the other women that their lovers have been fought with, put to flight, indeed, laid low by the bold stranger. Lamentation and imprecations: they rush at Parzival. Their threats, reproaches, lamentations are mollified at the sight of the hero and the realization of how handsome, how child-like and artless he is. Some mock him, others invite him to make reparation for their lost lovers: soon he is being flattered and petted. Amazed, but wholly artless, Parzival abandons himself to what he takes to be a childish game without any thought of there being a serious side to the situation. Soon jealousy and argument arise amongst the women: some, having withdrawn into arbours, now return with hair charmingly adorned, and in daintily neat attire; they are scorned by the others, but imitated. The coquettish game for Parzival's favour degenerates into quarrelling and wrangling. Parzival still responds as if to childish play: refuses to understand anything and treats nothing seriously. Their derision turns against him: their scolding and mockery make him almost angry: he is about to flee. Then he hears the loud, loving sound of a woman's voice calling him by name. He stops, shaken, believing it to be his mother, and stands, greatly affected, rooted to the spot. The voice admonishes Parzival to stay: here he will experience great happiness: she orders the women to leave the youth; he is for none of them: their lovers have been preserved: they would fain return and urge them to be at peace. Hesitatingly the women obey: dejectedly they leave Parzival, each secretly preferring him to her own lover: gently and flatteringly they leave him and go separate ways. Parzival, now sure that he is dreaming, gazes timidly to see where the voice has come from. Then, in a grotto, upon a couch of flowers, he sees a young woman of the greatest beauty, Kundry, in new, wholly unrecognizable guise. Still standing far off, he asks in amazement if it was she who called. Kundry: Did he not know that she had long been awaiting him here? What then had brought him here if not the wish to find her? Parzival, wondrously attracted, approaches the grotto. His emotions are mingled with vast unease; his earlier cheerful artlessness deserts him; a deep seriousness descends upon him, a vague feeling of there being a most momentous decision at hand. The wonderful woman knows how to stir the tenderest chords of his emotion by touching intimately and solemnly on his memories of childhood; evening, morning, night – the complaints, fond embraces of his mother; the longing of that distant, forsaken woman for her son, her languishing, despair and death. Parzival, overcome by fearful emotion and overwhelming melancholy, sinks weeping at the beautiful woman's feet: he is tormented by dreadful remorse. Bending over him, she puts her arms gently about his neck. Soothing and chiding of his immoderate grief. Not all that could make him happy was contained in his mother's love: the last breath of motherly longing is the benediction of the first kiss of love. Bending her head above his, she now presses her lips to his in a long kiss. Suddenly the youth springs up with an expression of utter terror. With this kiss a dreadful change has taken place in him: he puts his hand to his heart; there suddenly he feels the wound of Anfortas burning; hears rising from deep within him Anfortas' lamentation. 'The wound! The wound is bleeding here! Miserable one, and I could not help you!' To the horror and amazement of the beautiful woman he responds with a cold stare: the mysterious happening witnessed at the Castle of the Grail claims him entirely; transferred wholly into the soul of Anfortas, he feels Anfortas' enormous suffering, his dreadful self-reproach; the unspeakable torments of yearning love, the unholy terrors of sinful desire, even there, beholding the wondrous Grail, permeated by the gleam of its sublime ecstasy, annihilated by the Divinity of its world-redeeming balm. He invokes the Grail, the Blood of the Redeemer: he hears Divine lamentation over the fall of the Chosen One; he hears the Saviour's cry for the relic to be freed from the custody of besmirched hands: and he himself has experienced this monstrous suffering, he himself has witnessed the agonies of the guilt-laden man: to his innermost being there has been a loud appeal for deliverance, and he has remained dumb, has fled, wandered, child-like, dissipating his soul in wild, foolish adventures! Where is there a man sinful and wretched as he? How can he ever hope to find forgiveness for his monstrous neglect of duty? – The woman, amazed and lost in passionate admiration, seeks vainly to silence him. He sees her every gaze, hears her every word, as if from Anfortas' soul: this is how the wretched woman looked, this is how she spoke, this is how she twined her arm about his neck; these are the fearful agonies he has had to bear away with him as his reward! 'Corrupter, depart from me!' Now the woman's soul blazes with insane desire. 'Cruel one! If you feel the agonies of others, then feel also mine! In you I am to find deliverance, in you alone to die! For you I have waited throughout eternities of misery: to love you, to be yours for one hour, can alone repay me for torments such as no other being has ever suffered!' – Parzival: 'You will be damned, with me, for eternity if for but one instant I forget my mission in your arms! I have been sent for your salvation also. Madwoman, do you not realize that your thirst is only increased by drinking: that your desire is extinguished only through lacking appeasement?' All the torments of the human heart lie open to him: he feels them all and knows the only way of ending them. The woman: 'So it was my kiss that made you see clearly? Oh, fool! Embrace me now in love, so shall you be this very day God himself. Take me only for one hour to your heart, and let me then be damned for eternity! – I want no deliverance: I want to love you!' Parz. 'I will love and deliver you if you will show me the way to Anfortas.' She rages. 'Never shall you find it. Let him who has fallen perish.' He persists. She demands as payment an hour of love. He repulses her. She beats her breast, calls madly for help. She is still powerful enough, she says, to lead him astray so that he will never find the Castle of the Grail: she curses the tracks and paths! Klingsor appears on the tower of the castle: men-at-arms come running: Parzival recognizes the lance with which Anfortas was wounded,[50] wrests it from the knight: 'With this sign I banish you. As the wound shall close that this spear made, let all here perish, and this splendour fall in ruins!' – He brandishes the lance: with a fearful noise the castle crumbles, the garden withers and becomes a desert. Parzival, from afar, gazing back at Kundry who has collapsed screaming: 'You know where you can see me again!' He hastens away through the ruins.

At Monsalvat there is grief and confusion. Anfortas can no longer be moved to preside over the office of the Grail. Tormented beyond all bounds, he wishes to obtain death by defiance: he no longer wishes to behold the Grail, which seems to have wrapped even its miraculous power in mourning, its gleam, since Parzival's presence, having grown steadily fainter. For long now, the sacred vessel has remained locked in its shrine. All are starving and demoralized. The knights are obliged to seek profane food; their strength is waning; they are no longer sent out. Titurel, deprived of the sight of the life-giving relic, himself incapable of still performing the office, has died. Anfortas longingly awaits his own death. The knights besiege his chamber, assail him, weeping and threatening: steadfastly he refuses: he wants to die. – Gurnemans, under such circumstances rapidly aged and become almost a childish old man, has retired to the sacred spring at the edge of the forest, there to die a hermit. Not long before, he has again discovered

Kundry, lying, as always, in death-like sleep; after again awakening her, he notices a great change in contrast to previously: awaking, she is not amazed, does not curse, but, on the contrary, attends him gently and constantly. But no word is to be got out of her: she seems utterly to have lost her tongue. – One beautiful spring morning Kundry is drawing water at the spring for Gurnemans who is lying before his hut in prayer. Slowly from the distance Parzival is seen approaching: he is all in black armour; with head bowed and lance lowered, he approaches dreamily and sinks down on a grassy seat near the spring. His visor is shut. Gurnemans notices and addresses him. To all questions, Parziv. only shakes his head sadly. At last Gurnemans, put out, rebukes him for stopping here with helmet closed and armed with shield and lance. Does he not know what day it is? – 'No' – Where does he come from then? He can hardly have lived amongst Christians not to know that today is most holy Good Friday? – Parz. is long silent. Then he opens his helmet, removes it from his head, drives the lance into the ground,[51] lays shield and sword before it, sinks to his knees, and fixing his eyes fervently on the blood-stained point of the lance, prays earnestly. – Gurnemans gazes at him with emotion, believes he recognizes him and summons Kundry as witness. She, with a quiet nod, affirms him to be the same who once appeared by the lake and killed the swan. Parzival is questioned. He too recognizes the old man and now tells how long he has wandered vainly searching for the Castle of the Grail where he has a great offence to atone for. He had despaired of ever again finding the way; by penances of every kind he had wished to partake of the grace to be guided aright: in vain: his works were not so powerful as the magic which condemned him to wander! Can the old man give him news? Gurnemans answers sadly that his tidings will not cheer him, and reports all the wretched events at Monsalvat. Parziv., tormented by remorse at not having alleviated this distress long before, chides his blindness, his childish foolishness, and, overcome with grief, falls back in a swoon. Kundry leaps forward: she fetches water in a large bowl. Gurnemans restrains her: there, by the spring itself, shall the pilgrim be bathed: he will, he suspects, today have a high office to perform; for that he must be purified, and all the dust of his long wandering washed from him. Both gently escort the revived Parzival to the spring. Parzival asks if the old man will escort him to Anfortas? Gurn: Certainly, we will go together to the castle today: the funeral rites of Titurel, my dear master, are being celebrated. Anfortas has vowed to expose the Grail once more for the canonization of his father who has died through his fault. Meanwhile Kundry has loosed his greaves and is now bathing his feet; he gazes at her with amazement and emotion, and then asks Gurnemans to moisten his head also with the holy water: the latter consecrates him for his appointed task, sprinkling his head with water. Then Parziv. sees Kundry produce a golden phial from her bosom, pour precious balm from it on to his feet, anoint them and then dry them with her hair. 'If you anoint my feet, so let Gurnemans anoint my head also: for I am to be King!' Gurnemans takes and anoints his head and pronounces the blessing. Softly and unnoticed, Parzival scoops water from the spring in the bowl and moistens Kundry's head with it: 'My first duty I discharge thus: be baptized and believe in the Redeemer.' – Kundry lowers her head and appears to weep. – With gentle delight Parzival gazes at wood and meadow. How wonderfully all is in bloom and speaking to him in soft colours, sweet shapes and gentle fragrance: never has he seen the meadow so beautiful. Gurne: 'It is the magic of Good Friday, lord.' Parz. 'The day of greatest grief? Ought not all creation rather to be mourning?' – Gurnem: 'You see it is not so: today all animal creation is glad to gaze up at the Redeemer. Not being able to see him upon the cross, it gazes up at Man Redeemed; who, through God's loving sacrifice, has a feeling of holiness and purity, the meadow flowers notice that man does not trample them today, but, as God took pity on mankind, spares them: now all that is blooming and soon to die, gives thanks; it is Nature's Day of Innocence.' Kundry, slowly raising her head, gazes up at Parzival earnestly and calmly beseeching. Parz. 'Today is the great Day of Innocence: rise up and be blissful.' – He kisses her on the brow. – Ringing of bells, chorus of men's voices approaching from afar. – Gurnemans: 'The hour is come: midday, as before. Follow me.' Parzival, armed by them both, solemnly takes the lance and, with Kundry, follows Gurnemans. – As the singing swells and the bells sound louder, the scene gradually changes as in Act 1. In the corridors – processions of knights in mourning garb. Nearer at hand – lamentations for the dead. – A funeral procession. – Then, return to the Great Hall. Dirges sung by bass, tenor and soprano voices: in place of the table before the baldachin, the catafalque. Enter procession of knights: from the other side, Anfortas, on his sick bed, behind Titurel's coffin: in front, the shrine containing the Grail. Dim twilight. When, with all in their places, the lid of the coffin is removed – a violent burst of lamentation: Anfortas raises himself from his sick-bed under the baldachin. Such is his despair that he condemns the knights for wishing to force him again to work the magic of the Grail, here, in sight of the father he has killed! His wound, since the ending of reanimation through the Grail, has moved fatally close to his heart: another day perhaps, and death will be assured. Why this fearful cruelty of casting him once again back into life? – He again refuses. Attempts at compulsion. Muttering and threats from the knights. Anfortas: 'Madmen, with what will you threaten me, when death is my deliverance?' – Then Parzival steps forward. 'Live, Anfortas, live in repentance and atonement. Your wound I close thus:' He touches Anfortas' thigh with the spear. Parzival goes on to describe to him his suffering, his error, his inner agony: from all shall he now be delivered: the magic to which you

60

succumbed is broken; strong is the magic of him who desires, but stronger is that of him who denies. 'Thanks be to your suffering: it has made me a fellow-sufferer; be thankful for my foolishness, through which I was able to attain to knowledge. I can perform the Office, and shall, so that you may be delivered!' – Anfortas, suddenly healed, has taken and elevated the Grail from its shrine: the Grail now gleams forth at its brightest; a halo is spread over all around; Titurel rises from his coffin and gives his blessing. Anfortas leads Parzival to his place beneath the baldachin: – Kundry embraces Parzival's feet and silently sinks lifeless before him. A white dove descends from the cupola and circles above Parzival. – Anfortas on his knees before him in homage. –

30 August (1865)

Well, that was help in need![52]

The entry for 31 August 1865 begins with a quotation from Tristan *Act III, 'The Ship' being also the name which Wagner had given to his Munich house in the Brienner Strasse to suggest the restlessness of his situation at that time. The King too knew this name and its significance. On 14 January 1867, desiring Wagner to return from Tribschen to Munich, he wrote '. . . again take up your abode in "The Ship" which henceforth shall bear you peacefully . . .' The quotation is a means of asking when Cosima is at last going to return, which was not in fact to be for another fortnight. In the entry of 31 August 1865, previously unpublished except for three sentences, his reproaches to her for not accompanying him (and Bülow) to Dresden to the funeral of Ludwig Schnorr von Carolsfeld are unjustified and unjust, and to be seen as the result of extreme emotional strain.*

31 Aug *[1865]*

[['The ship – do you not yet see it?' –]]

As long as I sat working at Parzival, my imagination helped beautifully: [[– whenever the red curtain at the door moved my heart trembled: – she is coming in! –]]

Now the ideal tension is dispersed. –

Reality has again to be overcome, whole and naked!

[[– Tomorrow she is travelling to Segszard[53] – for four days, – then to Venice[54]: wherever they take her to. – And she does not understand me! Amidst all the explanations for me it doesn't occur to her how fearfully bitterly I suffer from her being far away. – And yet how long is it since she also failed to understand me. I was going to Tristan's funeral, to see the Dear One once more: quite automatically I assumed <u>She</u> would accompany me. As she is not to, I too declare myself unwilling to go for some reason or other: she comes and cleverly and amiably tries to persuade me, putting this and that to me: I became furious and violent, argued the futility of the reasons adduced. <u>Nothing</u> did any good: in the end I had to tell her, actually tell her that I was not going to be parted from <u>her</u>, and would even abandon seeing my departed friend once more if <u>she</u> would not accompany me! – That would never have occurred to her! Only when she hurries home to insist on coming too, do I finally resolve to perform my precious

62

duty towards my friend. – In the end I do have to go without her: separation from her makes me more miserable than grief for him I have lost! Thus it was. I was obliged to tell myself every instant! – And she? ? – I come back and have to count the days until it shall please another to leave her to me. – She goes away, and not to a gloomy funeral – no! – She lets herself be taken here, taken there, – and when all has been settled, she will, I suppose, come back again too. –

Dear wife! I know that you suffer through this! But that you cannot so much as imagine my suffering, does tell me that man's love is deeper than woman's! –

And now I am suffering because of you! Your misunderstanding must in the end only cause me fresh sorrow on your account. – Ah, heavens! You cannot do otherwise, – I must not! It is misery! –

But – I do love you more than you me! – this sad conceit you must leave me! – Oh! –]]

Wagner's entry dated 1 September below is one of those rendered illegible by Eva's pasting over. Now recovered, it confirms facts hitherto only guessed at relating to Cosima's association with Wagner in the summer of 1864. In his biography of Cosima, Max Millenkovich-Morold wrote in 1937: 'For Cosima the tugging of her heart had become the voice of fate which she did not for one instant hesitate to follow. Her husband she left in no doubt of this; her father too seems soon to have become party to the secret.' This was in August 1864 which suggests that Bülow was also in the know by then, although whether through Cosima herself or on the basis of his own experience, must remain open.

Wagner writes subsequently, on 1 September 1865, that 'a year ago', that is, in the summer of 1864, Liszt was doubting the genuineness of his love for Cosima, and saying it would come to his treating him with contempt. That was on 30 or 31 August 1864 at the Villa Pellet by the Starnberger See when Liszt, returning from the Karlsruhe Music Festival, paid Wagner a brief visit.[55] Cosima had also been to Karlsruhe and returned to the Starnberger See with her father. In Karlsruhe, Liszt had taken her seriously to task as well, she having probably told him of her relationship with Wagner (v. p. 75 note and text). Liszt had no doubt thought by intervening to make them see sense and save Cosima's marriage. Certainly he could not have known the fateful nature of Cosima's bond with Wagner, otherwise he would hardly have advised Bülow to accept Ludwig II's summons and move from Berlin to Munich.[56] He did, however, take obvious care to separate Cosima and Wagner for a considerable time. Three days after Liszt's departure from Starnberg on 31 August 1864, Bülow and Cosima, together with their daughters Daniela and Blandine, set off back to Berlin to put their move in hand. It was not until seven weeks later, on 24 November 1864, that they arrived at Munich and moved into rooms of their own at 15 Luitpoldstrasse,[57] *whereas previously, in July and August 1864, they had lived with Wagner at the Villa Pellet. Wagner meanwhile had moved from the Starnberger See also to Munich, and was living at 21 Brienner Strasse. Cosima now had her own house to look after but, her work done, she would go to Brienner Strasse to look after Wagner's too.*[58]

When, a year after Liszt's first intervention (at the end of August 1864) the relationship still persisted, Liszt made a second attempt to 'divert Cosima's thoughts'. On 8 August 1865 he got her to come, with her husband, via Vienna to Budapest where, on 15 August 1865, he was giving the première of his St Elisabeth.[59] *Cosima and Bülow did not return to Munich until 13 September 1865. He thus kept Cosima from Wagner for over five weeks, although of course without achieving the desired result.*

The realization of this by Wagner explains his deep ill-will towards Liszt which, in the entry below, extends to hated and unjustified accusations. But Wagner was far too fond of Liszt ever to have repeated words prompted by the exceptional emotional strain of the time. Eva knew it too, which is why she ought not to have undertaken the senseless pasting over. There was subsequently, it is true, a cooling-off in Liszt's attitude towards Wagner, and towards Cosima in particular,[60] *but no actual break took place. Wagner's affection for Liszt was genuine, and his gratitude towards him almost boundless. He showed this at Bayreuth in 1876 at a celebration banquet after the* Ring *première when, before an audience of some 700, he said, indicating Liszt: 'Here is the one who first had faith in me when I was as yet unknown, and without whom you would perhaps not have heard a note of mine, my dear friend – Franz Liszt!' (Glasenapp, Vol. V, p. 298.)*

[[1 September *[1865]*

No! It is not until tomorrow that is she going to Segszad.[61] – 'Father says we are staying on till Saturday in Budapest.' Father says 'I need to recover'. 'We are going to Venice.' And at the same time keeping on making herself believe I wanted to hurt her; probably didn't love her at all! In the end your father's right, – he told me a year ago of course 'it would turn out like this, – He would treat me with contempt!' –

Oh, to have to bear this insanity ! ! – It is so ignoble, so unworthy to brood over such things. But what is left to him who is abandoned, lonely, childishly misjudged? –

I know, – you'll realize it, violently, passionately, and beautifully! – But it was possible, and will again become possible! – And from Rome[62] will come letters again, – and everything will be just so again – and me? – I shall finally come to hate my Friend completely! I do not believe in his love. He has never loved. He who loves can complain, and does not enter into special relationship with the Good God. The pious man does not love: what matters to him is simply domination. I know what I am saying. To me all this Catholic rubbish is repugnant to the very depths of my soul: anyone who takes refuge in that[63] must have a great deal to atone for. Once you revealed it to me, speaking in a dream: it was dreadful. Your father is repugnant to me. – and when I was able to bear him, there was more Christianity in my blind indulgence than in all his piety. – You need recuperation, also distraction – don't you? – Don't talk to me of your love ! ! –]]

2 Sept. *[1865]*

What to do about the blood-stained lance? – The poem says the lance is supposed to have been produced at the same time as the Grail, and clinging to the tip was a drop of blood. – Anyway, this is the one which has caused Anfortas' wound: but how does this hang together? Great confusion here. As a relic, the lance goes with the cup; in this is preserved the blood that the lance made to flow from the Saviour's thigh. The two are complementary. – So, either this: –

The lance has been entrusted to the knights at the same time as the Grail. When trouble presses hard it is even borne into battle by the Keeper of the Grail. Anfortas, in order to break Klingsor's magic, which is so fatal to the knights, has taken it from the altar and set off with it against the arch-foe. Succumbing to seduction, he let shield and spear fall, the sacred weapon was stolen from him and used to wound him as he turned to flee. (Perhaps because Klingsor is anxious to have Anfortas in his power alive, he commands the lance to be used against him, knowing that it wounds but does not kill. Why?) The healing and deliverance of Anfortas is now logically only possible if the lance is rescued from impious hands and reunited with the Grail.

Or this: –

On being entrusted with the Grail, the knights were also promised the lance: only it must first be won by hard fighting. Were it one day to be united with the Grail, then nothing more could assail the knights. Klingsor has found this lance and is keeping it, partly because of its powerful magic – it is capable of wounding even the godliest of men if any fault attach to him – and partly to withhold it from the Community of the Grail, for, by winning it, they would be invincible. Anfortas has now gone forth to deprive Klingsor of this lance: seduced by love, he is wounded by Klingsor's hurling the lance at him. – The continuation now remains the same: it has got to come into the knights' possession. – Klingsor hurls the spear at Parzival: he catches it; he knows about it, knows its power, its significance. –

Which is better, Cos[64] – ?

Oh, anything, anything is better than to be so Godforsaken as I was yesterday! – How I 'complained'! –

– I expect I had been working too hard. I am, I'm afraid, still always too passionate in all that I do, – even my work: I had merely finished a day too early: now I was having to atone for it. My suffering had got very much worse. –

Well, today you are going to Baron Augus! He is someone I have also come to know. It is the affable who are dangerous; one credits them with depths, with a divine needs-must, and then, occasionally, is ashamed for having gone much too far. Only one have I found with this divine needs-must in his soul: my Parzival, my son in the Holy Spirit. –

Oh, if only the magic word could be found to enlighten your people concerning you completely! What they know of you remains defective, only half complete. Now they're dragging you around. I am deeply humiliated by their being allowed to! But that you should not really be letting yourself be dragged but, to deaden your suffering, your weakness, should now be trying to make yourself believe that it is all right like this too, and this and that has indeed its own truth too, and everything that I know of, and what they say to you: – then I could, and can, not look on any more: then nothing has any sense for me any more, and my love seems weakness even to me. To me you then seem wholly lost, completely unfaithful.

Oh – to work ! ! –

3 Sept *[1865]*

[['It must be so!' – [65]

It cannot be otherwise! – Our love can only be suffering! – Let us suffer then, but let us suffer gently! I cannot cope with the storms any more. – Let us be close, let us stay close – that is all! Let us control the suffering: let us assuage it! Perhaps the sharp quills will now soon be blunted; they have stabbed enough; let us, with artistry, grind away at the points so that they become rounded and slide. That is a good form of labour, and with each effort the rough edges are smoothed! –

I am so tired, so tired! But I know now I can still succeed: I learn it by holding out now.]] At last I have written to Malvina[66]: I have written not a word to her of

Tristan. Not to speak of him is for me a necessity. I notice that I have been put into a dream-like state by this death. If I remain in this state I dream, and like that it is fine: In it I am inviolable and at home! To speak, to hear, any word of him rouses me from that dream, and the awakening is fearful: [[I am not able, and do not care, to endure life; I cannot exist. All is madness to me! – See, I am doing it now with you! I cannot speak of you. As no one gets shown in to see me that is tantamount to my not being allowed to think of you; i.e. to not conceiving that you really exist and are now merely far away from me, worshipping your father daily and doing this and that: but this I can only not – conceive thus when I do not think at all of your person. I have, concerning you, to end up wholly in a dream; my whole day, my waking has to be a dream: then it is fine; then, inside me, I am profoundly at peace with you, then there is no disturbance at all and I am united with you completely. Then I delight in what I am doing, delight in the sky, the garden, my house, the deep peace around. A letter from you banishes the dream. Write what you will, I feel miserable; I can then no longer deny the reality of separation; everything that is supposed to gloss over it excites my wrath; scorn and shame on all that is supposed to comfort me! – Oh, from this dream no awakening! –

And so – I must turn all of life into a dream for myself! It can be done, and I shall write all my works provided I am never dragged out of my dream concerning the world. I must not truly see its reality: I cannot any more. But – in the dream it looks bearable, and the dream state itself is fine precisely because it is a dream. In this dream I now enclose myself together with you, my Cosima! Be ever with me, ever dreaming with me. Suffering but always dreaming. No talk any more, ever, no talk of love, of our love, ever, – but loving and – dreaming. And in this dream, let us create what shall rock the world into a dream. How wonderful dying, falling out of this dream into sleep, will be! –]]

4 Sept [1865]

Yesterday I was stirred out of my dream. Mathilde Maier[67] sent me the picture you had forwarded for me of your father, the latest photograph, in abbé costume, with unwrinkled face, youthful, defiant and bold. Do those things go together? More in keeping would have been a sword. Strange aberrations! You your father seems to like making old: his favourite way of arranging your hair makes you ugly and quite alien to me: it doesn't suit you, – God knows why he likes it. To me you ought not to have sent this portrait. I am leaving it in the Brown Book too. Of the portrait of your father M.M. wrote that this was the first thing she had not liked sending me. I sent it straight back.

Now I must try to lose myself in the dream again. Oblivion! – Perhaps Siegfried will help. –

5 Sept. *[1865]*

Yesterday I was in Grosshesselohe. I rambled again through the wood by the Isar. It was there that my head rested on your lap! – With the evening light and a beautiful sunset the journey back was splendid: I gazed at the distant city growing closer – No feeling of home at all! The city itself no facial expression either! And should I say where I should like better? – Nowhere! It's all the same where I am – If I can only dream: dearest to me is what disturbs me least in that. –

Dreaming and – sleeping! –

The entry dated 9 September 1865 which follows, was pasted over by Eva. No reason can be seen unless she regarded the 'childish' applied to the King, as a lèse majesté. Wagner explains here his disinterest in the monumental Munich Festival Theatre to be built at the King's desire by Gottfried Semper, and says he thinks the King childish for persisting so passionately with this plan; his friend Semper's approaching visit on this matter was therefore disagreeable to him.

To understand Wagner's attitude it should be borne in mind that on 26 November 1864, Ludwig II had decided to build a great stone theatre at Munich for complete performances of Wagner's Nibelung's Ring. *A month later, on 29 December 1864, he commissioned the architect Gottfried Semper, an old friend of Wagner's from Dresden days, now living in Zürich, whom Wagner had himself suggested for the task, to produce drawings. In his decision the King was following an idea of Wagner's expressed by him in 1862 in the foreword to the edition of his* Ring *poetry. But Wagner was writing only of a temporary theatre, 'as simple as possible, perhaps only of wood' (Collected Prose and Poetry, Popular Edition, Vol. VI, p. 273). To that he held, and the King's plan failed to please him from the outset, although he encouraged Ludwig in his enthusiasm. The King wished the theatre to be ready by 1867 so that the* Ring *performances could take place in it. Wagner on the other hand, declared that it would be better first of all to build a temporary theatre in wood and possibly brick, in order 'first to solve certain problems experimentally'. From this the plan was developed for building a provisional theatre into the Munich Glaspalast, a great exhibition hall of iron and glass erected in 1854 (and destroyed by fire in 1931). The King gave his consent on 15 February 1865, but insisted that his plan for the monumental theatre with which he was becoming increasingly captivated, should be further elaborated at the same time. The building of the magnificent festival theatre was of almost greater importance to him than Wagner's performances.*

When, as soon happened, the commission to Semper of 29 December 1864 to produce drawings became known, an opposition front was immediately formed within the cabinet, the royal family and amongst the public. To erect a costly monumental theatre merely for the performances of one man was considered absurd. And as the building was to be financed out of the royal civil list, court officials were especially angered at the threat they could see to allowances they received from savings effected in this budget. They made efforts to rouse public opinion against the building, and against Wagner whom they imagined responsible, and these first found expression on 19 February 1865 in the Augsburger Allgemeine Zeitung. *At this the King temporarily abandoned the plan for the monumental theatre, and contented himself with the building of a provisional one beneath the roof of the Glaspalast. He insisted, however, on the grand project's being continued, and on 15 May 1865 wrote to Wagner: 'I hope the plans for the monumental building of the future will not be too long in appearing! – All must be fulfilled: I shall not weaken! – The boldest dream must be realized!'*[68]

Wagner's reserve towards the royal plan is explained by his considering the monstrous project inopportune. At the end of 1864 when Semper received the commission, he had begun scoring Act II of Siegfried *only in first draft, thus being unable to guarantee completion of the whole work until 1867, especially as in Munich he had no peace for composing. Besides which, for the time being, he was without singers suitable for the new tasks posed by the* Ring. *Light is thrown on this by a letter to Mathilde Maier*[69] *dated 31 December 1864. This, in the context of Mathilde's hearing trouble, states that Wagner himself has a 'longing for auditory peace' and would prefer to hear his works not at all rather than inadequately. For which reason he opposed what was 'unready, inadequate and distorting'. He goes on: 'Despite the enthusiastic determination of my young King, and the fact that he has summoned Semper in order to agree with him the commission for building my theatre, I still do not yet believe I shall really produce my works for myself and for you, because my lack of faith in the performers is too great.' He had first to train these performers for himself, and for this he demanded the setting up of a special music school, which the King also agreed to. In a letter to the King dated 30 July 1865, however, he complains about the building of this school being delayed by the court officials, and writes: 'I now regard this school . . . as the first and most important point of attack for the work of the future. . . . The opponents and attackers of your noble project regarding the Festival Theatre building are quite right to object and ask who, then, is to perform in it when it is ready.' And on 20 August 1865 he writes to the King that he must first be put into a state to complete his work in peace, that the music school must be established, and that 'consequently there is no hurry even for the provisional theatre'.*

Wagner was also sick of the public attacks against him personally which had sprung up and increased since the royal project for a Festival Theatre had become known towards the end of 1864. The reproaches against him concerned a matter which was not of his willing but of the King's, and which was even opposed to his own artistic interests. Of sole immediate importance to him was the music school for preparing performers for their future task in the Ring. *The carrying through of this involved difficulties enough. Why expose himself to attack on account of the King's senseless building project, especially as, in this form, it did not agree with his own ideas at all? On 13 September, four days after the* Brown Book *entry below, he writes to the insistent King pointing out that it would require four to five years to complete the Festival Theatre and referring him back to the provisional theatre in the Glaspalast.*

But even after Wagner's forced departure from Munich on 10 December 1865[70] because of the attacks against him, the King did not rest. Wagner meanwhile, on 12 January 1866, had resumed work on the Mastersingers' *score, interrupted in 1863, and had reached the orchestral sketch for Act III when, on 2 January 1867, he wrote bluntly to the King: 'Without the school, the theatre will be a piece of childish frippery.'[71] But the King did not react, and persisted with his plan for the monumental festival theatre unimpressed. It was not until March 1868 that the project was abandoned. For this there were several reasons of which the most important was that the King's passion for building had found other objectives in the raising of palaces: Linderhof and Neuschwanstein, on which work was begun in 1868. Also Wagner himself now asked him to abandon the building of any theatre, finally recognizing the impossibility of ever overcoming the Munich difficulties, and having, in the peace of Tribschen, returned to his old idea of producing his* Ring *in a simple theatre of beams and boards in some small remote town, such as he had long had in mind. In short, a Bayreuth.*

Some explanation must be offered of Wagner's reference in the entry below to his 'last Dresden journey'. His remarks about the building of the theatre applied to the King but were not directed against Semper. Quite the contrary, for he writes that if Cosima is not there, he can and will see nobody, not even the 'dearest' one, who here is Semper. Cosima had already experienced this reaction on 22 July 1865 when he had not wanted to attend the funeral of Ludwig Schnorr von Carolsfeld[72] in Dresden because Bülow would not allow her to make the journey with him. Then Cosima attempted to talk Hans von Bülow round, but did not succeed. Since Wagner could not absent himself from the funeral (which he in any case arrived late for), he was not able to persist in his refusal to travel and had to go to Dresden with Bülow alone and without Cosima. It was therefore all the more annoying to him when, two weeks later, on 8 August 1865, Cosima went with Bülow to Budapest to see Liszt, and was away for over a month. Her inability to go against her father's wishes was something he could not understand. But that in no way alters the fact that the reproaches made to her concerning her journey to Hungary and expressed with especial vehemence in the entry dated 11 September 1865 (v. pp. 74–75 and note) were without justification.

[[9 Sept. *[1865]*

Good morning! – Things are not well with me. My poor nerves! – A shock: Semper is here! Franz,[73] I'm afraid, has admitted to him that I am not away. I have got to the point of finding Semper's visit odious. God, what does a provisional or a definitive Festival Theatre matter to me, or all the architecture in the world! Cos is different. She has a heart full of wounds, and yet at the same time looks at pictures, people and buildings, listens to music, enjoys torch-light processions, etc. All of that can still exist for her, can, for she attends to it with mind and heart. That is what women are like! They can do anything. Not men. I at least quite certainly not. – You learnt that over my last Dresden trip. Now learn it again. I am not able, and do not care, to see any human being, not even the dearest and most intelligent when Cosima is not there: anything that happens when she is not there is torment to me. How I hate this projected theatre, indeed, how childish the King seems for insisting on this project so passionately: now here I am with Semper and supposed to deal with him, talk about the senseless project! I know of no greater torment than this which now faces me. – You see, – that is how I am! –

Yet what can you do about it: you have your father there too, of course. That, it goes without saying, is different! – Good! If only, in his proximity, your joy were pure and untroubled! Then I would <u>have</u> at last to be glad for you, as I love you. But like this? – Oh, oh! – It means having a great, great, very great deal of patience! – It is what I have <u>got</u> to have now! – Wicked one! –]]

10 Sept *[1865]*

'Everything in life repeats itself.' – Old proverb. Awareness of this grows clearer and clearer the longer one lives. On the one hand it is the basis of bad conscience, and on the other, of despair, of satiety with life. – Even this separation together with many of its torments I have lived through before – a year ago.[74] I shall live through it again. In a year's time Cos will have forgotten it all, what sufferings she has inflicted on me now, what torments of inner strife she has made for herself, and she will suddenly find that there is absolutely nothing for it but once again to obey some new decision of her father's, and – it will be the same all over again! –

One ought therefore to get used to it!! –

In the end, a life art form will emerge. This tendency of life is expressed incredibly positively and meaningfully by music. – The common life of the ordinary person is represented in the 'canon': a theme, unaltered, constantly repeated, complementary to itself solely through itself: a character that remains ever constant, so keeping all around it constant. But now comes the 'fugue': the theme remains basically always the same; but it has free contrapuntal counterparts which cause it to appear always in a new light: the theme itself shortens and extends itself, and modulates; the course of the fugue does not let itself be determined in advance, as that of the immutable canon does – and ends only on the pedal note of death. The great, rich character does not take it beyond the theme of a fine Bach fugue: and at best, as far as a splendid counter theme; that is then the triumph, and if the double fugue always shows both themes equally recognizably and significantly then life's finest course has been achieved. They interlace, part and unite; like a dance. But the piece remains always the same: it becomes highly varied but always repeats itself. – We two are living in just such a fine Bach double fugue. –

Your father's life's course is stated for me in the 'variation'. Here one has before one nothing except the theme, repeated ever anew, but always somewhat altered, adorned, decorated, in different clothes, now virtuoso, now diplomat, now martial, now spiritual, always amiable, always him, at bottom incomparable and for that reason presented to the world only in variation form; personality ever to the fore, noticeable above all, always so placed that the latter is shown to advantage, as under a prism, – ever unique, repeatedly astonishing, but always the same, and – following each variation, it goes without saying, applause. Then comes the peroration, the apotheosis – the coda of the variations. – I have nothing against this form: I think Beethoven has wrested great things from it: the adagios of his quartets, the Fourth Movement of The Eroica, the Andante of the C Minor Symphony are all built on variation form. For that sort of thing I am absolutely useless: I cannot produce even one variation on a theme! –

(Today in front of St Marks's![75] –

Even Ferry,[76] the good fellow, is here and plaguing me, and that too is fine and part of the fugue.)

72

The Illustrierte Zeitung has published a report about the Students' Association Jubilee at Jena, together with drawings. Amongst the three Nestors of the still-surviving, founders is a Pastor Riemann: his head appeals to me very, very deeply. I should like to get to know this man. The banquet, the Old German costume, many things – strangely! – touched, indeed – moved me in a most inspiring way! I gave way to gentle tears. – Heavens! I was overcome by something akin to <u>hope</u>! I wonder, is it possible? – Can something still come of this German nation? Are the seeds really present, I wonder? My heart told me what noble, quite incomparably beautiful things must come of it, if it became the uniquely right thing. See this head of Riemann's. That is the <u>German</u> ideal. Quite indescribable! Little emotion, no Hungarian, Polish or French flexibility, somewhat ponderous, ungraceful: but that thoughtful disposition! The naïve gaze, the strange faith it contains, the fanaticism! This Student Association! Is there anything more peculiar? Whatever is there in the world to compare it with? Thoroughly unique. Everything borders so close on the ridiculous: and now – here there are placid, almost philistine men, – they believe in it! And, we mustn't mock them. Behind the enthusiasm of the French when, in 1793, they let themselves be recruited into army camps and to the frontiers, the family hearth was hedged with horror, the scaffold and misery. The Frenchman is bloodthirsty: having served his Fatherland he has remained, de gaité de coeur, a soldier, made himself a soldier emperor and swaggered about the world. Anno 1813 in Germany it was different: there 14-year-old boys, and 60-year-old men, went running to camp! It was a fervent, sacred cause: to which were sung songs that sounded almost pious. That was hope! A Germany was to come into being. What that was supposed to be was shown after victory and betrayal. Then came the Students' Association. The League of Virtue was founded. All so fantastic that no human being could grasp it. But I did. Now it is <u>me</u> no one grasps: I am the most German being, I am the German spirit. Question the incomparable magic of <u>my</u> works, compare them with the rest: and you can, for the present, say no differently than that – it is <u>German</u>. But what is this <u>German</u>? It must be something wonderful, mustn't it, for it is humanly finer than all else? – Oh heavens! It should have a soil, <u>this German</u>! I should be able to find my people! What a glorious people it ought to become. But to this people only could I belong. –

Take a look at 'Riemann', and the Students' Association members there in Jena! – That's where I ought to be living, in a German university town like that! – Away with your Rome – and Hungary! – All that's gibberish! – [77]

The entry below dated 11 September 1865 is the last of the pages pasted over by Eva but recovered in 1974. It reveals that Wagner's depression had, by Cosima's return from her protracted journey to Hungary on 13 September 1865, developed to the point of fatalism. In this entry, Wagner no longer believes that the happiness he has found in possessing Cosima will continue, he doubts the genuineness of her love, asks himself what he means in her life, and is prepared to give her up. What we find here is no theatrical pose, but the real despair of a man who feels himself abandoned and betrayed. Wagner, in his despair, goes so far as to reproach Cosima with having 'run away' from her and Wagner's daughter Isolde, only four months old, in order to go 'adventuring'; next time, he says, he will take charge of the child himself. Cosima had indeed left Isolde with her two sisters from the marriage with Bülow, $2\frac{1}{2}$-year-old Blandine and Daniela, soon to be five – certainly under good care in her rooms at 15 Luitpoldstrasse, the young, 27-year-old wife being unable to evade her father's summons to be present at the première of his St Elisabeth. *Moreover, Wagner had reassured himself concerning his daughter's health by visiting Luitpoldstrasse immediately after his return from the Hochkopf hunting lodge. On 23 August 1865 (v. p. 43) he writes: 'Yesterday I visited the children. But merely saw Boni [Blandine] and Isolde. Isolde was asleep, but woke up at once . . . then she gave me a laugh.'*

Wagner's reference to Cosima's arriving back 'a year ago' from being with her father refers to Cosima's journey to Karlsruhe to Liszt, already examined on p. 63, on the occasion of the music festival there. The 'frail, miserable, lacerated' may be taken as some indication of the forcefulness of Liszt's reproaches concerning Wagner on that occasion, and Wagner was afraid that she would return from her trip to Hungary in a similar state, and that it would then go on like that. But in this he was wrong, and Liszt, for his part, failed to appreciate Cosima's steadfastness. The greatest of the difficulties concerning her relationship with Wagner were not to occur until after September 1865, but Cosima overcame them by her courage, diplomatic skill and – it must be said – true love for Wagner and unshakeable faith in his artistic mission, which it was the decree of fate she should assist to fulfilment.

[11 September 1865]

[[Your letter, my love! Again, sheer madness! Madness and no end to it! – In the midst of pure bliss, love, adoration, nature, music – and full of horror and trembling, crying out aloud and pining! – There's nothing more I can say. If it must be, then let it: I surrender. Perhaps that is what you need: your father will be pleased: he likes having you there, you like being there. Why me there too? You have too much! – I can't keep up any longer, except in feeling! God knows how you will come back. I know how you arrived back a year ago from being with your father: restless, faint, frail, miserable, lacerated! It was dreadful! I felt an anguish beyond all compare. So it will be now again. And in a year's time? – The Bach fugue – the same dance. – How do I appear to myself in the process? – And you go running away from little Isolde, for five weeks now – : That is how you deserve a sweet child! If you again go adventuring I shall take charge of the child myself, and you[78]]]

Following the entry of 11 September 1865 two pages have been cut out by Eva. This explains the great gap of six weeks until the next, still unpublished entry on 24 October 1865. In the interval Cosima, on 13 September, had returned from her five-week journey. On 23 October Wagner had to travel to Vienna for dental treatment. He took the Brown Book *with him. In Vienna he met his friends Dr Standhartner, Julius Fröbel and Heinrich Porges. With Fröbel, an editor on the Viennese journal* Der Botschafter, *he negotiated concerning a publication planned in Munich that was to promote his artistic and national ideas. Also he was trying to win over Porges for Munich.*

[[Vienna 24 October /1865/ the Brown Book again.

Oh Cosima! All the things I now know about! – Florence, Rome, Naples, Sicily, Spain – all is a matter of indifference to me, they will be nothing to me without you, and only by virtue of your being included in it all! – Oh foolishness still to try to seek salvation outside harbour when to run to harbour was the final salvation! – How easy death is: for me almost all is dead already. Am I the ghost, or is the world? Again I've grabbed at broken glass: the merest glimpse of this Vienna, and then tell myself it was her I once wanted to build my harbour! I'll give something, my love, not to see Paris again either: I'll have to feel hideously ashamed to tell myself there that there too I once wanted to be at home, – always with the glass-grabbing sensation! – Oh! –

My love, my love! Things really have gone nice and differently with us. There were a couple of stars which came together in constellation only every leap year: then they looked at each other in amazement, and did not know what next. Not a word they said, – they set, shone here and there, floated in broken glass – ether – and so it had to be. Then came death: they wanted to die. The spasm left hold, the crazy orbits reached out no more. As the sail, when the mad wind eases, trembles, falters and flutters, so I hung upon your lips, – ready for death ! And we knew all. And now the orbits are changed. – Now the eternal leap-year has been won. And now – you grow ever more beautiful to me ! – Everything I have lived away so quickly: nothing has held, no illusion. With us everything was willing. You are coming ever more beautifully to life again, so that less and less can I understand how I wandered distant from you for so long. Oh Cosima! Certainly you cannot see, looking at me, how I love you, how I respect and honour myself because you love me! Now I expect you will look shrewdly at me and laugh? –

No, imagine me now here in Vienna. I've been out, once, quite briefly, and now I've sworn only to drive out on my errands. I am now so hideously ashamed at having once run around here looking as if I fancied I'd make something out of it for myself, if not even find something in it. Fine nonsense! – Besides, certainly now after three years, the people here have become much more brutish. – No – my propylaea – quiet, peace – my Parzival and – and –and – high above, deep inside – who then? Probably you? – Ask! – Franz has just come and only just brought me your letter which you gave him – : yesterday, after our arrival, he was quite giddy with Vienna, and forgot it. My love, I thank you! – You do, don't you? Love me? –

Yesterday evening Standhartner was with me: we've put a lot in order. Today it's off with him to the dentist – it's that monster who will now decide my existence – that is to say, in Vienna. – This evening at Fröbel's. – Yesterday settled business. Received Porges III. Am being clever and awaiting chances. –

Oh heavens, now into my house – and never again any further than to the Nymphenburg and the English Garden ! And write pages and pages, no 'learned papers' – that goes without saying, for then I get a telling off – always music, nothing but music![79]

My love! I've slept well. How about you? And Isolde? –

Now I shall telegraph to you so that you have something for the witching hour. Dear Cosima! Cosima! Cosima! – – And once more – Cosima! – Shall I now be angry with your begetter, – that won't do? But that's what he's out for! The devil! – Adieu! –]]

The entry below 'At night, before bed' calls for more detailed comment. Cosima knew the part played by Mathilde Wesendonck in Wagner's life, knew that he had loved her, and was anxious lest the memory of her be still alive despite his having meanwhile become united with her, Cosima. At the end of April 1864, whilst staying with the Wille couple at Mariafeld in Switzerland before proceeding to Stuttgart (where, a few days later, he received King Ludwig's call to Munich), Wagner wrote Mathilde Wesendonck 'a final, sacred letter', of unknown content or, rather, no longer extant, whose purpose was to bring their

one-time relationship to an end. This letter he left with Frau Wille to be passed to
Mathilde Wesendonck. She, however, refused to accept it then, but did
accept it later, in October 1865, when redelivered by Frau Wille, and at once
expressed her opinion of it in a reply to the latter. This Frau Wille immediately
sent to Wagner in Munich. He first read it through briefly, and then once again
together with Cosima. After that (according to Cosima, on 22 October 1865) he
wrote Frau Wille the following letter: 'Herewith, Dear Lady, Mathilde's letter
returned. It could be more natural, less flowery: but only the true power of love
could give it the beauty it lacks. A disquieting fault of our friend has always been
the tendency to gloss over her own weaknesses, or – as it is vulgarly put – to
whitewash herself! A free, loving Forgive-me-I-have-sinned – never passes the
lips of him who is weak! I wish her well, happy woman! – ' This letter, together
with Mathilde Wesendonck's letter attached, was not, however, sent off,
presumably because Wagner was travelling to Vienna on the evening of the same
day (22 October 1865). Cosima found it next day and immediately wrote
reproaching Wagner who received her letter in Vienna on 24 or 25 October. In
the entry below, and then again for 28 October 1865, on page 80, Wagner
defends himself against Cosima's reproaches. (The abbreviations M.W., Fr. W.
stand for Mathilde and Frau Wesendonck respectively.) – Wagner's unposted
letter of 22 October 1865 to Frau Wille is in the Wahnfried Archive; of Mathilde
Wesendonck's letter to Frau Wille it is safe to assume that it, like other
letters also from Mathilde Wesendonck, was destroyed by Cosima.[80] In My life
(1963 edition, p. 853) Wagner has only the following on the subject of his letter
at the end of April 1864 which Frau Wesendonck did not at first accept: 'Frau
Wille . . . had initiated an agreement with the Wesendoncks, under which the
latter should make available to me a monthly subsistence of 100 francs; receiving
knowledge of this, I had no alternative but to notify Frau Wesendonck of my
immediate departure from Switzerland, and to request her most amicably to
regard herself as relieved of all concern on my account, I having ordered my
affairs entirely in accordance with my wishes. This letter, which she may have
considered compromising, was, I learnt later, returned by her to Frau Wille
unopened.'

[24 (or 25) October 1865]
At night, before bed.

Your letter has come from Munich. – you are right, my love! I myself cannot
understand how I was able to show you the letter from Frau W. Seeking now to
explain it to myself, I find that the sole explanation that I can find will, at the same

time, have to reassure you. Reading through the letter with you, I was truly shocked too: I had not even read it correctly or properly to myself; so preoccupied had I been while assimilating it that I was now first astonished at its contents. What you are to gather from this strange preoccupation I will excuse myself from explaining: it is too natural. Certainly now also for the first time it dawned on me what _my_ letter might then have contained: even of that my recollection was still only very vague. Whatever it may have been, I only know it was my beauty-urge ideally to cover up an indescribably disagreeable frame of mind from that time, in order – to save myself. I knew only that this letter from that time had been an external sign of the magnanimity of my heart, and must therefore have regarded it as a strangely veracious fate that _this_ letter was not accepted. I ought now to have demanded it back: over that you are right, my love. That I did not, is explicable to me only by my having in the end forgotten it in its wording, and ultimately by the bitterness having vanished completely from my heart. I did not demand of Frau Wille that she should give the letter to M.W., – but simply mentioned, by the way, that, if it had not yet been asked for, Fr. W. should certainly take it that she would also, through her, have nothing more to learn of me: this in order to explain my not sending her any greetings. Secretly I was malicious enough to wish her the humiliation that reading this letter ought once again to cause her. That may all have been unclear, unattractive and confused: the main thing in this matter was my preoccupation. You do me total and wicked, wicked injustice when you say that I wrote the unposted lines _for you_. – With that I put up only because I think I can see that I have deserved to suffer injustice, having in the whole matter acted with an unattractive preoccupation, of which, I am afraid, I became aware only – as I said – on reading Frau W.'s letter through again _with you_. – But never mind ! – Don't brood over it any more. It was not nice of me, but really only lack of thought. There is nothing, nothing else behind it! – But it has been a useful lesson to me. I thank you for it! –

26 Oct *[1865]*

Leafing through the Brown Book just now, I read a bit of Parzival. How that time lies once more like a sacred dream, – once more like a lost paradise behind me. – Oh Cosima! Will it ever come to my quietly completing my works and entering with you the promised land of peace? – How storms rage ever and ever anew! I desire – so it seems – the most unnatural state of affairs which the world just will not accede to. My trouble is great. Always something new hounds and oppresses. From within and from without. This love of the King's does seem a veritable martyr's crown. Treachery lurks within with an intensity which our tender longing for peace is no match for.[81] [[From without I hear the cry: it is high time, the catastrophe is in preparation; Germany must know what it has in the King, otherwise it will be too late: all is pressing for decision. [82] That, I consider, is not to be taken so literally. Yet I can well see that in no direction is one able to rock oneself to sleep in peace: how taken unawares we always are! How shall the work of all these troubles prosper? – My sole comfort now is that I know how pessimistic I have become, and that accordingly, in my pessimism, I exaggerate and may now and then be pleasantly disappointed. Sweet comfort! –

Oh, my love, my love! – Ought we then not soon to set out on the quiet way to the cooling couch? –

And what devil suddenly has me in this Vienna! My dentist finishes today, but I am not to travel on the same day because the slightest cold could cause me great trouble. But tomorrow will be Friday. To stay until Saturday merely to avoid Friday is too crazy. But as I am superstitious I shall, against this, let it depend on an omen: if today or tomorrow I receive a good letter from Monsalvat,[83] I shall defy Friday: if not, I shall avoid it. The day that I live I'll gladly give over to at last once properly preparing for myself the day that I shall live. –

Yesterday, as the result of a very, very poor night I was in a bad way: a tooth operation was undertaken; [reading] Balzac brought balm – in the evening an hour at the Standhartners'.[84] From Frankfurt I have good business news. Now today I'll just make ready to go to Rotsch.[85] to see what might come of it.]]

Oh heavens, would I could still be happily with you and little Isolde! 'Happy'!! Yes, we could be: [[I have the most incredible talents for being favoured: one only needs to pack me up properly and wrap me up a bit soft and immediately the gas inside becomes willing and rises freely into the air where then is smiling and bliss. – Ah! My love! My love! – Cosima – Cosima – Cosima!!]]

28 Oct. *[1865]* Morning

[[So, my sweet wife! That seems to be that then again, and done with. Tomorrow at this time I shall be resting in my beautiful bed and awaiting the witching hour. – I know now that I shall find peace: I know, you see, that without this peace being found it cannot go on at all any more. All my suffering is but lack of peace. Now let all conspire, – my peace they are to leave me: the first assault on that will drive me for ever from any connection with the world. Parzival is again wrapped round in a web: but I believe in him and do not budge. He will come, or I shall go. Peace I must have, and will! –

Ah Cosima! – how every nerve pains me! The speaking, the anxious brooding – they are killing me. –]]

Your letter was beautiful, but really sad: what a mean opinion you have of my delicacy of feeling! Shall my comfort always only be that, within I feel myself to be better than I appear to you! What now of your love if it has so little faith? Why do you so often so misunderstand my words! Why immediately interpret 'lack of thought' in a sense so disadvantageous to me! Did I mean by that that I was not aware of what I did, why apply this to my communication of the letter, and not, more correctly, rather to the fact that I was not paying attention to <u>what</u> I was communicating! But that is how it was! If I read a book, a newspaper, it constantly happens to me that some passage so powerfully engages me that for quite a time I read everything further merely quite mechanically, not being in the slightest aware what I am reading, for which reason, when reading seriously I very often have to go back again, having read whole pages while completely preoccupied, i.e., while concentrating on something else. Right on the first page of that letter, it was the bit about the 'gala humiliation, – if not', etc., which impressed me so completely as fundamentally typical that I read all that followed in a state of complete inattention. This – once again – was my 'lack of thought' – also the fact that I communicated the letter to you without having read it over calmly once again, which would probably have kept me from the foolishness of imparting to you this quid pro quo of an infirm vanity. Now you are so hurt, and tell me, tell me that you are unchanged, yet also that I am a really evil person. – Ah! –

[[From the formation of my teeth, the dentist promises me long life: we'll see what we make of it. What I am able to endure is unbelievable: and this dentist has again taught me. There is ultimately about all these pains something which merely passes around me and does not penetrate into my inner life: this remains often and constantly in secure, unassailable peace: to being only lovingly active the obstruction is from outside, and for that reason I am so unhappy because I am quite aware of this yet cannot substantiate it. God, what heavens I wanted to build up for you and Parzival! – Really, only one thing should strike at my life's nerve, only my beloved should be able to do it. But I believe that only your loss, your death, could. Misunderstanding and error which make you blind and unjust against me, touch me only as life's other distresses do, but for a different reason: whilst I know that these do not touch me to the core because they cannot reach to it, I feel that you do not either, because you brush by and take hallucination to be what is real. But then I know that you are helped by love, and the glorious clarity of your gaze will soon make you recognize what is right. That I know – for I <u>believe</u>. And so I believe also in Parzival: my dreams show me dangers, but it is not me they can strike, only him, and he must be protected by his faith – or else – . No, He will do it! –

And now peace! Peace! Peace! As it is peaceful deep, deep inside me I want to gain the peace from within for outside. Want to, for I must! You will help, and will lead the way for Parz. with your fine example? Won't you? – But example means – not forgiving – but being sorry that you could suffer on account of me? Is that bold? – But only thus is it true! Do not suffer! Do not suffer! – Just love!]]

The following, previously unpublished lines of music, as well as the also unpublished note on despotism, were written on scraps of paper and presumably do not belong in the Brown Book. *Of course, the possibility cannot be excluded of Wagner's having inserted them in the* Brown Book, *perhaps with the intention of entering them later. Eva stuck the three pieces of paper on page 14 of the original which she had already pasted over. Following the recovery of this page (v. Introduction, p. 16), the three pieces of paper had to be accommodated elsewhere, and were stuck on page 84 of the original which Wagner had left blank. The second motive is a study for the Prelude of* Parsifal, *Act III. – Of Wagner's pencil-written poem 'Above the Abyss I Stand' (v. pp. 30–31) Eva made an ink copy using a double page of four sides; the first three sides are written on, the fourth, blank side was pasted to what was originally page 15 of the original. As this page 15 (continuation of page 14) has also been recovered, Eva's copy of the poem has been pasted in at the end of the original book. In the present printing of the* Brown Book, *Eva's copy has not been included.*

[[

Despotism goes only for as long as the submerged, unheroic subjugated ones are impressed by the <u>heroic</u> nature of the dominators: – but for no longer.]]

Hohenschwangau.[86]
12 Nov. *[1865]*

Thus it sounds from one tower and is answered from another: the clearest sky, the sun golden; the castle gleams – That is magic! – Nothing, nothing is more inventive than love: to no ill-disposed man can so many ideas occur for the damaging of another, as he who loves has for the delight of the loved one. –

My Cosima! Who thinks today that the daemon must be paid for this beauty! – [[When I look like this out of my grand Crown-Princely window at the beautiful country: hear Lohengrin's greetings reverberating at me from the battlements, feel the joy, the gratitude of a kind King which I earn myself by a warm word, – I think of the wonderful woman who lovingly awaits me there, – who should fancy me not to be upon that peak which would put me beyond the reach of even the daemon? –]]

13 Nov. *[1865]*

Good morning, beloved!

Yesterday evening I read Parzival the beginning of the biography:[87] in preparation for further reading, I have just been reading the whole through again, and feel infinitely cheerful in my mind. My love, we are producing there something quite unique: believe me, such a thing has not yet been chronicled. Parzival listened with extraordinary seriousness, and again and again could not help a splendid laugh. Indeed, only now have I become conscious of the whole sublimity and beauty of his love: I admit that my imagination had been too blunted by the repulsive rasp of my life experiences to be quite suitably sharp and alert to such a revelation. He exceeds everything imaginable. He is Me, in a new, handsome, youthful rebirth: wholly Me, and only so much He as to be handsome and powerful. But there is not a wrinkle: a love that is only love. My final glorious task in life is now, in achievement, to rise completely to this wonderful trust. [[Oh, my Cosima! We shall be happier than mortals have ever been, for we three are immortal. Death cannot loosen our bond, and yet I hope I shall, through great age, make up for what might differentiate us in life span. O Cosima! Now there are just the works to be created. We can never again be happier. It is not possible. The spring of triple-life is in full blossom: the summer can only ripen the fruit! –

Believe me, I cannot write much more in the Brown Book for you. I lose consciousness of what has been experienced, and the content of it is neither to be spoken or written about. Just to talk intimately, to joke, – as about my earlier life: just to create, to work, to be genuine, fine, true and good. There's no longer anything else to be done. Believe me, we are in heaven!

Oh, peace! Peace! – How happy we are, and how wonderfully blissful we shall now always be! It is no longer possible any other way! –

See, I can't get anything else out. – We can only gaze at each other, be busy and thorough, love each other and – silence! We are not of this world, – You, He and I. We can only marvel at finding ourselves so, because it is the world we find ourselves in. But now there's no sense even in marvelling any more: now we know, soar, and make each other mutually happy. –]]

15 Nov *[1865]*

Die Sonne von Hohenschwangau

Zwei Sonnen sind's die Licht den Welten
geben:
Des Tages Stern, wie sähen wir sein Licht,
erleuchtete aus tiefstem eig'nen Leben
die Weltnacht uns die inn're Sonne nicht?
Was er bescheint, ist wechselvolles Weben;
doch ewig strahlt was aus dem Inn'ren bricht.
Ein Wunder nun! Aus unsrer Seelen Wonne
lacht heut' ob Hohenschwangau hell die
Sonne.

The Sun of Hohenschwangau

There are two suns that to our worlds give
light:
the star of day, how would we see its gleam,
did not, from its own profoundest life,
our inner sun illumine the world night?
What it shines upon is movement, change;
yet what breaks from within, shines out eternal.
A wonder now! From out of our soul's bliss
the sun today laughs bright on Hohenschwangau.

18 Nov *[1865]*

Abschiedstränen

Vereint, wie musst' uns hell die Sonne scheinen
durch bange Schleier, die das Sehnen wob:
der Trennung heut' wie muss der Himmel
weinen
ob eines Glückes, das so schnell zerstob!
Wollt' uns des Tages Wonneglanz vereinen,
nun werde auch der Himmelsthräne Lob!
Aus Sehnen, wie aus banger Trennungsklage
entblühten Hohenschwangau's
Wonnetage.

Parting tears[88]

How bright had sun to shine for us united,
through the uneasy veils that longing wove:
how has today to weep the sky of
parting
for happiness that was so swiftly scattered!
If the day's blissful lustre would unite us,
praise be now to tear of heaven too!
From yearning, as of parting's dread lament,
Hohenschwangau's blissful days have
blossomed.

[18 Nov. 1865]

[[It's a bad diary, isn't it,

Cos? and nothing at all to be found in it? –

Oh my Cosima! –

Today I am coming to you! I was only able to be happy even here, knowing my beautiful wonder-
woman to be there! –

Oh Cosima! Oh Ludwig! You are splendid! – United with you both, how mighty, how splendid am I! –

Pray for poor Hans! –

Greetings! Greetings ! My wife!

I am redeemed – I am happy!]]

The happy days at Hohenschwangau from 11 to 18 November 1865 were followed by grave events which put an end to Wagner's stay in Munich. On 26 November 1865, the Munich Volksbote *published an article containing serious attacks on Wagner partly based on truth but mainly libellous. Wagner defended himself in a counter-article which he caused to be published anonymously in the* Münchener Neueste Nachrichten. *His reply contained sharp attacks on persons of the royal cabinet and of the court secretariat. This made the situation worse. On 3 December 1865, the King wrote to him: '. . . That article in the Neueste Nachrichten . . . has without doubt been written by one of your friends desirous of doing you a service by the same; I am afraid that he has harmed you instead of helped.' The officials under attack fought back and finally compelled the King to order Wagner's departure from Munich. He was requested to leave Bavaria for a few months. The King's letters to him state: '. . . Believe me – I had to act as I did . . . I could do no other . . . After all, it's not for ever . . . For your own peace I had to act as I did' (7 and 8 December 1865). It was, however, to be for ever, at least in so far as a permanent stay in Munich was concerned. Thus the Munich period had lasted for less than two years from 4 May 1864 to 9 December 1865. Wagner left the city on 10 December. He was once again homeless, but at least financially assured for the future by an annual salary of 8,000 florins. Now it was a question of seeking a new refuge. Wagner travelled first to Geneva, then to France and again to Geneva. It was on his travels in France that he made the entry below, the first for many months.*

<u>Lyons</u>. 22 Jan. 1866

Good signs, Cosima! – in dreadful spirits I stepped out through the window on to the balcony. Night. – Slim crescent moon! – on the left, the sword of Orion with the point turned towards north-east. Cut, cut, my sword, so that a King's heart may feel what real sufferings are! –

– I felt ill – and believed myself unable to continue my journey. – Now I am making up my mind, and shall travel into the night – tomorrow by the sea;[89] –

<u>You</u> it was who first mentioned this refuge to me. What a feeling I have to be seeing this Lyons again – I saw it in 1850! – Ah, I ought finally to have become wise, – these childish monstrous cities – like a thousand-voice Italian unison opera! Not a trace of life! – How shall I endure turning up at such places again and again! – yet, Orion's sword! – It must be! –

The despair felt by Wagner in his situation at that time may be seen from the following entry 'Roland's Death' in which he draws parallels between his own fate and that of the legendary hero Roland. The figure of Charlemagne corresponds to Ludwig II, the traitor Ganelon to King Ludwig's cabinet secretary, Pfistermeister, Roland's beloved, Corisande – to Cosima, and Roland himself – to Wagner. The allegory is a kind of final appeal by Wagner to King Ludwig for aid, which is confirmed by the fact that Wagner sent it to the King on the same day, 28 January 1866, in somewhat altered form.

<u>Marseilles</u>. 28 Jan. *[1866]*

Roland's Death – once again he sounds his horn – the fearful lament of the echo travels afar – Olifant[90] bursts. Charlemagne becomes fearful: the traitor Ganelon reassures him – it is nothing, all is well with Roland, he is out hunting, that's all. – the King – does in fact calm himself. 'Then it cannot be so bad' – Now the hero's last strength deserts him: resting his head against the rock, he silently awaits death. But his sword 'Durandal', – that must not fall into base hands: with his last strength he attempts to shatter it; in vain he strikes it against the rocks – the rocks crack (his last works of art!) but the sword does not break;– then he hurls it high over the mountain peaks before him: it falls into the mysterious depths of an inaccessible mountain lake – none will be able to find it. Now he is calm. The sun sets – the hero breathes Corisande's name – and expires. –

And ultimately Charlemagne arrives at the truth. Needless to say it <u>now</u> goes ill with the traitor also. He is duly punished. Also vengeance is taken. Four hundred thousand unbelievers fall, and 300 cities are destroyed by fire. – Only Corisande understands: she embraces her beloved's body – and dies. –

– A fine model. So it is – and ever was. – The horn is not heard, the traitor remains close to the King, – the hero languishes – only love redeems. – Childish, foolish world! –

[[7 Feb. /1866, Geneva/

Spring sun! – I sat on the seat outside the house – great warmth: first budding of the shrubs. On the right, in the firs, the finches calling: beneath them, Pohl's grave.[91] –

Day comes on. –
Or is it night? –
There rots my wife –[92]
there languishes my beloved! – And here? –
Spring! –]]

*

Day – Night. –
The Hellenes had a fine sense of the sanctity of night. The profoundest sense of it must have been revealed to those attending the great performance of the Oresteia of Aeschylus. This began in daylight: Agamemnon – complete human error – crime – desire. Afternoon: Electra – revenge – expiation – punishment. With the Eumenides dusk falls; at the end fully night: the young men escort the appeased, reconciled daemons of revenge in torchlight procession to their nocturnal place of rest. –

Now the sanctity of the night feeling gives birth to playful merriment also: fauns and satyrs tease each other by torchlight, jocular dismay and disappointment – drunks scrambling for resting-place. The world lightly sheds its burdensome seriousness, and – peace becomes possible. – Here sleep – there death! –

Frühlingssonne! — Ich sass auf der Bank
von dem Hause — grosse Wärme : erste
Knospen der Gesträuche. Rechts in den
Tannen rufen die Finken : unter ihnen
Pohl's Grab. —
Der Tag bricht an. —
Oder ist's die Nacht? —
Dort wandelt meine Frau —
dort sieht die Geliebte! — Und hier? —
Frühling! —

———

Tag — Nacht. —
Eine schöne Gefühle von der Nachtheit
Recht lachen die Hellenen. Der tiefste
Sinn musste daran dem sich offenbaren,
welche der grossen Aufführung der
Oresteia des Aeschylos anwohnten.
Diese begann am hellen Tage : Agamemnon
— voller menschlicher Bosheit — Ver-
brechen — Begehren. Nachmittag : Elektra —
Rache — Sühne — Strafe. Mit den Eumeniden

That was fine – :

and it was at the approach of spring that they played it! –

Wagner now made no further use of the Brown Book *– apart from one page which has been cut out – for over a year. This may be because, except for a few weeks in April and September 1866, he had been living with Cosima in Switzerland. She had joined him on 8 March in Geneva, where he was looking for a new home. Soon Tribschen[93] was found, by the Vierwaldstädter See, and on 15 April Wagner moved in. On 12 May Cosima followed him there to run the house, bringing with her her three daughters, Daniela, Blandine and Isolde. The Munich accusations continued and were now publicly directed against Hans von*

Bülow also who, on the grounds of spiteful press attacks upon himself, Cosima and Wagner, tendered his resignation to the King, and on 10 June, while retaining his Munich apartment, joined Wagner at Tribschen. He stayed for almost three months, but could stand it no longer, for the ménage à trois *proved intolerable, and he needed solitude in order to compose again, as Liszt had recommended, and play the piano, for which Tribschen offered no opportunity. A chance presented itself for a stay in Basle where he could resume teaching. His second wife, Marie, records in her book* Hans von Bülow in Leben und Wort (Hans von Bülow, his Life and Words), *Stuttgart 1925, p. 109: 'He decided to try Basle, leaving wife and children with Wagner . . . To Munich, he was "on leave", waiting for it to become "habitable" again.' Bülow moved to Basle on 15 September, and Cosima remained with the children at Tribschen. Six months later, on 5 April, King Ludwig II appointed Bülow Court Kapellmeister in Ordinary and Director of the Music School yet to be founded. Bülow accepted the appointment, and on 16 April returned to Munich, with Cosima but without the children. In the entry below, Wagner expresses his emotions at this separation from Cosima which was to continue for fifteen months.*

Triebschen. 16 April 1867
6 p.m.

In my whole life I do not think I have ever been so sad as I am now!! – How easily that is said, and how unspeakable it is –

– I walked home, and sank down from exhaustion. A brief, leaden sleep such as often drives out a cold fetched up all the misery of my life as if from the depths of my soul. – I yearn for major illness and death. I have no inclination any more, no will! –

Would there were an end to it, an end! –

Today she has left. – What this leaving has said!

What is the use of any seeing each other again?

The leaving remains. It is wretched! –

Concerning the entries below for 22 August and 16 September 1867: since 16 April 1867 Cosima had been in Munich with Hans von Bülow who was anxious for the children to return from Tribschen to Munich also. But Wagner wanted Cosima, who had borne his second daughter Eva on 17 February at Tribschen, to rejoin him there. Hans was against this, and Cosima, also difficultly placed on account of her father's opposition, tried to convey as much to Wagner. Disagreements ensued, of which the entry for 22 August with its reference to 'mathematic proof' is evidence. On 16 September, Cosima, who had been at Tribschen 'for 2 nights and one day' for the purpose of collecting her children, left for Munich. Eva, however, just six months old, remained at Tribschen, which may be seen as an acknowledgment on Bülow's part of Wagner's paternity, although an acknowledgment of which only the three of them could have been aware.

[[Sie hört nicht meine Stimme mehr
wenn ich Ihr Alles sage –
Sie sieht nicht meine Blicke mehr
wenn ich ihr Alles klage –
Auf mathematische Beweise steht
ihr Sinn –
Geb' ich sie ihr, wär' dann nicht
Alles hin? –

[[She hears my voice no more
when I tell her all –
She sees my looks no more
when to her I pour out all –
On mathematical proof
her mind is set –
Were I to give her it, would not then
All be gone? –

22 Aug. 67.]]

The lines below were written by Wagner for King Ludwig II's twenty-second birthday. Monsalvat means Hohenschwangau, Parzival is Wagner's name for the King. – This entry is followed in the original by a blank page.

25 August 67

Und wieder hör' ich ahnungsvolle Glocken,
von Monsalvat dringt weihlich ernst
ihr Ton:
Grüsst Parzival des Volkes Heilfrohlocken?
Jauchzt Deutschland seinem königlichsten
Sohn?
Es tönt und hallt, erfüllt die nahe Stille:
so schwillt der Muth, so wächst ein
Königswille! –

And again I hear portentous bells,
from Monsalvat their sound comes, holy,
solemn:
Greets Parzival the people's jubilation?
Exults Germany for its most Kingly
Son?
Sound and echo fill the immediate stillness:
thus courage swells, thus a King's
will grows! –

16 Sept. a.m.
(1867)

As life's circle draws ever tighter: all blood towards the heart. To die in love. The limbs grow pale. Life drops from me. – What love is a man can discover only at my age: the grave of life. – For me the world lives on for as long as the brain obeys the heart. How weary I am! –

Christ, after his death, wandering the earth for another 40 days – appearing now and then to his own, joining them in the familiar way. The most moving touch in the founding of a religion. –

It was thus that you came once again: for 2 nights and one day my house sheltered you. Now gone, wholly gone? – Gone where? – – where I am, I know: in the grave. –

Little Eva sleeping. – And so now I'm experiencing the old Paris 'dors, mon enfant'[94] – Very moving! – – [[Yesterday I dreamt of a bird that wouldn't leave my writing desk but kept clinging to it. – Went to bed in a very sad, solemn mood, the theme being roughly: 'I am the last.' – I do not wish a swift unconscious death. –]]

*

[[Oh Cosima! How proud and happy I am! – Your Day![95] – I had a beautiful dream about you. – But to be aware of you, aware, – to be quite clearly conscious that you are, are, for me! Ah! That merits a lot of 'distress' – . But how should I not be aware of it? I can, after all, see and grasp it!]] Every day the thrill of emotion I feel, approaching little Eva increases. Lying, living and laughing there is the clear proof that 'I too was born in Arcadia!' – Dear, dear wife! – Behold, all has succeeded and succeeds: child and work! – Whom would we envy? –

The five-month interval between the entries of 27 September 1867 and 17 February 1868 is explained by Wagner's spending almost two months of that time in Munich. Back in Tribschen on 9 February, he sent the telegram below to Cosima for Eva's first birthday on 17 February. The previous year, 'at the approach of Eva's birth', he had played the 'Morning Dream' motive from The Mastersingers *in the adjoining room. Now, to this 'birth music' he added the 'Apprentice Boys' Dance'. This is the final entry addressed to Cosima. The première of* The Mastersingers *was now imminent, taking Wagner to Munich again, this time for two-and-a-half months. When, after the première on 21 June, there was a renewal of the attacks against her, Cosima left Munich, and on 22 July joined Wagner at Tribschen, now, apart from an interval in Munich from 14 October to 16 November in connection with the separation arrangements, never again to leave him. Her divorce from Bülow followed on 18 July 1870 and her marriage to Wagner on 25 August of the same year.*

91

Daniela and Blandine remained with Bülow in Munich and were looked after by his mother. When he gave up his Munich post to go to Florence, and his mother departed for Wiesbaden, he placed his children in the care of Cosima, with whom they remained. In a letter to Wagner dated 8 April 1869 (of which the original is in the Richard-Wagner-Gedenkstätte) he writes: '. . . This evening you will see my children . . . Their mother will, I think, be pleased with them, and that joy I grant her with all my heart. – Mother is now leaving me in a few days' time to go to Wiesbaden. Then I shall be completely alone . . .'

1868!
17 February.

Telegram:

'Was die Weise mir gebar,
mehr als Morgentraum nur war:
vom Parnass zum Paradies
sie den Weg dem Leben wies.'

'What unto me the music bore,
was more than just a Morning Dream:
from Parnassus heights to Paradise
it showed the way for life to go.'

[[(Van Dyck: St Anthony of Padua.
Michelangelo: Madonna. –)

Eva, sitting on the piano, listened very attentively and happily to the birth music, then to the Apprentice Boys' Dance.]]

From 17 July 1865 and until 1880, Wagner dictated his autobiography My Life *to Cosima using as a basis notes in a red pocket-book of which only the first four pages are still preserved. Having dictated from these up to Easter 1846, he wrote fresh notes in February 1868, presumably using the 'Red Pocket-Book' which was supposed to have been kept up to 1856. These are the Annals reproduced below, and those for the period 1846 to 30 (29) April 1864 have not previously been published and contain many things not used in* My Life *or presented differently. The Annals for the period 5 May 1864 to the end of 1868 are important in that they provide the sole authentic continuation of* My Life *which ends at 4 May 1864. Explanatory notes to the Annals have been kept to the minimum to avoid extending the scope of the present work disproportionately. Clarification for the period 1846 to 3 May 1864 is provided by* My Life,[96] *and thereafter by Otto Strobel in* König Ludwig II und Richard Wagner, Briefwechsel, *Vols I and II. Here the Annals from 1864[97] are printed for the first time and amply annotated.*

Annals *[1846–1867]*

(February 1868)

[[1846

Easter. – Petition to King of Saxony. – Sponsored by Lüttichau. Advance from Theatre Pension Fund (5000 thalers) at 4% against life assurance. Latter procured with great trouble. Doubts about my health. Certificate from Pusinelli. So to Leipzig. Much tormented. Settlement: have to pay 300 thalers annually just for interest and assurance, which always deducted from salary at source: accordingly draw only 1200 thaler still, and remain owing the 5000 thaler. – 3 months summer holiday. May to Gross-Graupen, 1 hour above Pillnitz. Must immediately to Leipzig again (because of life assur.): there meet Spohr, by whom invited: at Mendelssohn's and Hauptmann's. Back in country: (last opera was Tell; lingers disagreeably; dispelled by 1st theme of 9th Symph.). Finally to work on composition sketches of Lohengrin: very rough. Outings: Borsberg, Liebetalergrund. Pirna – to bathe. (Pilgrims' Chorus whistled.) Visits. H. von Bülow with Lipinsky. Fr. Schmitt. Röckel with father. Heines with Müller. Sketches completed. – August back to Dresden. Trouble: question of debts not fully settled; opera publishers still demanding sacrifices: must try anew to help

93

myself. – Begin more detailed composition of Lohengr. with Act III, don't get far: break off to recast Gluck's Iphigenia in Aulis. Complete this by end of year. –

1847
Hiller's concerts. (Schubert's symph. Gade. – Minuet of 7th Symph. Ruins of Athens.) Social life: Club. – Schumann. – Lohengrin Act III completed. (Iphigenia performed. – Easter repeat of 9th Symph.) Move to Friedrichstadt: Marcolini Palace (rent 100 thalers.) Hähnel. Large garden. Greek antiquity. (first Gibbon: then classical historical works. Aeschylos – fearful impression. Droysen's Alexander, Hellenism. – also Hegel's Philosophy of History.) – Glorious summer. Hide in shrubbery reading Aristophanes. The Birds. Pleasant evenings. Visitors. Rapprochement with Ed. Devrient. – Sister Cäcilie on visit. Dry fountain bowl with Neptune. Memories of Napoleon. At theatre perf. of Tannh. and Rienzi. – Very excited and in good spirits. Complete detailed composition of Lohengrin, Acts I and II (August). – Circumstances tight owing to salary reductions. Decide to summon Berlin to my aid. Queen Marie of Saxony. (Audience) request to recommend Rienzi to her sister of Prussia. Following which, invitation from Küstner. – September to Berlin for Rienzi rehearsals. – Meyerbeer (departing and remaining) Redern. – Werder: apartment overlooking Gendarmenplatz. – Frommann: evening visits. (Lohengrin.) Countess Rossi. Sontag: Also Lohengrin (breakfast). – Sans Souci trips: no getting to the King. Cabinet Minister Illaire. – Tieck: Lohengrin. – Taubert: – jealousy; also dinner. – H. Franck (also brother Eduard Fr.:) pleasant and instructive. Lohengrin. Gaillard. Kossak (genial.) Truhn (Lutter and Wegner). Rellstab. – Küstner: Stawinski. (Werder – Stawinski.) Dinners – Meinhardt (C.C.) Dinner – Redern (Littolf. Fonton.) No King to be had. – October: Minna's arrival. Meinhardt: oyster-evening. Wretched rehearsals. (Wieprecht.) Recovery at Franck's. (Desperate nature of political views: defunct United Landtag.) – – Marx and wife (also dinner!) – Even Cläre coming to the performance from Chemnitz. These two repeats finally at end of October (previously J. Lind.) – minus King. Prince and Princess of Prussia. – Feeling low. (Learnt at Redern's of death of Mendelssohn.) Return to Dresden with Minna. Criticism on train. – There Hiller's Konradin von Hohenstaufen. (Johanna and Tichatschek: – scheming.) 4th perf. of Hiller's opera: latter to Düsseldorf. – Petition for increase in salary: disgraceful report by Lüttichau; on my part, misunderstanding of Royal Decree. Capitulated. – Previously: November, Tannh. in presence of King of Prussia (on visit). Arranging of orchestral concerts at theatre. (Major memorandum concerning orchestra going ahead.) – : gratuity of 300 thalers.

1848

Orchestral concerts at theatre. (Seb. Bach. Palestrina!) Great success. Ed Devrient closer: ideas for reform of theatre. Growing dissension with Lüttichau. – Orchestration of Lohengrin. – Old German studies. – Beginning Feb. Death of my mother. To Leipzig for funeral. Intense cold. Dreadful state of mind. Returning from cemetery conversation with Laube. – Return. February Revolution. Events of March. (Röckel in Floridsdorf.) 3rd orchestral concert. New Ministry. Illuminations; me in the streets. – End March Lohengr. score completed. – Visit of Frau J. Laussot. Karl Ritter. – Kietz junior (Peps.) – Poem: Appeal to the Germans (sent to Auerbach: nothing further heard). Politics, socialism, communism, – Papa Fischer. – Liszt comes from Vienna. His entry at Marcolini. Evening at Schumann's (Walk home with Schubert:[98] Liszt in tails.) – Poem to the Viennese, following events of May. (Österreichische Zeitung.) Societies.[99] Ed Devrient, Röckel. – Vaterlandsverein. Republican essay in Anzeiger: read to Verein. (Blödl. Klette.[100] Röckel always.) Dreadful effect. Rienzi cancelled. Anger in Anzeiger. Agitation at Court. King kind; reconciliation with Lüttichau on strength of latter's apparently first-rate conduct. Ed. Devrient good counterbalance to fuss. Beginning July short holiday: to Vienna via Breslau (Mosewius). Professor Fischhof with Beethoven and Bach manuscripts. State Councillor Fonton: interesting disputes. Uhl.[101] Agitation for theatre reform. Dr Pacher (†). Franck etc. Meeting and lecture. Club. – Vesque von Püttlingen (Hoven). Old acquaintances. Academic Legion, German tricolor waiters at theatre. 'Die Freiheit in Krähwinkel'. Grillparzer. Back via Prague. Thence with Hähnel (and Count Nostitz) to Dresden. – Explanation of Lüttichau's behaviour towards me. Exigency financial operations. August to Weimar to Liszt: no assistance possible. No significant reminiscences. Disputes with Princess Wittgenstein. – Old German studies. Sketched out in my head Barbarossa in five acts. Passed on to Siegfried by way of a prose work on his historical significance: *Die Wibelungen*. – Detailed plan for organization of Theatre: presented to Minister Oberländer. (Casually to Pfordten.) – Solitary walks. Edda: Mone's researches. – Events of October in Vienna. Pressure of situation. Much with Ed. Devrient. Fresh dissensions with Lüttichau on account of reorganization plan. Definitive financial arrangement with my creditors. Restrict myself to fixed salary of 800 thalers. – September. 300th Anniversary of the Orchestra. Pillnitz. – Concert. (Lohengrin finale.) Banquet: speech. Marschner. Weber's grave. On account of Lohengrin performance: order to Heine junior for scenery again withdrawn. Comes to see me – break decided. – Isolation: communistic ideas for shaping mankind of the future to be promotive of art. (Theatre: Martha. Favourite!) November: Poem of Siegfried's Death. Read to: Semper, Heine jun.,

Karl Ritter, Bülow. – Röckel dismissed: Deputy; arrest and release to ovation. Great disorder. Wild confusion. Ed. Devrient's lectures.

1849

New Testament:[102] sketch of 'Jesus of Nazareth' in 5 Acts. – Theodor Uhlig increasingly intimate. Orchestral Players' Union: my visit and address. Reported to Lüttichau. Big scene: expect him to apply for my dismissal; Ed Devrient sent to see me: breach avoided. Dull, hopeless wasting away of position. – Michael Bakunin in hiding at Röckel's. Extensive association with him in secret. Many Poles. Czechs. – Told him about Jesus of Nazareth. Nothing of Siegfried. Poem 'An die Not'. Also 'An einen Staatsanwalt'. Ideas for an 'Achilles' in 3 Acts. Beginning of new year, walks with Bakunin. (Schnapps. Sausages between bread.) Polish countess. Haimberger. German Catholic priest (Viennese refugee: of whom heard first of Feuerbach.) Strange acquaintances: Viennese Calabrians. Refugee demagogues. Evenings at Hempel's: Röckel and Todt. 'Volksblätter' – Ministry of reaction. Everyone making ready to fight. – Beginning May Landtag closed. Röckel flees: Volksblätter. 3 May. Sultry heat. Fatherland Committee: Kleine Brüdergasse. Dr Gerber: reports, conferences. (Shrapnels.) Painter Kaufmann: with him in the Postplatz, hear alarm bell from tower of St Ann's Church. Yellow-brown atmosphere. Frau Tichatschek. To the Neumarkt: encounter wounded; Calabrians rubbing their hands. Barricades. Town Hall. Communal Guard: Semper as a citizen guard. Enormous confusion. Marschall von Bieberstein. Defence committee. 4 May (Thursday) Town Hall. Provisional government: parade in Market. Köchly proclaims and administers oath of allegiance to Imperial Constitution. Bakunin in tails. Promenades between barricades. Brühl Terrace to bridge. Agitation against expected march-in of Prussian troops. 5 May (Friday) continuing truce: provisioning, preparations. Leo von Zychlinsky. Bakunin – Polish officers. Semper. (Frau Schröder-Devrient at Heines': seen for last time.) Wilh. Devrient and Heine jun. over barricades each evening and cosily home to Friedrichstadt. There found Ottilie and Clara Brockhaus (Luise's daughters): longish time every Sunday. Good spirits. 6 May (Saturday) Prussians march into New Town. Midday, battle begins. Up tower of Church of Cross: schoolmaster Berthold and others. 2 o'clock heavy attack with cannon: retire. Town Hall: Bakunin a Heubner enthusiast after attack on Frauengasse –Neumarkt barricade, under Marschall's command. Todt and Tzschirner disappear. Church of Cross tower again, in line of fire. Spend night there. Clock tower. 7 May (Sunday) glorious morning through mist. Nightingales in Schütze garden. Marseillaise from Plauen direction. Sun: columns of volunteers; Altmarkt bivouac. Battle continued without decision. Conical bullets: Mattress. Tower occupied by armed

96

gymnasts. At about 11, burning of Old Opera House and part of Zwinger Gallery: 'stuffed noblemen'. Tower under cannon fire. Very difficult getting home in afternoon: wife's reproaches for being out all night. The two Brockhauses: much excitement and hope. Hähnel reactionary. Frau Röckel. 8 May (Monday) Morning once again by roundabout route via barricades to Town Hall. At St Ann Barricade guard shouts 'Well, Mr Conductor, joy's beautiful divine spark's made a blaze.'[103] (3rd perf. 9th Symphony at previous Palm Sunday concert; Opera House now burnt down. Strange feeling of comfort.) Meet Hiebendahl – dissuasive: Röckel, back from Prague, searching houses with guards for muskets. Plauensche Gasse. Gymnast reinforcements; led by Röckel. Don't see latter again. Town Hall. Bakunin, Heubner. Plan: retreat to Erzgebirge and join up with Thuringian reinforcements. Prussians in Ostrallee. Home: quick decision to take Minna to Chemnitz to Cläre. On ahead and hire carriage in first village: over ground of old walks; glorious morning: larks. Very heavy musket and cannon fire in town: long in my ears. (Roar and motion of sea in London.) Minna arrives with Papo and Peps. Journey via Tharand and Freiberg. Company of marksmen. Irregulars; encouraged. In Oederan to Town Hall: HQ of Chemnitz Municipal Guard: bad position for me. Then on: Chemnitz, Wolframs. – 9 May (Tuesday): early back to Dresden alone. Freiberg: hear of reinforcements. Evening reach Town Hall with difficulty (via broken-through houses). Situation there: Tzschirner brought back. Heubner. Marschall, Zychlinsky. All hoarse. Bakunin well: on mattress smoking cigar with young Haimberger. Röckel (jittery) presumably captured. Plan, as blowing up of Town Hall not accepted, for energetic fighting to cover retreat. Reports of reinforcements. Undertake to speed their arrival. Marschall offers to accompany me. To his home: warm clothing. Carriage. By night to Freiberg. 10 May (Wednesday) Reinforcements urged on; march-off promised. Morning turn back alone by special mail coach. Meet the retreat. Government carriage. Bakunin, Heubner: the hirer out of the carriage! – Approach from Chemnitz Municipal Guard on hill: wheel about. Freiberg. At Heubner's: his wife. Breakfast with Bakunin. Discussions. Compositor Born. Bakunin's sleep. To Heubner at Town Hall. Situation there. Shouting, unheard-of confusion. Withdrawal to Chemnitz decided on. Departure of post coach delayed by march-off of irregulars (drum). Twice back to Heubner's so as to travel with them to Chemnitz; miss them or they sleeping. – Finally off by post coach: more frequent attempts to halt by shooting. Night in Chemnitz inn: brief sleep. Out very early to Wolframs. Morning, news about state of things: Heubner, Bakunin etc., arriving shortly after me, arrested in Chemnitz. Disintegration. Troops expected. Reversal. Wolfram accompanies me in his carriage to Altenburg: night 11 May from Altenburg to Weimar by post. – Liszt. Previous performance of Tannhäuser: Repeat of work. Rehearsals.

Liszt's nervousness. Princess Wittgenstein. Altenburg: dogmatizes. Outing to Eisenach – Liszt on to Karlsruhe. Stör; Kimstädt. Wartburg – visited for first time. Wilhelmstal. – Grand Duchess of Weimar at Eisenach Castle. Beaulieu. – Letter from Minna in Dresden says warrant out for me. Liszt back. Prof. Wolff. Sybel. Minister von Watzdorf. Zigesar. Dress rehearsal of Tannh. (Fr. Haller.) By one-horse carriage to Magdala, 3 hours from Weimar: as Prof. Werther from Berlin – on account of Camerliis. Expeditions on foot: irregulars: National Assembly. 22 May (36th birthday) Minna via Weimar to Magdala to see me. (Dante.) Next day on foot to Jena: there at Prof. Wolff's again met Minna. Very miserable parting. With passport of Prof. Widmann (Swabian) by post via Rudolstadt, Koburg, Nuremberg, Lindau (anxiety over passport) – to Rohrschach; evening at 6 o'clock (last day of May) from Oberstrass to Zürich in glorious weather: lake and alps for first time. Excellent spirits: great moral well-being. Schwert Hotel. Alex. Müller (Würzburg). Willh. Baumgartner (Dresden visit). Sulzer. Hagenbuch: passport to Paris. Strassburg – Paris. 3 June. Letter of recommendation to Belloni. Rue Notre D. d. Lorette. Cholera. Low spirits. Desplechin: Semper. W. Heine. Liszt: Journal d. débats. – Meyerbeer at Schlesinger's. – After a week, with Bellonis, to Laferté-sous-Jouarre (Rueil). Monsieur Raphael: Marchand de vin. (Consumption. Caterwauling.) Fishing. Hiking. Lamartine: Histoire des Girondins. In Paris 13 June (Ledru-Rollin). Uprising and collapse in Baden and Palatinate. Attempt poem. Communist studies.[104] Unpleasant letter from Carolyne to Belloni: ingratitude. – Very unpleasant letter from Minna: she against our re-uniting. Liszt remitting 100 thalers for her (from unknown donor). End June: Paris. (Alb. Franck) Kietz. Beginning July to Zürich: completely without money. Two months at A. Müller's. am amenable to everything. Strohhof. Sulzer, etc. Reading of Siegfried's Death. Winterthur wine: banquets at Cantonal Secretary's. Arrival of Baden refugees: of Dresden refugees. Marschall. Zychelinski. Also schoolmaster Berthold from tower of Church of Cross. – Schröder-Devrient at Schwert Hotel: never meet her again. – (Görgey near Villagos.) Great despondency. Hopes for France. Increasing excitement despite calm outer and inner composure. Out of touch with Minna. – Feuerbach: Death and immortality. – 'Art and Revolution'. Sent to Leipzig, to Wigand. – Revise 'The Wibelungen' (Many acquaintances: Prof. Fröhlich from Bern.) End August: letter from Minna. Conciliatory. Announcing arrival. – Beginning September to Rorschach via Toggenburg, St Gallen, on foot: Lindemann's. Welcome Minna together with Natalie, Peps and Papo. To Zürich. Lodgings at Kaufmann's. Dolder. Sulzer helps. Spyri. From October move to Escher-houses rear. Miserably furnished: piano, title page of Nibelungen follow: becomes quite bearable. Friends often at our house. Conduct A major Symphony at Music Society Concert. For which

100 francs. November and December write 'The Art-Work of the Future'. Eduard von Bülow in Zürich: visits, discussions. Growing nervous disorder. Writing to Dresden for help. –

1850

Liszt points to Paris. Idea for 'Wieland the Smith' – for Paris. (G. Vaëz) – Jessie Laussot's letter from Bordeaux. Frau Ritter sends me via someone 500 thalers from Dresden. Decide to travel to Paris. Very ill. Nerves overwrought, loss of voice: wrong treatment. Minna refuses to agree to abandoning Paris: nasty presentiment of the futility, the useless sacrifice of money; great weariness. Minna inconsolable over Zürich future. Set out in profoundly bad humour. Travel beginning February. – Paris. Rue de Provence. Very ill. (Dr Meding). Seghers about Tannh. overture. Comes to nothing. Belloni. Semper. Kietz, Anders. Agent from Ministry. – Wieland elaborated in greater detail. – 'Art and Climate' (Art-Work of F. published. Only half my payment.) Greatest aversion to any Paris undertaking. Ambigu comique: 4 fils d'Haimon. Notre Dame. (Genre premier). Another letter from Laussot. Pour out my troubles to her. Invitation to Bordeaux; revelations concerning Ritters' interest in me. Mid-March by diligence to Bordeaux. (Orléans. Tours. Angoulême: – Gironde steamer.) Eugène Laussot. Cours du 30 juillet. Jessie: Mama Taylor. Relief. Sympathetic element. Become aware of marital dissension. Inquire of J.: – whether I ought to depart? 'No' – Music. B major Sonata (Beethoven). Lohengrin. Acquaintances. Wieland received with sympathy, Siegfried's Death with horror. 12 Muses. Frau Taylor reveals agreement with Frau Ritter to provide me with constant financial aid. Very uneasy farewell after three-week stay. – Back to Paris: much troubled by nerves. Hotel Valois. Not sleeping and filled with despair. Minna's last letter to Bordeaux: beside herself at my wanting to return to Zürich without having achieved object. Whole affair brought up. Mid-April told Minna of decision not to return to Zürich at all: assign to her half the aid guaranteed me by Taylor and Ritters. Inform Bordeaux of this. At same time Jessie responds with decision to leave Bordeaux and put herself under my protection. Struggle to compose myself. To Montmorency: 'Homo' – family of hens. Letter to Liszt about Lohengrin. Minna said to be in Paris looking for me. Kietz as axis of world's misfortune. (A. Franck.) Departure. (Clermont Tonnère.) Beginning May in Geneva. Villeneuve: Hotel Byron. Karl Ritter looking for me in Lausanne: get him to come and see me. Letter from Bordeaux reporting tragedy there. Decide at once to travel there: Letter to Eugène L. that I'm coming, and at same time to Jessie but saying nothing of my arrival. Mid-May three days by diligence via Lyons, Auvergne (Puy) (Dordogne) to Bordeaux (where fire burning). Passport difficulties at frontier. Hotel Quatre

Soeurs. Wait in vain for Eugène. Summons to police station. Situation understood. Two days' stay to recover from dreadful weariness. Letter to J. – now vigorously advising her to break with Eugène. House deserted: Leave letter in work basket in boudoir. Evening star anxious too.[105] Back same way. Lyons. At Hotel Byron, K.R. waiting. 37th birthday. Frau Julie Ritter comes to Villeneuve with daughter Emilie. Great, new impressions of high-minded interest. Week of excursions. Part, after the leaving of assistance. Beginning June, with Karl to Valais, Vispertal, Zermatt, Matterhorn. Lengthy stay abandoned. After two days (Corpus Christi) by way of Lausanne – Geneva – Bern to Thun: attempted to settle. Karl melancholy. Odyssey gives great pleasure. Letter from Liszt: Lohengrin performance decided. Much Proudhon: propriété. End June, Jessie L. to K.R. about me. Very bad feeling. Hear at same time of Minna's receiving ill-natured report about me from Madame Taylor: furious, decide to explain. Karl sent to Zürich: returns and reports in good, conciliatory terms. Leave for Z. Villa 'Evening Star' at Enge, by the lake, with Frau Hirzel. Minna in bed in morning: 'Not out of pity?' – Papo, Peps, cheerful accommodation; garden. (Beginning July.) Old acquaintances: Sulzer superb. Money returned to Madame Taylor. – Kolatschek. Holzer. – Herwegh. – Attempts at composition of Siegfried's Death. – Very loyal and intimate correspondence with Uhlig. Brendel: Zeitschrift für Musik – 'Judaism in Music'. Dreadful sensation. – K. Ritter staying: moves out; goes to Weimar to Lohengrin. – With Minna. Rigi, Lucerne; 28 Aug: days of Lohengrin performance. – K.R. back. Wants to become music director. Engagement with Kramer. (September: 'Opera and Drama' begun.) October: Theatre. K.R. at Piano and conductor's rostrum. Enormous spectacles. Freischütz. Send off for abduction of Hans Bülow. Both walk from Lake Constance in storm and rain. Hans reports for work: vaudeville. Good mood. Papa Eduard: avoids seeing me. (La Dame Blanche. Zauberflöte.)

1851

'Die Stumme von Portici'. Quarrel with theatre. Hans and Karl to St Gallen to direct music at theatre. Visit them there. Finish 'Opera and Drama'. – 12 February. Death of Papa. Mood of immeasurable sadness. Nervous trouble. Conducted symphonies at three concerts. Karl and Hans come to 'Eroica'. Hans plays Tannh. Overture by Liszt. – Enge-evenings. Always: Sulzer, Baumgartner. Spyri. – also: Kolatsch: Solger (soon to America) then Herwegh. – Readings of 'Opera and Drama' in room of coffee house where also earlier club with piano. Swiss attentiveness: Köchly. 'Siegfried's Death' also read. – New year, skin eruption: sulphur baths. – In May: 'Young Siegfried' written. – Much correspondence with Liszt. Zigesar, commissions 'Young Siegfried' for Weimar for 500 thalers in instalments over a year. Aversion to dealing with music until health improved. – Uhlig: Brendel. – July: to St Gallen where Karl R. alone (Bülow having gone to Weimar to see Liszt at Easter.) With him to Rorschach: there arrival of Uhlig. With the two of them Appenzell: high Säntis. Adventure with Karl who has to go back. Return via Toggenburg. Uhlig to stay. Piano score of Lohengrin. Dreadful news about Meser's business. Swiss journey with Uhlig: Brunnen; Grütli. Beckenried – Stanz: St Christopher in the Aa. Engelberg. Surenenpass: waterfall, to Amsteg. Maderanertal: Hüfigletscher. Great fatigue. Back via Flüelen. Beginning August Uhlig leaves. – 'Communication to my Friends' as preface to three opera poems. – Hydropathic reading: Rausse's health radicalism. – Middle September to Albisbrunnen for water-cure (to Minna's great sorrow). Karl also summoned from Stuttgart: H. Müller (Schröder-Devrient's former lover) also comes for the cure. Minna visits. Water-Jew. Ignatz the Executioner. Liszt on subject of Lohengrin and Tannh. Press. Water torture. – Against which growing inclination for pleasant furnishings. House plans. Genesis of 'Valkyrie'. Plan for complete realization of 'Nibelung's Ring' with 'Rhinegold'. Much stimulated. – Ritter's uncle dies: family inherits and offers me regular 800 thalers of financial aid. Inform Liszt of my decision to execute the whole Nibelung plan, return to Zigesar (with Karl's assistance) the payments received for Siegfried and revoke this commission. – Drag on miserably with unsuccessful cure. Karl lapsing. Whist. After nine weeks, back to Zürich at end of November. – Minna has accomplished removal: Escher-houses, front, ground floor; very small but comfortable; some luxury. Desk with green silk curtains (later sold to Blandine Ollivier-Liszt in Paris and taken to St Tropez). Dreadful nervous state: very thin and pale. Total insomnia. Continue cold hip baths: Minna's distress; lights with lantern for early morning walk. – Karl too turns up. – Wesendoncks seek my acquaintance through Marschall: old lodgings, Escher-houses, rear. Karl to Dresden. 'Opera and Drama' in print: great agitation on re-reading. Preface to 3 Operas. Alterations during printing. – (Figaro as Messenger) 2 December.

1852

Deny onset of supposed year of upheaval: carry on: 32, 33 Dec., etc. – Letters: to Liszt (Goethe Foundation). To Brendel (Music Journal). Herwegh closer. The Wesendonck house: German Americans, Lösching, Stütmer, Christen. – Symphony conducting: Tannhäuser Overture with descriptive programme. Music for Egmont. – Theatre: Conductor Schöneck. Performance of 'Flying Dutchman' end April. – Tannh. in German Theatres. Schwerin (Henr. Röckel-Moritz) – Julie Kummer (Ritter) and husband arrive for water-cure. – Beginning May summer home on Rinderknecht estate[106] – Frau Julie with boy. Cold, nasty. Valkyrie written. – (Herwegh. – Herzen scandal.) Also newspaper verses against review of Fly. Dutch. Birthday in open. End June town again. Modest income from royalties. Mid-July Alpine journey. Lucerne, Oberland: Brienz, Interlaken; boy for guide, Lauterbrunnen, Jungfrau, Scheidegg. Grindelwald. Faulhorn (wretched eagle) Meiringen. Haslital: Grimsel. (Rash menial as guide.) Sidelhorn. (Glissade) Obergesteln (Valais). Herwegh awaited in vain. Griesgletscher (sick cows): glacier crossed after nevous debility. Descent: Bettelmatt. Pomatt. Formazza Valley. Tosa Falls. Passo. Crodo. Domo d'Ossola. By carriage to Baveno (with rejected officer). Lake Maggiore. Borromean Islands. To Locarno and Bellizona. Monte Cenere Lugano. Hotel. Heat. Telegraph to Minna. – Late arrival. Dreadful thunderstorm. – Dr Wille, Herwegh, Prof. Freudenberger following. Expeditions. Turn back to Palanza, Borromean Islands ('General Hainau'). Prof. Freudenberger's fear on boat. Men back to Z. Baveno with Minna: (Italian one-horse carriage) Simplon. (Martigny: night without accommodation.) Chamonix. (Fête noire.) Mer de glace. Flechère: Minna's fall, twisted ankle. To Geneva. Difficult journey by post home to Zürich. – – Theatres after 'Tannhäuser'. Wiesbaden. Breslau. Prague. Leipzig. Frankfurt. (Berlin: negotiations; Liszt to direct. This declined.) – Guide to performance of 'Tannh.' – October, November: 'Rhinegold' poem. November (in mild weather) excursion with Wille and Herwegh to Klöntal: very weary and poorly; insomnia: night at Näfels. Wallenstadt. (Loge's closing apostrophe.) Revision of 'Young Siegfried'. Completion of whole 'Nibelung's Ring' poem. – Immediately read at Wille's: first evening Rhinegold and Valkyrie; morning: Siegfried. Evening Twilight of the Gods. Great over-excitement. Frau von Bissing. (December.) –

1853

3 January: Death of Uhlig. Papa Fischer's account. – Printing of 'Nibelung's Ring' (50 copies). Doctor retained: Dr Rahn-Escher. Reassuring treatment. Family life. Symphony perf. and rehearsals. (Coriolanus.) – Vieuxtemps. Belloni. – Mid-February: reading of Nibelung poem on four consecutive evenings; Baur assembly room. (Cold: weak tea.) Many people. Beginning March: 'Wagner Week' in Weimar. – Efforts to vitalize Zürich Music Society. 'A Theatre in Zürich'. – More commodious apartment, Escher-houses, front; beautifully furnished. – Silk furniture and curtains. Liszt: 'petite élégance' – Frau Stocker-Escher. Wall-papers. Grand performance of my fragments, with descriptive programme: 18, 20 and 22 May (40th birthday). Frau Heim. Becher. – Banquet: Ott-Usteri. – Emilie and Julie Ritter. Wesendoncks away on travels. Sonata. – June: outing with Minna and Peps over the Brünig (rain) Brienz, Interlaken: Ritter's visit. Otto Kummer. Bad weather; everything gone wrong. 1 July back via Bern: glorious weather. Liszt come to Zürich on visit: stays ten days.

Symphonies. Poetry. Herwegh. Outing; Grütli (3 springs). Beds at Brunnen. – After his departure torch-light procession in the Zeltweg. Speeches. – End July with Herwegh via Chur to St Moritz (Julier). Engadine. Unpleasant spring-cure: Goethe's Elective Affinities. Letters about Wiesbaden performance of Lohengrin; excursions: Maloja. Bernina, Poschiavo. Rosegg Glacier. – Trouble with Herwegh. – Mid-August back with Herwegh by same route. – Wesendonck back. Project for Italian journey progressing. Mood for it. End August: Geneva. (Gen: Klapker. Adler.) Chambéry: special post coach. (Village of cretins.) Mont Cenis. Turin. – Railway to Genoa. Prince Sgaradine and wife; recommend her Liszt's writing on Tannh. and Lohen. – Genoa: Fresco Palace. Sea bath in harbour. Brignole Palace: Van Dyck. Villa Palavicini. Solitude: snow-water. Theatre: Ristori. Purchases for Minna. 3 days: then dysentery. Steamer to Spezia: nasty. Bad accommodation. Ill. On second day attempt walk; pine hill. Afternoon nap on sofa: awoke with conception of instrumental introduction to Rhinegold (E flat major triad): sinking amidst rushing of waters. Resolve immediately to turn back and begin work. Post route along Riviera: (Hungarian officer from Naples). Eight white bullocks: red rocks; bright green pines; deep blue sky and sea. At Genoa form hope of continuing journey: immediately ill again. Direct via Alessandria (dreadful post journey to Novara!). Lake Maggiore (glorious morning: Monte Rosa) home over St Gotthard. Mid-September. Minna at Baden am Stein: hot baths. Visit her often. Beginning October: Karlsruhe concert; rendezvous in Basle. Drei Könige Hotel. Entrance: Liszt, Bülow, Joachim, Cornelius, Pruckner, Pohl. – Next day: Princess Carolyne with daughter Marie. Reading: Siegfried. – To Strassburg. Cathedral. Some reading. With Liszt, Carolyne and Marie to Paris. Splendid rail journey: glass out of the window. (Macbeth.) – Hotel des Princes. Confusion of arrival. Boulevards. – Reading of Nibelung's Ring continued. In between: Berlioz. J. Janin. Dinners. Theatre: nervous trouble; withdraw. – Rue Casimir Bovier. Liszt family. 'Twilight of the Gods' Act III. Madame Patersi. – Theatre: Sept merveilles du monde. – Erards: Muette. Opera. – Quartets in E flat major and C sharp minor. Maurin-Chevillard. Departure of Liszt, 'Conductress' and 'Child' after a week. Remain another week: Hotel des Italiens, boulevards. Minna comes. Kietz. Anders. (Tyszkiewicz jun.) – Wesendoncks. Dinner with me. Embarrassment for return journey. Dr Lindemann: laudanum; metals. Bad state of health. – End October back to Zürich. – Beginning November straight down to composition of Rhinegold: difficulty in sketching orchestral overture. Immersion; much joy: state of health better. –

1854
16 January: Rhinegold ready sketched in pencil. – Symphony conducting.

Overture to Iphigenia in Aulis. Rehearsals. Kirchner. Quartet studies. Family life. Insufficient income. Financial embarrassment. Much about me in German press: Robert Franz. Agitated, ill. – 28 May: orchestration (pencilled pages) of 'Rhinegold' completed. (In Klindworth's possession.) – Money worries. Trouble with Meser. Assign publishing of my operas to my creditors in Dresden. Hiebendahl's proceedings against me. Also Kriete. Dresden solicitor. Bad position. – Article on Gluck's overture to Iphig. – Scene I of 'Valkyrie'. End June: Minna (onset of heart trouble) to Seelisberg for milk cure. Beginning July to Sion (Valais) for Swiss Music Festival: at Karl Ritter's (married) in Montreux; with him to Sion. En route Hornstein. Dreadful mood: bolt, leaving note for Music Director Methfessel from Bern: alone to Geneva in very ugly frame of mind: back to Montreux, where Karl and Hornstein also reappear. An odd marriage. 'Alcibiades' (with me as Socrates). To Seelisberg via Bern, Lucerne: end July back to Zürich with Minna. – August: Act I of 'Valkyrie' composed. Wessendoncks back from travels. – Beginning September: Minna on visit to Saxony and Weimar. (also Waldheim: Röckel.) First reading of Schopenhauer's 'The World as Will and Idea'. 26 September: complete fair copy of Rhinegold score. Excursion with Wesendoncks: Glarus, Stachelberg, Klöntal, Pragel, Schwyz, Brunnen; at Goldau separate: they to the Rigi, I to Zürich. – Very short of cash: – Sulzer empowered by Otto Wesendonck; arrangement; Sulzer administrator. Makeshift order. – Tristan conceived. – November: Minna back. Music Society once again requested by me to do something for the orchestra. Once again promise to conduct symphonies. Gloomy, difficult life: less to do with people. Composition sketches of 'Valkyrie' continued and finished 30 December. Quartet in C sharp minor rehearsed. –

1855

Orchestration of 'Valkyrie' begun. – 'A Faust Overture' revised. – Mr Anderson in Zürich: Accept invitation of 'Philharmonic Society' in London for fee of £200. – February: Tannhäuser at Zürich Theatre: my extraordinary words of farewell at curtain call. – Again conduct (for last time). – 26 February leave for London. Paris: Kietz, Lindemann; Zychlinski. – 2 March: London. Präger and wife. 22 Portland Terrace. – Klindworth. – Sainton and Lüders. – Anderson. Hogarth. Costa. First concert (2 symphonies). Second concert: excerpts from Lohengr. (holy Graal!)[107] Ninth Symphony: (hail thee joie)[107] – Times (Davison). Athenaeum (Chorley). Anderson's despair. – Easter; outings: Brighton. Richmond. Eduard Röckel: fish dinner Gravesend. Crystal Palace Sydenham. Dr Gerber and Eschenburg. Klindworth ill. – Semper in Kensington; little contact possible. – Dr Franck (from his son at Brighton) visit; remarkable conversation. Take leave of each other – for last time! (His fate.) – Präger.

Sundays. Sainton – weekdays. Have perpetual cold. L. Napoleon in London (digs in ribs). Haymarket Theatre: 'Romeo and Juliet'. Miss Curshman from New York. Adelphi Theatre: Fairy stories. 'Shoal for tigers'.[107] Olympic (?): 'Yellow Dwarf'. – Marylebone: 'Merry wifs o. W.'[107] City of London Theatre: 'Bandits' – Corsican Brothers. Audience. Henry VIII at Princess's Theatre not possible. Covent Garden: Italians; ballet. – Bad cold. Suffer from climate – Change of concerts in view of press disfavour. Mr Lucas. Wyld. (New Philharmonia: C minor Symphony.) Exeter Hall: oratorios; Paulus. Messiah. Mr Potter (?): Macfarren symphony: steeplechase. – Benedict. – Ellerton. Dinner in University Club. – Berlioz (and lady) – Dinner at Sainton's. 7th Concert with Tannhäuser Overture. Queen Victoria and Prince Albert. Lord Chamberlain. conversation. – Evening meal at my place with Berlioz. Since decline of London situation, after every concert: Sainton, Präger and Fr. Lüders (Lobster salad. Punch.) – Reading: Indian fairy stories. Dante. (Letters to and from Liszt.) (Ferd. Hiller at Rhine Music Festival.) – Very poor health; comfort: Orchestration of Valkyrie to half Act II. Klindworth arranging. – Night walk: policeman. Regent Park path. Zoological Garden. Hindu. – Merchant Beneke and family in Camberwell; dinner. (Mendelssohn's 'rich mind'.) Encounter Meyerbeer at Howard's (Fétis. Gazette Musicale.). 8th Concert: hearty farewell. Family banquet: 26 June, evening, departure with hangover. (Crossing.) Paris. (Pleasant impression.) Kietz. Wesendonck: journey back with him. Basle – heat.) – 30 June: arrival in Zürich. Highly pregnant state. Very poorly and ill tempered. London profit 1000 francs. – Decide to go to Seelisberg: Peps frail; severe agony, moving devotion. Dies 10 July, 1.10 a.m. – Burial in Frau Stocker-Escher's little garden. – – Next day to Seelisberg. Hornstein. Fair copy of Valkyrie orchestration; cheering. Schopenhauer. Liszt's visit postponed. Mid-August back to Zürich. – Tannh. in Munich. Dingelstedt. – New study of Schopenhauer, also minor writings. His opinion of me (Poem of Nibelung's Ring sent previously.[108]) Berlioz's letter. – Karl Ritter arrives and settles in Zürich. Unpleasant and capricious. Nasty, erratic state of mind, especially towards Wesendoncks. Sponsorship refused because unlucky. Since autumn frequent recurrence of erysipelas. Ask Liszt not to pay visit as constantly unwell. – Complete withdrawal from concerts. – With great breaks, through illness, work on Valkyrie. – Tristan conceived in more definite form: Act III point of departure of mood for whole. (with weaving in of Grail-seeking Parzival).

1856

Tannhäuser in Berlin. Illness: all the time fresh relapses of erysipelas. Evening at Ritters': Golden Pot.[109] – with difficulty complete 'Valkyrie' (with fair copy): last page. Scene with Wesendoncks. Minna mediates. – Scenes from Valkyrie with

Fr. Heim: Kirchner piano. Buddhism: Introduction à l'histoire du B. – 'Victors' conceived, after Buddhist legend in Burnouf. Conceive new ending for Twilight of the Gods on sick bed. – Birthday morning with adagio from E minor Quartet. Tichatschek's visit. (Lohengrin.) Excursion to Brunnen: fresh relapse; collodium. Föhn. – Change of air decided on: beginning June to Geneva via Neuenburg: Fips, Peps' successor accompanies me. Dr Coindet. Mornex: conflict with church service in garden room. Dr. Vaillant: water-cure from 15 June to 15 August; first-rate treatment and successful. Isolated. Morning tea. Walter Scott. – Negotiations with Härtels for publication of The Nibelung's Ring: first hopeful, then shattered. Ideas of building a house; plans. – Karl R. and wife on a visit from Lausanne where they are for the summer. – Also read Byron. – Return via Lausanne (Night at Ritters') Bern (Wesendoncks from Thun to rendezvous). 20 August in Zürich again where I find my sister Cläre (also Math. Schiffner). Outing with them to Brunnen: glorious sunset with milking of cows and yodelling. Serenade by Brunnen brass band on two boats. Colonel Auf-der-Mauer. Rough trip on Vierwaldstättersee. – Mid-September Wesendoncks back; good, peaceful family life; Cläre very agreeable. (Scenes with Minna.) – 22 September composition of 'Siegfried' begun. Much troubled by nearby tinsmith: explode. musically: G minor. Siegfried. Cläre happy. – 13 October Liszt arrives. Plays: 'Dante', 'Faust'. Row with Karl Ritter: baboon. Jesuits. Académie. Much discord from this. Carolyne and Marie follow. Hotel Baur: plenty of life. 'Child's beauty gone. Professors (Moleschott). Evenings at my house. Tell of sketches for 'Tristan' and 'Victors'. Pretty group: Cläre. – Tannhäuser at Josephstadt Theatre in Vienna (J. Hoffman). Carolyne very popular. (Winterberger.) 22 Oct.: Liszt's birthday (Herwegh's bass-falsetto: Fallersleben.) Musical performance: Act I Valkyrie and scene of Act II with Frau Heim. Daube. Festive sounds. (Sulzer.) – Liszt ill. (Egmont.) Cläre departs. Stirring, swelling moods. Work interrupted. Willes, Mariafeld. Mid-November: Wesendoncks to Paris. With my friends to St Gallen: Szadrowski. 23 November: joint concert. 'Orpheus', 'Preludes' – 'Eroica'. Banquet with speeches. 'Princess service'. – 24 Nov: 20th wedding anniversary: large gathering; bridal procession from Lohengrin performed. (Bourry.) – Suffer at night: Carolyne and Marie! – 27 accompany Liszt and ladies to Rorschach. Back to Zürich with Minna: cold weather, ill, low spirits. – 1 December: composition of 'Siegfried' resumed. Threat of trouble with Ritters over Karl: bad things legion. But no more erysipelas: swear by Vaillant.

1857

Jan. and Feb. Siegfried Act I completed. (Full write-out of composition.) Cure: wet-packs once a week: exhausting. Wesendoncks back from Paris: acquire small property for me; building of Villa Wdk. Good Berlin royalties.

Understanding with O. Wesendonck; ending of Sulzer administration. – Frau Dressler Pollert and daughters: sing Rhinegold and Valkyrie: Kirchner. A year since Semper called to Zürich. (Kern.) Pleasant contacts. Herwegh. – Getting better and better acquainted with Schopenhauer. Also Walter Scott. – Invitation to Rio de Janeiro. – Suffer from piano; also one flute. Heims. – No contact with K. Ritter. Furnish cottage: much trouble in process. – Letter to Marie Wittgst. on Liszt. – (only later) letter from Grand Duke only after Devrient's visit. Grand Duchess of Baden: for her album (Wotan's Farewell). Letter from Grand Duke Friedrich. – Vienna negotiating over Lohengrin. – 20 April: Move from Zeltweg: Hotel Baur. Ill. 28 April: Move into cottage: cold and damp; bad. Nice weather coming: kind letter from Frau J. Ritter. Good signs: Good Friday. Imagination at peak: conceive 'Parzival'. – Furnish, with ardour: last Asyl. What to call it? – Good spirits: 9 May 'Siegfried' Act II begun. 'Fafner's Rest'. Birthday: 'Rhinegold'. Three Pollerts. New negotiations with Härtels over Nibelungs: My hopes of Grand Duke of Weimar for it destroyed by Liszt's letter. Concern for continuity of domestic peace. Out of sorts with execution of Nibelungs. Recovering from bad cold: Tristan afresh and decisively. Possibility of its first performance in Strassburg. About mid-June decide to break off 'Siegfried' for 'Tristan'. – Parcel to Emperor of Brazil. (Italian – Brazilian Tristan!) – Beginning July: Eduard Devrient from Karlsruhe. Also reading Herwegh, Semper etc. – Composition Siegfr. Act II. – Beginning August: Präger from London: Rhine Falls. Wesendoncks move into villa. – Robert Franz. – Also F. Hiller. – Summer restlessness. Begin 'Tristan' poetry. (Calderón.) – Hans Bülow and Cosima married: Hotel Bellevue. Three weeks with me. Got through Nibelungen to end of Siegfried Act II: C. – Tristan poem completed. Read aloud 18 September. – 1 October begin composition. Negotiations with Härtels about publishing. – Anxious days. – Confusion. Read through my diary: when peace? – American money crisis: Calderón evenings. Autumn. Winter. December: Act I of Tristan ready; also Prelude orchestrated. Morning-music with Bär's musicians.[110] – 31 letter to Alwine Frommann. –

1858

Neighbourly embarrassment. January: trip to Paris decided on: development there over Tannhäuser (Carvalho). Money difficulty: Müller. Semper. – Liszt: dismay at Altenburg. 14 depart. 15 Strassburg: at theatre Tannhäuser Overture. (Conductor Hasselmann.) Orsini's attempt. 16 Paris: Hôtel du Louvre. – Concerned about money: urge Rienzi at German theatres; arrangement with Härtels for Tristan. – Emile Ollivier. Blandine. (Liszt: Carolyne.) Conservatoire: Seasons. Herolds. Erards. Théâtre Lyrique. Dame d'honneur: de Charnal. Concerts Arbau: Tannhäuser Overture; rehearsal: performance with Blandine.

Gounod's: Médecin malgré lui. (Zychlinsky. Lindemann.) Power of attorney for Ollivier for protection of my copyrights: Palais de Justice; Tannhäuser and Crémieux. – Berlioz: reading of his 'Aeneas' (Trojan Women.) Blandine: two hours of Tristan. – 2 February to Epernay. Kietz. Paul Chandon and wife. 2 days. Strassburg (Hasselmann). 5 February: back in Zürich. Evening party: best of bad job: Herwegh; Semper – grumpy at things going so well with me! – After a week: Otto Wesendonck's visit. Low spirits. Thought much of leaving Zürich. Business bad: Orsini as pretext against Rienzi. Feb. Mar. Orchestration of Tristan Act I. Poems composed. – Easter: house concert at Wesendoncks: movements from Beethoven symphonies. Baton after Semper. (Fr. von Muralt.) 3 April: Tristan Act I ready and sent to Härtels. – Letter on Faust to Mathilde Wesendonck. – intercepted by Minna. Much confusion; propose going away for my sake, against which, promise of silence. Minna at Frau W's. – 15 April: Minna taken to Brestenberg for cure. Bad state of affairs: to Wille's 2 days. Tolerable order achieved by Wille. Beginning May: Erard piano arrives. Soft tone of instrument invites composition of Act II. Wesendoncks go away. More frequent trips to Brestenberg and to Mariafeld to Willes. 20 May: Karl Tausig's arrival. 30: Minna for 2 days on visit. Bad night: my explanations; she humble and beseeching: kisses hand; compassion decisive. – Breakfast morning: hope to get on top of the trouble, and be able to stay. Continue composition sketches for Act II. Compromise, reconciliation in way. – June: Hülsen (Berlin) negotiations over Lohengrin. – Esser (from Vienna) comes about Lohengrin: Contract (Eckert). Dresden: Tannh; again received with enthusiasm. Friendly, hopeful situation: summer ardour. Act II. (Tausig. – quartet etc.) – Beginning July: sketches ready; begin composition. Tichatschek's visit (very burdensome). Philistine: 'You will never find peace!' Also Niemann (with Fräulein Seebach). 15 July: fetch Minna from Brestenberg. At same time Bülows arrive: three days later dreadful scenes (Friedrich: garlands). Visit to M.W. with Cos: – Departure from Zürich decided on and announced. Bülows in house: little music. Klindworth too. Also Karl Ritter for a week. Constraint and agony. Countess d'Agoult. National Song Festival: Franz Lachner. – August: Cosima to Geneva. Many leave-takings: also of Klindworth and Tausig. 16 August: Bülows away. 17 5 a.m. take leave of Minna: clear cheerful sky; no tears. Evening in Geneva. 18 Maison Fazy. Passport difficulties cause delay. – 24 Karl Ritter at Lausanne: takes leave of wife. Travel via Simplon: Lake Maggiore. Isola Bella (beautiful morning). Karl's confidences. – Sesto Calende: Milan. Venice. 29 August. 30. Apartment: Palazzo Giustiniani. – Eliza Wille. Diary. Calm. (2 September: Minna leaves Zürich; noisily, with evil consequences.) News of Lohengrin in Vienna. (28 August.) Karl closer. Gondola trips. Albergo St Marco: Lido. Comet. (Schopenhauer.) Piano: drawing-room, furnishing. Money worries.

(Rienzi rejected Karlsruhe and Munich.) Prince Dolgoruki. (also Count Zichy.) Winterberger. – October: resume composition sketch of Act II. Dysentery. 18 Guido Wesendonck dead: letter from his father with news; my reply. Decide to make winter visit to Mariafeld. Ardent wish to know all at peace: wholly undemanding. Solely to make it possible to work. November: bad dysentery; difficulties with apartment. Bad letters from Minna. Dr Wille's letter re Christmas visit: answered. – Book of Tristan printed. Write to Cosima. 21 November: Karl to Dresden and Berlin. – Tessarini. – Violent illness: leg ulcer. Suffer much for three weeks: Pietro carries me to bed. Dr Minitzch. In addition: money worries; but Minna grateful. Very alone: dreamy. No work. Daru: Histoire de Ven.[111] – Schopenhauer. Parzival much in mind: shepherd's melody in F minor. Cosima's letters, diaries. December: again by gondola to the Piazetta; difficulty walking. Dolgoruki: Albergo St Marco. Lonely Christmas: work troublesome. Push Rienzi at Weimar so as to have money: – lonely New Year's Eve. – Good sleep. – Addendum: Princess Galitsin (not visited). Gr. Wimpfen.[112] – Painter Rahl from Vienna. Architect with him. News of Karl R. –

1859

Very quiet: sole concern uninterrupted work. – Unpleasant letter from Liszt: misunderstanding (Rienzi money); cleared up by Marie Wittgenstein. – From Vienna second payment for Lohengrin. – Beginning January: Karl Ritter back: confused news concerning C.[113] – Instrumentation of Act II: Act I already engraved. Winterberger, Karl, Tessarin: Musical evening with Dolgoruki. – Minna still difficult. Otherwise social life peaceful. (W. von Humboldt. Pasqué: Biography of Schiller. – Schopenhauer, constantly.) Sheet of Tristan to Liszt. Stiff further correspondence. – February: Lohengrin Berlin also. (Flop.) Karl's 'Armide'. Attempted expulsion from Venice: apply to Archduke Maximilian in Milan; order by telegraph. Apply to Minister of Justice, Behr and Lüttichau re return to Germany. In vain. Return abandoned. – Offer from New York: again comes to nothing (Klindworth suggested). From Moscow: Saburov; bookings: no good. – Outing to Treviso: (dust, tormented animals). – St Marco. Good evenings with Karl. Theatre: Malibran: 'Le Baruffe Chioggiote'. – Comploi: more often; Goldoni. 'Semiramide' (Karl sleeps.) Venice: opera and ballet (Mystères de Paris). Piazetta. Campanella of St Marco. Giardino pubblico. Church with Veronese. – Decide to settle in Paris for good. With Minna, bearable. (Frau El. Wille not kind.) Decide on Lucerne for Act III. March: Winterberger to Rome. (Gondola singer.) 17: instrumentation completed. Piano packed. Good deal with Vienna for Tannhäuser. In good spirits for departure. Threat of war: disembarking of troops. 24. Karl, Tessarin (also Schneider) Railway. Evening Milan: 3-day stay. Brera (Van Dyck. Crespi.) Ambrosian

Library. (G. Reni. Drawings by da Vinci and Raphael.) Last Supper. Ascend cathedral. Scala: Cleopatra Ballet. Zezi from Dresden. Teatro Re: Goldini. – Beautiful spring: via Como, Lugano, Gotthard (sleigh) Lucerne. 28 March. Dreadful weather. Schweizerhof Annex. Joseph. Vreneli. 2 April (snowstorm) Zürich. Wesendoncks': sleep one night there. Dream-like. 4 April: piano arrives. Settling in. 9: beginning of Act III. Fatigue; low spirits; restlessness. Bad weather. Liszt: Grand Duke re Nibelungs worse and worse. – (Karl Ritter: vanished, remain without news.) – Composing agony. – May and June: visit Wesendoncks in Lucerne. All tolerable: occasionally very bad moods. Corpus Christi. Kissinger water. Riding. (Liese.) Rigi (bad: bull) – Dresden Opera Publishers: Lawyer Schmidt. Sale. Tannhäuser score engraved; – visit to Zürich: night at Hotel Baur. Italian war: Beautifully hot. Move into main building of hotel. Good work. – Draeseke. Also Baumgartner. Wesendoncks again. – Beginning August: Tristan completed. (Horn duets on lake. Cow-bells at night.) Negotiations with Karlsruhe about settling there; to no purpose. (King of Saxony refuses Grand Duke of Baden.) Firmly decided on Paris. Franz operation necessary. – Pilatus, also Brunnen and Grütli – with Draeseke. – Serov. – Hang on in corner room: piano unpacked again. – Agreement with Otto Wesendonck re Nibelungs. 7 September: packed; 3 days in Zürich at Wesendoncks. (Herwegh. Gottfried Keller. Semper: bad argument about politics.) Winterthur: Sulzer's boy. – 15 September: arrive in Paris. Avenue de Matignon for one month. – Rent small house in Rue Newton. (Nervous trouble.) de Charnal. Carvalho: Tannhäuser – Leroi. Gasperini. – Berlioz (shock at door). From Karlsruhe: Tristan abandoned. Servant taken on. October: Mad. Charnacé. – Belloni. Giacomelli. – Great irritation over arrangement of house. Wesendoncks to Rome. – Roger (Villa) re translation of Tannh. stay with him. 17 Nov: Minna's arrival. (Fips, Jaquot, Therese.) Herolds: Josephine for Minna. My silence. – Negotiations re place for three concerts. Letter to Louis Napoleon. (Monsieur de Lucy – Mocquard. – Ollivier, Blandine. – All the time new recommendations: no good. – No replies. – Bois de Boulogne. Stiff correspondence re projected German performance. – Gasperini. – Monsieur Villot. Flaxland. Ferry. – Baden Ambassador (Herr von Schweizer). Swiss Ambassador (Kern). No answer from Kaiser re opera theatre for concerts.

1860

Schott's inquiry through Esser: negotiations re 'Rhinegold'. Good business. – Hall of Opéra Italien: Calzado; acceptance. Preparation of concerts. Copyists in house. Belloni, Giacomelli for orchestra. Berlioz: his wife. (Meyerbeer.) Chorus (Choral society: Ehmant.) – Hans Bülow arrives and helps. Rehearsals: Emente. Herz Hall; double rehearsal with breakfast. – From Dresden: silver work as present from Weiland. – 25 Jan: first concert. – Perrin. Auber. – Berlioz. – Franck – Marie. – 1 February: second concert. 8 third. (Erard. Lucy. Stürmer. 10,500 francs expenses.) Press. – Champfleury. – Baudelaire. – Berlioz: letter to him in Journal des Débats. Saint-Saens. – Malwida von Meysenbug. (Memories of London: Althaus, Schurz.) Hans: déjeuner for Prussian Ambassador. Count Pourtalès. Count Hatzfeld. (Paul) No Fould. No L.N. – Marshal Magnan: summons to Rue Newton. – Wednesday evenings. Acquaintances: Count Foucher de Careil. – March: von Seebach. – Rossini (Fish and sauce. Visit.) – Halévy. – P. Hatzfeld. Intrigue around Empress Eugénie. – Count Barchiochi. Royer. – Emperor's command for performance of Tannh. Princess Metternich. Count and Countess Pourtalès. – Mimi Buch. – Hans' concerts. – German company impossible. – Prospects bad as regards money. – Letters to Serov – Saburov; Tannhäuser: for St Petersburg. – 19 March: Brussels. Théâtre de la Monnaie: two concerts. Giacommelli. Fétis. – Antwerp. – Privy Councillor Klindworth and daughter Mme Street. Franz Coudenhove (Kalergis). Not the price of my journey. 29 back to Paris. April: Wednesday evenings. (Madame Bronsart-? Ingeborg Stark) Fräulein Hund. – Fräulein Meysenbug: Widow Schwabe. Some help. – Royer: indecisive negotiations. – May: crippling worries. 47th birthday: Jupiter. June: severe financial straits: General Saburov. – Michatte: Stephens. – Decline collection by Madame Schwabe. P. Hatzfeld. – Madame Kalergis. – Oh: Klindworth from London. Tristan with Paul. Viardot. Berlioz. – July: – Niemann. – Translation: Roche (my acquaintance with him.) Lindau. – Minna to Soden – Bois de Boulogne: Fips. – Czermak: riding. – Seebach: Concessions by Saxony. – August: eight-day excursion. Cologne, Rhine. Soden. Frankfurt. (Liszt doesn't come.) Brother Albert and Wife. Darmstadt: Schindelmeisser. Heidelberg. Baden: Princess of Prussia. Return via Cologne: also Mathilde Schiffner with Minna. – Beckmann: Emil Erlanger. – Truinet: translation. New scene for Tannh. ballet – September: rehearsals for Tannh begin. – Vauthrot. Dietsch. Cormon. – (Metternich – Fould – Kaiser.) – October: Luise Brockhaus with husband and daughter Ottilie. – Rue Newton excavated. Litigation: Picard. (Dinner: salmon without caper sauce.) Removal to Rue d'Aumale. Great excitement: Ottilie helps. Drive to Meudon. Cold. November: typhus fever: (Garibaldi fantasies. Also Tuileries: Kalergis, Metternich household.) Gaspérini – also doctors. Very long recovery: drag myself to Opéra. Scenes for Tannh. completed with difficulty. December: 4 poèmes d'opère: preface. 'Music of the Future.' – Rehearsals: Sax. Morelli: Tedesco. – Prince Poniatowski. – Metternichs, Pourtalès (often) – Erlanger. Meysenbug. Hopes of rehearsals. Purchases for Minna for Christmas. No New Year celebrations. (Bavarian beer.) –

111

January and Feb.: – orchestra and theatre problems. Cercle artistique. Meetings at Comte d'Osmond's. Auber-Gounod. Polignac. (A major Symphony) Ballet scene complete and orchestrated. (3 a.m. Minna from ball.) Szemeres. – Meysenbug. – Niemann critical. Tedesco. – Chorus master Massé. – Leborue (copy.) Cormon (direction). – Gaspérini. – Here for performance: O. Wesendonck. Kietz. (Präger.) – Bülow. Growing concern. – Walewski – Dietsch. – March: Repeated efforts against Dietsch: conference, useless. (Dealings with Flaxland over publications: quarrel.) Legal action. (Ollivier's Etoile du soir.) – Renewed dress-rehearsals: orchestra. 13 March First performance. (Pifferaro.) Dreamy Song Contest. Great Uproar in Act III. 'Il prend encore sa harpe.' Morelli. – After performance: Hans beside himself, embraces Minna. – 18 March: Second performance. Good: to middle of Act II. Huntsman's whistles. Niemann in Act III. – 25: (Sunday.) Third performance. Stay at home. Great uproar. – Liszt does not come. – Letter to Royer: score withdrawn. Truinet. Roche. – Aufmordt. Stümer. – Comtesse Gasparin (from Geneva). April: Frau von Löwenthal: matinée. Viardot. St Saens. – Gounod. – Metternichs. Pourtalès. Erlanger withdraws. – Hans from Karlsruhe: Rhinegold. 15 Apr: travel to Karlsruhe. Grand Duke and wife. – Kalliwoda. Eduard Devrient. (Durlach.) After 6 days back to Paris. – Much distress. Meysenbug. Lorbac. – Gaspérini (Lucy.) – Opéra-comique (de Beaumont). – Baudelaire. – Frau von Seebach. – May: via Karlsruhe (Grand Duke) to Vienna. Rehearsal and performance of Lohengrin. Esser. Dustmann. Ander. – 'Flying Dutchman' – Some intoxication; more exertion. – Cornelius. Tausig. Standhartner. (Students refused.) Lanckoronski: Tristan decided on. – Via Munich, Winterthur ('Years of travel') 22 May Zürich. Karlsruhe; Grand Duke. – With Tausig (Strassburg) to Paris. – There: Liszt. – June: Déjeuner at Gounod's. Soirée at my place. (Liszt.) Hesitation on all sides. Blandine. Flaxland. Mlle Eberty (dinner Bois de Boulogne). – 22 June. Fips[114] dies (like Peps,) to save travel difficulties. Buried, with some difficulty, in Stürmer's garden. From domestic and matrimonial point of view, intolerable. – July. Hatzfeld. Metternich: help. 12 July. Minna to Soden; invitation from Countess Pourtalès. Same day move into Prussian Embassy hotel. Black swans. – Fly. Dutchman translated with Truinet. Album pages: soirée with Saint-Saens: Neapolitan princess. (Dr Schuster.) Bethmann-Holweg. Countess Pourtalès: tea evenings. P. Hatzfeld. Count Dönhoff. Diplomatic dinners: Prince Metternich on legitimacy. – Prussian passport. (Count Pourtalès' efforts in Berlin thwarted. Hülsen.) – August: via Cologne to Soden. Minna (Schiffner). Frankfurt (Schopenhauer dead). Take leave of Minna. – Weimar: 2 a.m. Pay respects to Altenburg which in process of being sealed up. (Edward Liszt.) Franz Liszt in cap.[115] Music festival. The

Brendel-ry. Great number of musicians. Marie's rooms: Blandine, Ollivier. Banquet (no torch-procession). Hans. Peter. Tausig. Gille and students. Damrosch. Tieffurt. Emilie Genast. Röckels. – Alwine Frommann. Faust Symph. – Prometheus. Weissheimer. Draeseke (March). Annoyance. – 9 Aug: left with Olliviers. See Liszt off by train: ('luxury'). Eisenach. Nuremberg. (Landlord: 'Margarethe'. German Museum: torture box.) Blandine during journey. (qu'est-ce qu'il dit?') Ollivier: ham. – Munich: antique buildings. Beer cellars. Hornstein. – Reichenhall: – Cosima. – (Adoption:) – Salzburg (Liszt's Sina cigars.) – 14 August: arrival in Vienna. – Kolatschek. – Dr Standhartner; Seilerstätte. Doll.[116] Rudi Liechtenstein. Cornelius. Tausig. (O. Bach.) Count d'Osmond. (Memories of Paris.) Difficulty with Ander. (Mödling.) September: – With Liechtenstein to Count Nákó's at Schwarzau. Tziganery and Van Dyck. Hungarian magnates. To Mödling: alone in the Brühl; morning; breakfast. Sparrows. Much cheered. – Ander – Affliction. – Dinners at Dustmann's in Hietzing. Reading, irritation. – Salvi. – Winterberger: Countess Banfy. (Karl Ritter in Naples.) Mösmer: harp. – Evenings with Doll, Tausig, Cornelius. Translation into German of new Tannh. scenes. – Esser: Schönbrunn. (– Minna to Dresden.) – Flying Dutchman. – Beck and Privy Councillor Raimond. – Chevalier Hebbel. His plays. – End September: Standhartner returns with family. Hotel Elisabeth. Ander declared unfit. Hunt for tenor. Persecution by critics. Hanslick. (Look back at.) – Laube and wife. Burgtheater (Goethe's Faust.) – Tenor: Morini (Lucia – Cornelius.) Peter up: Tausig down. With Dustmanns: Reichenau. – Grand Duke of Baden's reply to my letter re small pension. Very dim prospects. – November: trip to Venice. (Telegram to and from Tichatschek and Schnorr.) Wesendoncks. Grey sky. Hotel Danieli: Luigia; also Tuski. (English widow at table d'hôte.) Dinner Albergo St Marco. Titian's Assumption of Blessed Virgin. Palace of the Doges. Tessarini. 4 days later: long grey journey back to Vienna. 'Mastersingers'. Overture in C major. – Return: gondola and Italian song for Cornelius. – Salvi. Rehearsal of extracts from Tristan. Metternichs. Dinner. Invitation to visit them in Paris. – Research for Mastersingers. Management: fee for Tristan; reject their proposal. Negotiate with Schott for Mastersingers. Draft of scenes: (Library. Wagenseil.) Cornelius in Floridsdorf. 24 November. Minna's silver wedding. – Bad telegram from Schott. Decide to seek deliverance in Berlin: mean to travel that evening; midday good letter from Schott. Doll: packing; at 4 o'clock to Mainz. ('Der Vogel der heut' sang'.) Cornelius happy at saving of Mastersingers which, with Berlin, would have been lost. 1 December: Mainz. Schott family. Weissheimer. – Difficult negotiations. (Paris or Karlsruhe?) – 3 December to Paris. Death of Countess Sándor: my quarters at Metternichs' occupied. Hotel on Quai Voltaire. Truinet. (Taverne anglaise.) Flaxlands. – Gaspérini. – Death of Count Pourtalès.

113

– Do not take up Metternichs' offer of hospitality. Countess Pourtalès. – Theatre with Czermak and Gaspérini. – Much correspondence. Olliviers. Blandine at Mama Liszt's. Dinners. – End December: begin writing poem of Mastersingers. Opposite Tuileries and Louvre. Omnibus. –

1862

Metternich (New Year visit) postponed. Hatzfeld. Appeal to Berlin: troublesome reply. To Brussels: negative. Zürich: lion of San Marco. – Avenarius: Minna intervenes. – Decide on Mainz area. – In spite of all, good mood for writing. Taverne: Truinet. Gymnase: 'Je dîne chez ma mère.' Flaxland. (Rienzi transaction.) Peter (Du:)[117] Doll. End January Mastersingers poetry completed. – Champfleury: evening. moonlight; accompaniment. Olliviers: Blandine enigmatic: no farewell. – 1 Feb.: dinner at hotel. Truinets. Gaspérini. Czermak. Departure. – Karlsruhe: two days. Kalliwoda. Grand Duke and Duchess: promise to return. 4 February: Mainz. Flood. 5, evening: Mastersingers reading at Schott's. Cornelius on dot of 7: back next day. (Surety.) – Weissheimer. – Biebrich. Wiesbaden. – To Biebrich: Europäischer Hof. Take rooms at Architect Frickhöfer's. Cold; ice breaking up. – Raff and wife. 15 February: move into new rooms: furniture from Paris. Piano. – Weissheimer. – Eight days later: Minna's arrival. Unpack and arrange furniture. Cushion (Christmas present from M.W.) old scenes. Days at customs house: evenings at home. Engage Lieschen. – Darmstadt: Rienzi (Niemann. Dalwigk.) 1 March. accompany Minna to Frankfurt. (Theatre: comedy; Friederike Meier.) Return to Biebrich. Deeply disturbed: mood for work gone. Telegram from Grand Duke. 7 March (Osthofen) Karlsruhe. Reading of Mastersingers. Tannhäuser at theatre. Eduard Devrient. – 10 March return. Minna urges writing to King of Saxony about full amnesty: hard battle. Mathilde Wesendonck pregnant. Letter to Otto Wesendonck. Letter to King of Saxony. – More often to Frankfurt. (Don Guiterre.)[118] Weissheimer. Lieschen. Gradual mood. – April and May: Countess Pourtalès. Prelude to Mastersingers. Work going well. Biebrich Park. Weissheimer ill: visit him in Wiesbaden. – Soirée at Schott's: Mathilde Maier. Pleasant spring: evening walks to Wiesbaden. (Gounod's 'Faust'.) Leo the dog on a chain: Frickhöfer. Visit Duke of Nassau: cigar. – Friedrike Meyer's visit: scarlet fever. Guaita. Strange circumstances. – 22 May: for my birthday: Mathilde Maier from Mainz. Luise Wagner. Städel. Dr Schüler. – Often between Mainz and Frankfurt. 'Das Schöne Fest, Johannistag' – maid's attack of hysterical laughter. – Bad exchange of letters with Minna: Pusinelli intervenes. Amnesty: former Court Musician. – Furniture to Dresden. June, Minna to Reichenhall. – Friedrike. Mathilde. – Guaita. – Mathilde: farewell on Rhine

Bridge; tired donkey. Concern; reassuring however. – Wiesbaden: Städel; gambling table. Weissheimer: demon. – Karlsruhe: Schnorr and wife in Lohengrin. Grand Duke: discord over Devrient. Return. Correspondence with Devrient: complete break with Karlsruhe. – Beginning July: – Bülow; Cosima two days later. Soon: Schnorrs. (Dustmann: Vienna Tristan.) Much music-making: Tristan; Schnorrs. Weissheimer. Willig for Wesendonck.[119] Dante profile. Röckel out of prison. Frankfurt Marksmen's Festival. – Evening in Bingen: Friederike. Rüdesheim. Wiesbaden frequently. Raffs. David. Law suit for Lieschen. Outing with Bülows, Weissheimer and Röckel's daughter to Rolandseck. Adventure with 100 gulden. Cross-move[120] with Friedr. Lohengrin in Wiesbaden. – August: bitten by Leo; for two months unable to write. – Five poems for Schott; latter starting to get difficult. Frankfurt: Tasso. Miners outside hotel. Bülows leave. Lohengrin planned for Frankfurt. Schott's refusals: September. Kissingen. Return journey via Frankfurt. Friedr. Guaita. – Weissheimer; L. Wagner.[121] Week in Frankfurt: direct Lohengrin. M.M. – Choral Society: Ignaz Lachner. Hopeless. Mastersingers laid aside. Furnishing Biebrich rooms. Tristan in Vienna; preparations for concerts. – October: (Blandine's death). Weissheimer in Leipzig. Sad time. Orchestration of bits of Mastersingers. End October: to Leipzig. Eisenach: underlings' pleasure. Wartburg. Hermann Brockhaus. Ottilie. Weissheimer concert: Bülow's 'Toggenburg'. The Sasha[122] Ritters. Reading of Mastersingers at Brockhaus's. Professor Weiss etc. Härtel. Lothar Müller. David. Franz Müller from Weimar with commissions and money from Grand Duke. Lassen. Pohl. – Leipzig: very bare. – Beginning November: Dresden (minus barricades). Fritz Brockhaus. Luise. Clara. Minna: Salve. Paris salon. Cläre Wolfr: with her. Heine. (Schnorr.) Pusinelli. – Minister: Behr. Beust. Court Musician Kummer. 4 days (reading of Mastersingers). No help or prospects. – Take final leave of Minna. – Back to Leipzig: Alex. Ritter. Weissheimer. 7 November: back to Biebrich: pay and seek rooms for Mastersingers. Math. Maier. – 2 days later: Nuremburg; Friedr. M. (Visit to Jammertal). To Vienna: night journey, cold. Hotel Munsch: 2nd day: Hotel Kaiserin Elisabeth. 15 November. – Esser; Tristan. Friedr. M. ill. Visiting performance at Burgtheater. Laube. Frau Dustmann. – Standhartner: reading of Mastersingers. (Hanslick.) Cornelius. Tausig. (Irritation with both since summer; Geneva.) Doll. Tea with me. Increasing sufferings of Friedr. Meyer. Inexplicable situation. Prevail upon her to go to Venice for her health. December: preparation for concerts. (Little concerned about Tristan rehearsals.) Weissheimer. Tausig and Cornelius help. Also Brahms. (Uhl: Der Botschafter: Mastersingers Act I in feuilleton.) (Herr Moritz cause of nasty letter from Cosima: Tausig's intervention.) Concert rehearsals: Helmesberger. Three Rhine maidens etc. Theater an der Wien: (Polish Faust). Liechtenstein: Countess

115

Zamoiska. 26 December: 1st concert. (Dreadful expenses.) Empress alone. (Unpleasant correspondence with Venice.)

1863

New Year's Day 2nd concert. 8 Jan 3rd. Madame Kalergis (Empress Elisabeth.) Baroness Stockhausen; Lady Blomfield (Soirée at British Embassy.) Evening at Madame Kalergis's, the Nákós (Liechtenstein and wife). Bulwer Lytton (with reading). (Egg punch with Cornelius.) Countess Bamfy. (Jaell.) Kalergis at court: Zamoiska (Archduchess Sophie). Könneritz (Ambassador of Saxony). No success. Standhartner. Kalergis helpful. – Little faith in Tristan after discouraging piano rehearsal at beginning of January. – Invitation to St Petersburg: Philharmonic Society. – February: Prague: concert (1000 gulden) Heinrich Porges. (Lieblein. Musil. – Marie Löwe-Lehmann.) Deal with Dingelstedt (Weimar). 8 days later back in Vienna. Very satisfactory piano rehearsal of Acts I and II of Tristan. – 15 to Biebrich – good weather: country villas. Plans to build. With M.M. and L.W.[123] Bingen, Rüdesheim. Full powers. – 2 days. – Berlin (Bülows – piano school). Boni[124] in mother's womb. – Alwine Frommann. – Königsberg (over night). – Journey to Russia. (Livland nobleman – Police – military: adventure with musicians. Fur caps.) End Feb.: St Petersburg. Station; committee. – March: Nevsky Prospekt: Frau Kunst. Serov. – 1st philharm. concert. (Tannh. Dutch. Lohengrin. Russian hymn.) Baron Vittinghof. – Dr Arneth. Frau von Rhaden. – Count Wielohorski. – Fräulein Bianchi Serov. – Conductor Schubert. – 2nd phil. concert. (Trist. Mastersingers) – Rubinstein. – Own concert in Grand Theatre. Merchants' Guild concert: small drum. Remarkable singers. – Soirée. – Grand Duchess Helen: Nibelung poem telegraphed for. Evening readings. Fräulein von Stahl. General Brebern-Lvov. – Moscow: ill. Old friends: Lutzau (from Riga.) Albrecht junior. ('doch einer kam'.) Prince Odoyevsky: Rubinstein junior. 3 concerts in 6 days. Banquet with musicians and Prince. Kremlin. (Telegrams re building of house in Biebrich.) – 10 days later back to St Petersburg. (Ritter: also family.) Concert for Schubert. Evenings at Grand Duchess Helen's. Fräulein von Rhaden. – Sent money to Minna: to Biebrich. – One more concert in noble hall. (2nd day of Easter. – Russian.) comes to nothing. 3 days later, concert for benefit of imprisoned debtors: General Suvorov. Silver horn. – Madame Abaza. Grand Duchess, for departure. Serov. (Nothing from Bülows.) Farewells. – End April, depart: Wirballen (frontier) telegram from Fräulein von Rhaden. (Not too bold!) – Berlin – Uneasy: Cosima safely delivered. (Splendid carriage.) Hans. Waitzmann. Letter from von Rhaden: country villa no go. Assets 4000 thalers. – Hotel de Russie: dinner. – Via Breslau to Vienna. – Tristan broken off: Dustmann ill. Old inn: forgo Biebrich. Cornelius in Munich. Tausig ill. – May: find rooms in Penzing: lease for 5 years. (Franz and Anna Mrazeck.) 12 May move in. – Math. Maier. – (Friedr. Mr. wandering about.) 22 fiftieth birthday. Students and merchants. Serenade. (Fritz Porges.) Hietzing. Schönbrunn. – June: difficulty with domestic arrangements. – Minna writes to Natalie. Rebuff. Great concern. (Munich asks for Flying Dutchman.) Correspondence with ladies. – Gold snuff-box from Moscow stolen. Pohl becomes my dog. – Help in house. Some orchestration of Mastersingers Act I. – Tristan given up. Very lonely. Tausig gradually recuperating. Furnishing: money finished. – End July: invitation to Budapest, two concerts at theatre. Remenyi. Rosti. Mosonyi. Countess Bethlen-Gabor. Danube trip and danger. Kaiserbad: tziganes. – Count Coronini (Ofen). – Baron Augusz. – Banquet: toasts, Rakoczy March. – Baron Rabatinsky. Tenor Steger. Radnotfay. – Beginning August: return. (von Seebach.) M.V. into house. Visit Remenyi with Plotenyi. Garden. Great heat. Rambles: Ober St Veit. Hütteldorf: Esser. Remenyi's offers for Budapest. False hopes. Concert trip for autumn. Some orchestration. Many refusals: e.g. Darmstadt. Karlsruhe difficult. (Correspondence with Grand Duke.) Keeping in suspense. Promissory notes. Plans in a mess. Give up – where to go? – (Duncker: History of Antiquity.) Tausig back in Floridsdorf. New world. Strauss. General hubbub. – Polish up-rising: Russia difficult. – Promissory notes. October. Cornelius. Also H. Porges. Outings: Brühl; fall.[125] – Niece of Ottilie. Laube. Peter every day. Desire to compose. Break off. Article for 'Botschafter'. Beginning November: on concert tour. Prague. 2 concerts: bad. (Kittl.) Via Nuremburg, Stuttgart to Karlsruhe; Kalliwoda. Will. R. Pohl. Mainz comes visiting. Kalergis–Mukhanov. 14. Concert. Ed Devrient. Grand Duke. Second requested. – Dinner in Baden. P. Viardot. Turgenev. Mukhanov. – Brief visit to Zürich: negative. – 19 November 2nd concert. Fur coat out of it. Present. – (Good link?) Raff. Em. Genast. Eckert. – Fatigue: revulsion. Dresden written off. By night: Mainz. Schott's proposition. The Maiers: Karthäusergasse; peaceful night. – Night journey via Frankfurt to Berlin: Bülows at station. Stay one day. Concert. (Frommann on the stairs.) Waitzmann. (28 Nov:) – Löwenberg. Conductor Seifriz. Prince Hohenzollern. Rehearsals. Concert. Henriette Bissing. Dinner: Toast. Present from Prince. Money to Vienna for bill. Schubert. symph. (C minor Beethoven.) 4 Dec. Breslau. Damrosch family. Blum. 1 concert. (Judea) Frau von Bissing. Plans for me. Against Russian tour: promises help. – M. Buch. – 9 Dec. back to Vienna. Franz at station. Pohl; Stritzel. Week of peace: Peter. Heinrich. Money deals. – Frau von B. hopeful. October: theatre article in Botschafter. Uhl. – Christmas. Everyone receives present. – 27 Dec. Tausig's concert in Redoutensaal (Freischütz Overture). Ottchen B.[126] Very low state: nevertheless consider journey to Kiev. Bissing correspondence: precarious yet hopeful. Much thought of death: instructions for this eventuality. Nevertheless decide to resume work. – New Year at Standhartner's: Ottchen Br. Peter's poem. –

1864

10 January: illness (chronic cystic catarrh). Correspondence with St Petersburg about Kiev and Moscow. Fräulein von Rhaden. Frau von Bissing, (dubious exertions). Growing difficulty over promissory notes. Plan to travel to Kiev and Moscow via Odessa. News overdue. With last hopes in Frau von Bissing, resume composition of Mastersingers. (Walter.) – Brahms. Tausig. (Liechtenst.) – February: new promissory notes. Unwell. – Russia silent. – Fr. von B: ('in God's name: no!') – Ed. Liszt: Frau Schöller. Keeping in suspense. Inquiry to Berlin re journey to St Petersburg. – Manuscript sent to Schott. – March: Rancé.[127] – Tausig vanishes. – Peter (Odyssey evenings.) H. Porges: O. Bach (also Count Laurencin). Standhartner. – Write to O. Wesendonck. (Negative reply.) Write to Pusinelli about Minna. 21 March: information from Liszt and Standhartner. Tuesday 22. Preparations for flight. (Peter: 'When is it to be?') Bequests. – 23 Gottwald from Breslau, negative. – Take leave of: Anna, Pohl. – Trunk, Franz – assistance. – p.m. to Munich. Very ill: two days at Bayerischer Hof. Good Friday: mourning for King Maximilian II. 'Here lies Wagner who never made good, or got so much as a beggar's knighthood; not even a look from a dog could get he, or from college as much as a doctor's degree.'[128] 26 Lake Constance. Zürich: Mariafeld. Frau W. alone; he in Constantinople. Annexe (formerly Frau von B.). Piano etc. from Green Hill. – Math. Maier. – Truinet: royalties (75 francs). Communications concerning Frau von Biss.) – April: visit to Wesendoncks. Appearances. Reciprocated. O.W. corresponds with Frau Wille: sustenance. Very cold and nasty. Ill. 'Hermann, mein Rabe!' – Fever. Idea of separation from Minna and going for rich marriage. Write to Luise Brockh: silly answer. (C.) – Berlin royalty (75 thalers!) To London (re Tannh.) – Stuttgart: (Lohengr.) – Reading: Siebenkäs. Frederick the Great. Tauler. G. Sand. W. Scott. Friday. – Felicitas. – From Vienna. (no Peter) Frau Wille: rent for Penzing. – Standhartner announces sale of furniture: outburst. (25 Apr.) Peter feels sorry for Tausig. Inform latter of my imminent return. – Dr Wille. Incredibly miserable. Write to H. Porges. (Tristan at piano.) Leave letter for Frau Wesendonck. –]]

30 April to Stuttgart. – May. Eckert and wife. (Singer. Abert.[129] h.a.w.) Gall. Weissheimer from Osthofen. (Dr Grunert.) Cannstadt for summer quarters: Schott negotiates. Frau Wille: obtuse; Frau Wsdck refuses[130] my letter. 3 May. Pfistermeister. 4 May his visit: ring and portrait from King. At same time bad report from Vienna (dinner at Eckerts': Gall pays for Lohengrin). Evening to Munich. 5 May: visit to King. 6. Revelations: letter from King. Vienna

arrangements. Rooms by Englischer Park. (Frau Kaulbach. Pecht. Lachner.) Near Starnberg for summer. – 10 May to Vienna. (Franz. H. Porges.) Detours to Praterstrasse to Dr Stern's (Porges.) Lawyer Trotter. Standhartner. 3 p.m. everything arranged. 11 Österreichischer Hof. Negotiations about furniture. Standhr. and Liszt not visited. Peter silly. Violent correspondence with Hans. Telegrams. Prater trip. Not Tausig. Take leave of Standth. 13. with Franz, Anna, child and Pohl to Munich. 14. King. 15 to Starnberg. King at Berg: mornings, almost every day. Letter to Cosima about Hans. – Invite the Vienna people and Eckerts to my birthday: 20. remain completely alone. – (Cornelius invited: no answer.) 22. Alone with Pfisterm. King's portrait. Readings. – End May: King to Kissingen. (Empress of Russia. – Beginning of intrigues.) – June: bad weather. Disquiet. Peter doesn't answer any letters. H. Porges does not accept my view. – Mathilde Maier refuses.[131] – Pfistermeister, King. Funds for settling my debts. 12 June once more: Vienna. Some furniture back: Franz packing. Lawyer Trotter: debts discharged. Cornelius rejected. Doll reasonable. 'Friendships'. – Visit Dr Liszt.[132] Standh. Porges 2. – 14 June back. Starnberg. Piano. (Hietzing ribbon-manufacturer.) 'On State and Religion'. – End June: Cos. with children. Beginning July: Eckerts ('Ass on the ice!') 7 July: Hans. Soon Klindworth. End July: daily with H. (also Kl.) to Munich to King. Dinners. 29. Hans' appointment. (Return journey: showing teeth.) – Zumbusch. – Kochelsee. H. taken ill: Klindworth's departure (?) August. – King at Hohenschwangau. Birthday music. (Streck.) 'State and Religion' dictated. Lasalle. – Cos. to Karlsruhe. Hans to Munich: ill at hotel and furious. – Füssen and Hohenschwangau (with Zumbusch.) No music: Queen Mother. 25 Aug: Augsburg station master. – Starnberg:[133] (September). Poem to King. Cos. across lake. To Munich: Liszt. (Grey man.) Accompanies me to Starnberg for one day and night. Praises my good sense. – Again Munich: Bayerischer Hof Hotel: Kaulbach. (Hans!) 3 Sept. departures: morning, Liszt; evening, Hans and C. – Quiet at Starnberg. Negotiations for 21 Brienner Street. Ottilie Brockh., Hermann and daughter on visit. Pleasant family atmosphere. (Sakokzen alpski.[134]) King's letters. – Cos. with father on travels. – 'To you'. – Letter about Nibelungs – Completion to King. – Dinner at Lachner's – Vreneli from Lucerne. – Beginning October to Munich: hotel. – Friedr. Schmitt. – Birthday music. (Nohl.) King at chateau (Marshal's uniform). Agreements. Cornelius appealed to. Pfistermeister (?) Brienner Street: the Ship. – Math. Maier with mother (news of illness false). 15 Oct. first night on Ship. Dinner with Dienersch and Maiers. – nodal haemorrhoids. Ulcer. Confined to bed. – Cos. (Hotel Marienbad.) Back from Marseilles. (22 Oct.: Liszt's birthday.) Departure of Math. (Cos. talks much in her sleep of Daniel.) Jour des morts. Much puzzlement. Monastery bells: Consuelo; 2 Nov. 6 a.m. – Slow recovery. Furnishing. (Anonymous letter from Zürich.) Good letters: tonic. Artistic decisions. (Augsburg railway official.) Kriete's demand for interest. – Lachner. Perfall. Pecht. Rehearsals for 'Fl. Dutch' – Blunder. – 20 Nov: Bülow's arrival (Marienbad). December 4 and 7 performance of 'Fl. Dutch'. 11 Dec. Concert at theatre. (Hymn for the North American Republicans. Ullmann.) – Dinner with Lachner, Perfall, Pfisterm. King inspiring. (Some orchestration.) (Tausig's marriage letter.) – Echter (Nibelung corridor.) – Fresh ulcer. Privy Councillor Gietl. – Semper: theatre. – Tristan planned: Schnorr correspondence. – P. Cornelius: (pince-nez). Christmas again. New Year in Bed. Foolish dreams.

1865

January: – Semper in Munich. Theatre project. Allgemeine Zeitung opposed. King: against music at Court. Hans difficult. – Portrait by Pecht. (Dreams.) Pecht's article on Semper and building of theatre. – 1 Feb. Musical performance in private at Residenz Theatre. ('Above the abyss!') 6 Feb.: Pfisterm. 5 morning visit ('My boy'). Conducted back from King's door; Pecht's portrait. Newspapers disfavour ('Fly. Dutch.'). Tannh. without King (12 Feb.). Allgemeine Zeitung. 'Associates'. 17 Audience. Assurance of innocence. Pfisterm. – 19 Allg. Z.: 'R.W. and Public Opinion'. Pecht's denial re 1000 gulden. My statement. 22 Feb. Frau Dangl: 'Providence of Bavaria'. 25 Feb. Allgemeine Z. again. Standstill. Privy Councillor Klindworth from Brussels. (later with Mme Street again.) Balzac. – Zahlberg from Karlsruhe: 26 beautiful Sunday with Bülows, Zahlbrg and Cornelius. Schnorrs arrive. – Pfisterm: away for 4 days. Tannh: with Schnorr. Arrangements completed for Tristan. 6 March Sch: back. – Letter to King: everything clearly represented: reply appealing for my trust. 'Shall I go?' – 'Stay!' – Preparations for Tristan. Hans' concert tour. – 'Report on Music School'. Dictated and presented. – April 2 Hans. 5 Schnorrs. Mitterwurzer (Zottmeier. Deinet). Piano rehearsals in 'Ship'. (Cornelius to Weimar: Cid.) – 10 April Isolde born. – 1st rehearsal. – The two 'lions'.[135] (Obliged to buy up house.) – Schwabe. Schwind, – Residenz Theatre. May: 'Swinehounds'.[136] 11. Dress rehearsal (H. Porges). 15 May – visitors. (My invitation in Botschafter.) Schwabe – Schwind. Schauss. – Frau Schnorr hoarse. No performance. (Gaspérini – Röckel etc., also M. Maier.) Delay. Receptions in garden. 22 M. Birthday (inebriated!) Peacocks. Lions. Berg – Possenhofen. Visitors depart. Schnorrs to Reichenhall – June 8 and 9 new rehearsals. (Dorn.) Al. and Frau Ritter. Gaspérini and Leroy. 10 June 1st performance of Tristan and Isolde. (Box. Reception. Prelude.) – 13 2nd perf. (Unwell: withdraw; walk during Act I.) – 19 3rd perf. (King Otto. Berg: Cos. Pfist. King.) Albert Wagner. – Tegernsee: bumble-bees.[137] (Cos. dreams of altar piece showing Day of Judgement.) Hans in Baden. (English Garden) 1 July: 4th perf. (royal.) Frau

Heim. Schuré. – 9 July: 'Fly. Dutch' with Schnorr. Thunderstorm. Dark. – 12th concert in Residenz Theatre: (Rhinegold. Valk. Mastersg. Royal March.). Tea at Bayerischer Hof Hotel. Take leave of Schnorr. (13 leaves early.) Berg: excitement. Pfistermeister at the boat. (15 July: Pecht pays for picture.) – Pfisterm. rebuffed. 16 July: Berg again. (Cos. and children; magic garden and maze.) 21 July: telegram from Dresden. Schnorr dead. 22 with Hans to Dresden. Choral festival: miss burial, which put forward. (Malvina's reception and look.) (23 July). Midday to Prague. (Jews; Schützeninsel.) 25 back in Munich. – 28. Berg. – Baron von Moy. – (Procrastination over Music School.) (Präger) Mid-August: Cos to Budapest. 'Hochkopf'. – Ramayana. 'Les Misérables'. Poem (Siegfried – Tristan). Capuchin visit. – King Hohenschwangau. 25 August: back to Ship. (Poem by telegram to King.) Sketch for 'Parzival'. September. Cosima back. Witching hour. 'What is German?' Siegfried Act II. Orchestration. 2 October: King in Munich. Cos. and Pfistm. negotiating. – 8 Oct. break with Pfistrm. – Lutz.[138] – 18 King in M. – 20 money bags. – To Vienna: – Fröbel. Dentist. – November: King at the Grütli. Invitation – Hohenschwangau. Week: Paul Taxis.[139] – Biesenhofen. – Back: Hans still away: at lunch with C. and children (Russumuck). – Tenor Vogl. (Frau Schmitt.) Volksbote: Cabinet. – (Engineer Bauer.) – Röckel. (About Neumaier.) Orchestration of Siegfried Act II completed. – Morning dream: spider's web. 6 December: King in Munich; evening visit: Lutz. Message. – Matthieu. – Grandauer. Reitknecht. Kilp.) 8 Distrainers' visit: Kriete. – Lawyer Freitag. Corresp. with King. The 3 nights. – 10 December: depart early. (Porges: also Peter.) Without a tear. – Pohl (coughing) and Franz. – Lake Constance again. – Bern: 2 nights. – 12 Dec. Vevey. Pension Prélat. Grand Duke of Baden. Looking for country house (Ratzenberger). Draeseke from Lausanne. – On 20 to Geneva with Vreneli. Métropole. 'Artichauts'. Cold and ill. Christmas. 28 Dec: move in. New Year: to South of France.

1866

Jan.: Letter to Ferry (Pohl worse: little coat).[140] – C. Frantz: books, letter. – Letters: sympathetic; anonymous. – Set about completion of Act I Mastersingers. – Never to return; misunderstandings. – 20 Jan. to Lyons. Toulon; Hyères, Marseilles. (Constellation. Bad finger.) 4 days: telegrams from King. Pusinelli: Minna's death. Undertaking to King. (Dr Bertoni – Morocco.) Pohl dead. – Beginning Feb.: back via Lyons. (Fur-journey.) Week's fatigue: Pohl's monument. (Pierre.) Montsalève: Mornex. Roland's death. Mastersingers orchestrated. – (May decided for Munich.) New agitation in M. – (Minna's starvation.) Plaintive letter from King. – C. announces arrival; delayed. March 7 Lausanne: C and Lusch.[141] (Biss)[142] 3 weeks 'Artichauts'. Biography. (Chatter-

Lusch.) Montsalève. (Russ.) – Lutz about Pfordten. – (Monsieur Adore.) (St Maurizio and St Lazaro.[143] – 27 March: Lausanne, Bern. (Memphis, Tunis.) Interlaken, Brünig. Lucerne (Eduard and Madeleine.) Grütli flowers. (Good Friday.) Night in Lucerne. – Zürich (Table helpings) Romanshorn: lighthouse; farewell. – Bern. Geneva. – April 3 to Lucerne. Triebschen leased. (Am Rhyn) Schweizerhof Hotel. (Jeanne d'Arc. Eg. Sue.) – Vreneli and Steffen. 15 move in; make shift. Some of the things from Munich. – Melusine: fontaine de soif. 'Every seven years'. Invitation to Hunting Lodge at Riss – declined. Cos. to Holland. Time of mourning. C. Frantz. – May: great distress; arrangements for my death. – Romanshorn: Cos., and Loldi; children and Agnes. Silent journey. Zürich: Zeltweg. 7 May – 9 Composition Act II Mastersingers begun. Biography. (E.E.) – Paul Taxis. 22 May: afternoon, King. 23 Alpnacht and Stanz. 24: Morning: spider above King's chair. King departs with Taxis. – Great agitation in Munich: telegrams. War brewing. (Roseninsel.) June. Röckel's visit. Company to Romanshorn. (Group of boys with flowers.) Zürich: Bellevue Hotel. Triebschen. Mid-June: Hans in Zürich; C. goes to see him. Letter to King. Letter for Hans. (C. to Munich to fetch letters.) Hans and C. to Triebschen. – Letter from King. – Also letter to Pfordten. Dr Wille (Bismarck.) – Semper. – Bavarian Politics. – Seelisberg. War (useful for Triebschen). – July. – Sadowa. (Roseninsel.) – (Opinione.) – 15 The Pilatus. – Telegrams of resignation. – Draeseke. – (Muse.) P. Taxis again: give up Munich house. August: C. Frantz on visit. (Also Ollivier.) Whist evenings. – (Beckenried.) (Order of St Hubert.) H and C. to Munich – Loldi. (Bad weather.) Letters: much confusion. September. C. suffering greatly. – 20 Sept. H. to Basle. Letter from Lake Constance. 23 Composition Act II Mastersingers completed. 25 evening: C. at Triebschen. – 2 October: Act III begun. Biography. Stolzing[144] arranged for Winter: Walther-act: – Hans Richter joins as secretary. 1 November. Malv. Schnorr and Ida Pfeiffer (venom concocter from Brauen). (King's journey to Franconia. Pfisterm. sacked. – Neumaier.) Dec.: Lutz. – Hohenlohe. (Basle journeys: melody of Prize Song – without text. By Christmas verses too: 24 December: 12 midnight distribution of presents.) New Year: Hans on visit. Cos: 'he wants to go back to Munich'. –

1867
1 Jan.: Zürich. (Semper. Theatre model. – Return journey: vow.) 7 C. with Lusch to Basle. – Composition. Text: final lines. – King urging return. Hohenlohe. Dr Schanzenbach. – Düfflipp. – Agreement. – 7 Feb.: pencil sketch of Act III ready! – 13 Feb.: 'Prussian Nobleman'. – 16 11 p.m.: midwife. Dr Suiter. Night. 17 Feb. 9.45 (Walther's song:) Eva's birth. – 2 o'clock: Hans. – Garden. (Russ.) (18. Parz. betrothed) Hans at meals. 19. Christening in Lucerne. (Richter. Agnes.) Dining room with door open. After 8 days H. back to Basle.

9th day. – 5 March. Composition of Mastersingers completed. King. 'Do not break with B.' – 9th Munich. (Röckel. Franz. Bayerischer Hof Hotel. – Schnaufer –) 10th with King. Düffl. Schanzenbach. Peter. (Hotel teas.) 12th Hohenlohe. 13th Hans from Stuttgart. – Princess Sophie. (At Pr. Ludwig's – Kammerdiener.) – 'Dear God'. (16 March.) 17. King again. Physiognomical change. 18th early, return home. Hans as far as Augsburg: Eva. – Cos. in Zürich: black fur coat. (Butterflies.) Orchestration Act II begun. Tausig piano score. (Horn solo) Duties towards 'the children'. Very serious. – 25 Alpnacht. – 26 Cos. to Basle. – Beginning April: from Munich; Röckel on Düffl. – Immediate departure: Cos. as far as Romanshorn. (Child's steps.) Munich: next day King; Hans furious telegram. – Düffl.'s apology. Hohenlohe. Tauffkirchen. Röckel. After 3 days. via Lake Constance to Basle. 3 Kings. Bad and good. Decision by telegram. Relief. – Concert rehearsal: Oberon aria. Em. Genast. (Merian.) Shopping with C. – 9 April back: Lucerne. Next day Cos. Differences. Points of obscurity. – Beckenried: boat to Brunnen; Axenstrasse to Flüelen. Night watchman. – Bürglen: Palm Sunday! – (Pifferari.) Boat to the Grütli. Watering. Brunnen. Evening, back. – 15 Apr. C.'s departure. (Extremely exhausting.) Work. Confusion. May – but no spring! Great anxiety. Little Eva's thinness. Debilitating gastritis. – 19 May. Semper on visit. C's telegram. 21st Journey to Munich: cold and rainy. 'Adolphe'. Benj. Constant. Cs and Hs at station: Bayerischer Hof. 22nd 10 a.m.: Starnberg; Villa Prestel. (C.) Then Berg: King. 5 o'clock back. C. at station. Telegraph to Lucerne. – Bad health. Vacillation. (Lang. Ovations.) King off riding and travelling. Few days Arcostrasse. Richter with Loldi and Koss.[145] – Luise and Ottchen Brckh. – Lohengrin: Tichatsch. – 30 May evening to Starnberg: Richter, Franz, Anna, Koss. (Mommsen.) Piano work table. 'Sail and Wind'. June: King Wartburg. – Piano rehearsals in Munich. – Tichatschek trouble. Düffl. – Hans furious. (Cornelius and fiancée) Starnberg – Munich. Laube's 'German War'. – 11 June: dress-rehearsal: puppet hubbub. Röckel with ill tidings: King opposed to Tichatsch. (Commands.) Riding party. – 13th Bülows with children Villa Prestele. King's letter to Düffl. 15 June departure: (Koss under coat: Augsb; Hohenlohe.) Triebschen: rebuilding and alterations. Letters of repentance from King. – Begin scoring. 22nd Act II finished with difficulty. (Nohl: Beethoven II.) Bad health. Trouble with building. – Meals in garden. Eva getting strong. (Fate!) Blue sky. (Mérimée.) Wallenstein: 'Bernhard von Weimar'.[146] July: Munich performances. (also Tannh.: with new scenes. Silent.) Work. – August: H. Porges. – Hans. Children (without C.). Misunderstanding. Hans to St Moritz. (Tausig in Ragatz.) About mid-August: Cs. (No outings.) Furnishing of Stolzing. Gallery. (Velasquez Visitors.) The Willes on visit. – September: Negotiations re 'Süddeutsche Presse'. (Röckel and Fröbel.) Düfflip comes. Grumbling. Finally 'friendship'. Presse fixed. Articles:

the K and the P. – Hans from Graubünden: letters. – Cos. to Basle: dentist. Much anxiety. 15 Sept. Farewell at my bedside: carriage rolls away. – Work. Richter daily at table: gallery. Continuation of articles. – October. (Schiller: Wallenstein. Also Faust Part II.) Liszt's visit: dreaded but pleasant. 1 day. Morning: awakening of sleeper. – My letter to Hans about nirvana: acceptance reported. – Rome. Points of obscurity; incomprehensible. Great fear. 24 October Mastersingers score completed. For week to Paris. Grand Hotel. Truinet. Exhibition: schoolchildren; butterflies. Shopping: pottograph. Polykrates ordered. Dinner with Truinet and father. (Very excited and weak.) Metternichs. Bad impression of city. Toutsaint.[147] – Royalty. – 3 Nov. back to Triebschen. – Proofs. (Golden pheasant.) Articles. Rest. – Furnishing. (Truinet deals.) Minna's fire-screen. – News of Fröbel. Royal 'indignation'. Articles suspended with XIII. – Goodbye to Eva. (Richter ahead to Munich at beginning December.) 23 December to Munich. C. at theatre. Violet-blue cage. Franz, Anna: Richter. – Christmas. (Things from Paris for children.) C.'s birthday. (Polykrates.) Hans to Prague and Dresden. Düffl: Royal warning to C. concerning legations etc. Next day to King: $2\frac{1}{2}$ hours. Reconciliation and apology to C. Suppressed articles sent to King. (later come back unsuccessful.) New Year at Cornelius's: mother-in-law, Porges family, Richter, Hungary and Poland. (Genelli's life.) The 'friendly man'. Punch. 12 o'clock: New Year. –

The previously unpublished note below was written by Wagner on a small envelope. This has been stuck to the otherwise blank page 138 of the original; whether by Wagner himself, or by Eva later, cannot be clarified with certainty.

[[Progress through railway, etc. – Materialism, – Godlessness – acceptance of decline of man to point of reversion to animal – even total destruction of globe – can leave belief in moral significance of world unshaken: 'God' is outside time and space.]]

It is of relevance to the three sonnets to David Strauss that Franz Lachner was General Music Director at Munich, and that there was a Lachner faction which intrigued against Wagner. A member of, or sympathizer with it, was David Friedrich Strauss (1808–1874), a Protestant theologian and writer. In 'On Conducting' (Collected Writings, Vol. VIII, pp. 377/378) Wagner reports having once lost patience with a 'venerable maestro' of the baton. This maestro, Lachner, had so mistaken a tempo during a Tannhäuser rehearsal that – as Wagner writes – 'I was then, for the sake of eternal justice and to restore the correct tempo, obliged most respectfully to intervene against my maestro, which caused some annoyance. It even led, I believe, in time to martyrdoms which even a phlegmatic Gospel critic [Strauss] felt himself compelled to celebrate in two sonnets.' The three sonnets below are in ironical reply to Strauss's. Cf. note pp. 193–194.

An David Strauss

I.

O David! Held! Du sträusslichster der
   Strausse!
Befreier aus des Wahnes schweren Ketten!
So woll' uns stets von Irr' und Trug erretten,
wie du enthüllt der Evangelien Flausse!

Wie schön Du nun, auch in der Kunst zu
   Hause,
es weisst mit wunderlieblichen Sonetten
aus Zweifel uns in holde Ruh' zu betten,
das Schöne rettend vor Zerstörungsgrausse.

Der Fabeln unerbittlicher Ergründer,
auf unächt Alter weisst Du leicht zu schliessen,
von falscher Gicht machst bäldlich Du
   gesünder:

Doch wer will jetzt um Läugner noch Dich
   schelten?
Blieb Christ, der Heiland, Dir auch
   unbewiesen,
lässt Du dafür uns doch Franz Lachner gelten.

To David Strauss[148]

I.

O David! Hero! Straussest of the
   Strausses!
Deliverer from delusion's weighty chains!
May us redeem from error and deception
your exposé of humbug in the Gospels!

How beautifully now, at home also in
   art,
you're able, with sweet sonnets made of doubt,
to make for us a bed of charming peace,
saving what's beautiful from dread destruction.

Pitiless researcher into fictions,
spurious age you can deduce with ease,
discover instant cures for pseudo-
   gout:

But who will now berate you a
   denier?
If, for you, the Saviour Christ's not
   proven,
you let Franz Lachner serve as well instead.

125

Nun kommt heran, vereint euch, edle Hunde,
die ihr die Katzen hasset treu und bieder!
Jetzt bellt und heult gerechte Klagelieder
nach revidirtem Text vom neuen Bunde!

Uns brachte König David selbst die Kunde,
dass auf leibhaft'ger Seraphim Gefieder
der Schönheit Avatar uns stieg hernieder:
nur leider bracht' ein Kater ihn zu Grunde.

Selbst Katerina konnte ihn nicht schützen,
obschon sie von Cornaro wahrhaft stammte,
und selbst ein Strauss ihr ew'ges Sein bewiesen.

Nun gilt's, das neuste Testament zu stützen:
O ihr, Davidische, Sonnet-Entflammte,
Ihr Hunde, auf! der Katzen Blut soll fliessen.

II.

Come now, join together, noble dogs,
true and worthy haters of the cat!
Now bark, now howl a righteous dirge
to the revisèd text of new alliance!

Regal David brought the news himself
that, upon corporeal seraphs' pinions,
the avatar of beauty had descended,
but he, alas, was brought low by a cat.

Protect him could not even Caterina,
albeit hailing truly from Cornaro,
to live forever, as proved e'en by Strauss.

Time now to back the Newest Testament:
O you of David now inflamed by sonnet,
arise you dogs, for feline blood shall flow!

11 March *[1868]* – evening

III.

Noch ein Sonett? Auf zweie noch das
    Dritte?
O David! Wer ermisst wohl, wie erhaben
In einem Vers Du tiefen Sinn vergraben,
Erfüllt' ihn selbst auch Lachner's neu'ste Suite?

Denn rufen wir zurück in uns're Mitte
Den Meister, wollen wir ihn wieder haben,
Und schrei'n darnach wie sieben Schwind'sche
    Raben,
Was hülfe uns die zart bescheid'ne Bitte?

Du trafst es wohl: denn selbst der König
    Nobel,
Er stammt aus dem Geschlecht der bösen
    Katzen,
Verführte Reineck selbst, den Witzereisser.

Den Königspelz von Hermelin und Zobel
Entreisst, ihr Hunde, nun des Löwen Tatzen:
Zum König wählet euch den Bullenbeisser!

III.

One sonnet more? The third to cap the
    two?
O David, who's to measure how sublimely
you have buried deep sense in a verse,
has Lachner's latest suite imbued it too?

For if into our midst we will recall
the Master, if we will have him back,
and cry for that like seven crows by
    Schwind,
of what avail the humble soft entreaty?

You've hit it well: for even Lion the
    King,
is of the genus of the wicked
    cats,
and led the joker, Fox himself, astray.

The Royal coat of ermine and of sable
tear from the Lion's claws now, dogs:
and choose the bulldog for your King!

12 March *[1868]*

Foreword to German Art and German Politics

The author here offers, connected and complete for the more precise information of the public, a series of essays which appeared piecemeal and without a conclusion in a political paper towards the end of last year. Those who have hitherto directed a more intimate interest towards his artistic and his theoretical works, will, he hopes, from this find cause to give his unremitting struggle of long years to win supportive ground in reality for the ideas he has in mind, its due. Becoming imbued with great and elevating reassurance at recognizing this ground uniquely and unerringly in that of the German spirit, he now feels able to compress the more extravagant pre-conditions that had obtruded themselves upon him earlier, in the direction of the clearly recognizable goal that is the notion of the Germans' noblest wishes and aspirations regarding the re-forming of their great, indeed boundless, fatherland. If, particularly in the state of modern public art which precisely through its decay, is exposed to the shallowest judgement, the exceptionally unwonted nature of the immediate juxtapositioning of the two aims has, above all and against an erroneously selected background, given rise to much misunderstanding and confusion, the author nevertheless believes himself permitted not to lose heart, and, on the contrary, to cherish the hope that for his ideas, too, it will be possible to find effective agreement amongst the German public.

Tribschen   RW
16 March 1868

Of relevance to the entry below is that Constantin Frantz (1817–91) was an important political publicist who gained Bismarck's interest. Wagner's own political views had been influenced and also confirmed by him since November 1865. Writing to the King from Geneva on 8 January 1866, he said of Frantz: 'His is the most efficient, truly statesmanlike mind I have ever encountered amongst Germans. In particular, the second, greater, book [Die Wieder-herstellung Deutschlands (The Restoration of Germany)] *is the correct, truly German politics such as I anticipate; the author wrote to me that the chords of my music had revealed to him the image of the German future.'*[149]

Foreword to Second Edition
of Opera and Drama

[[For Constantin Frantz.]]

About the same time last year when a letter from you informed me in such gratifying fashion of your impression of this my book, I learnt that the First Edition had for some time been out of print. As I had been advised not long previously of there being a fairly large number in stock, I inquired in amazement as to the reason for the obvious interest in recent years for a literary work which, by its nature, was not really intended for a wide public. Experience to date had shown me that Part I, containing a critique of the opera as an art-genre had been flicked through by newspaper critics, and that certain jocular remarks occurring there had claimed some attention; the contents of this part had been read more seriously by a few real musicians, as also the constructive Part III. Of real attention being paid to Part II, devoted to the drama and dramatic material, I received no note: obviously my book had come into the hands only of music specialists. To our literary writers it remained entirely unknown. From the title of Part III, 'Poetry and Music in the Drama of the Future', a 'music of the future' was extracted to designate an ultra new 'direction' in music, as founder of which I have, in inadvertent fashion, been brought to something approaching world fame. It is to the previously wholly unnoticed Part II that I probably now owe the otherwise inexplicable increased demand for my book that has occasioned a Second Edition of the same. That is to say that with people to whom I was of no consequence at all as poet and musician, an interest arose to seek out in my

128

writings, of which strange things had been heard, the insidious bits dealing with politics and religion; to what extent these people succeeded to their own satisfaction in judging my tendencies to be highly dangerous I have no means of knowing; still, it did however become possible for them to induce me to attempt elucidations of what I understood by the 'downfall of the state' that I called for. I confess that this really put me in some embarrassment and that in order to extricate myself tolerably, I gladly condescended to confess to not having intended anything so bad, and to having, on consideration, really no objection to its continued existence.

From all my experiences with this strange book, what emerged to me was that its publication had been totally unnecessary, incurring me only vexation, and providing no one with agreeable instruction. I was inclined to consign it to oblivion, and shrank from concerning myself with a new edition for the reason that for this I should have to read it anew, something that, since its first appearance, I had felt a great reluctance against. Your so expressive letter soon changed my mind. Your being attracted to my musical dramas, whilst I was imbuing myself with your political writings, was no coincidence. Who will realize the significance of my joyous amazement when from the much-misunderstood heart of my difficult book you cried to me with understanding: 'Your downfall of the state is the founding of my German Reich.' Seldom probably has there been such complete mutual integration as had its preparation here on the broadest and most comprehensive basis between politician and artist; and this German spirit which, proceeding from the extreme antithesis of the accustomed view, has so surprisingly brought us together in deeply felt recognition of our People's great mission, is something which we may now believe in with increased courage.

There was however need for this faith to be strengthened by our meeting. The eccentric aspect of my opinions as still published in this present book was certainly occasioned by contrary despair. The reasons for opposing doubt might still be of small force if we were merely supposed to draw them from the declarations of our public; any contact with it can only bring those imbued with our faith into immediately regrettable associations, against which complete isolation, with all its sacrifices, alone offers salvation. The sacrifice which you made in this sense consisted in renouncing more general consideration and recognition for your noble political writings in which, with convincing clarity, you direct the Germans to that sole salvation which lies so close to them: slighter seemed to be the sacrifice that the artist, the dramatic poet and musician had to make, whose works speaking loudly to you out of the public of all theatres so animated your hope that you already saw all-powerful nourishment being fed to faith. You found it difficult not to misunderstand me and recognize even infirm hypertension in my resistance to your confident assumptions when I attempted

129

to instruct you concerning the small compensation of my successes before the German theatre audience. You yourself, however, finally supplied yourself with this radical instruction by taking precise cognizance of this volume, now dedicated to you, concerning opera and drama. Certainly it disclosed to you the wounds, concealed from all the world, from which, prior to my unerringly certain inner feeling, my successes as German 'opera composer' suffered. – In truth, even today nothing can mollify me for the fact that these successes rest, in one most all-important part, upon a misunderstanding, which actually directly obstructs the real, uniquely achieved success.

The explanations of this apparent paradox I set down, now almost 18 years ago, in the form of an exhaustive treatment of the problem of the opera and the drama. What, above all, I must admire about those who apply careful attention to this work is their courage in not allowing themselves to become wearied by the difficulties of presentation which were forced upon me by precisely that exhaustive treatment. My desire to get completely to the bottom of the matter and to shrink from no detail which, in my view, should render the difficult subject of my aesthetic investigation intelligible to simple intuitive understanding, misled me into adopting in my style that pertinacity which, to the reader out for entertainment and not immediately interested in the subject, will in all likelihood seem perplexing diffuseness. In my present revision of the text I did however decide to make no essential alterations, as in the said difficulty of my book I did, on the other hand, recognize the special quality that would commend it to the serious scholar. For that, even an apology must be considered superfluous and misleading. The problems which I have felt urged to deal with, have never been examined in the context which I recognize, and apart from that, never by artists whose feelings they most immediately represent, but only by theatricalizing aesthetes who, even with the best will, cannot avoid the abuse of applying a dialectic form of representation to subjects like music, which in their essential form have hitherto lain so remote from philosophy. Shallowness and ignorance find it easy to expatiate on matters not understood, drawing on traditional dialectics in such a way as to seem, again to the uninitiated, to be of consequence: he however who is not willing to toy with such concepts before an audience which itself possesses no philosophical concepts, but who, as regards difficult problems of erroneous concepts, sets store by addressing himself to the correct feeling of the matter, him let kindly learn from me, and perhaps from the present volume, what exertions one has to make in order to cope with one's task to one's inner satisfaction.

It is then in this sense that I commend my book anew to serious attention: where it encounters it, it will, as was, my honoured friend, the case with you, serve to fill the alarming gap between the misunderstanding-filled spirit of the success of my dramatic-musical works and what, to me, seems the solely correct effect of the same.

Lucerne, 26 April 1868.   Richard Wagner

The following 'Order for Complete Edition of my Writings' of 26 April 1868 has not previously been published. Wagner mentioned it, however, in a letter to King Ludwig of 27 April 1868. The order was altered in the Complete Edition *as it later appeared. What is striking is that the plan of 1868 had not yet envisaged the acceptance of Rienzi, Das Liebesverbot and the 'Communication to my Friends', whilst in the printing of the first ten volumes, the 'Agape of the Apostles' was left out of consideration. Cf. note p. 195.*

[[Order for Complete Edition
of my Writings

Vol. I   – Biographical Sketch (Zeitung für die elegante Welt.)
            Two Novellen: A Pilgrimage to Beethoven
                            The End of a Musician in Paris.
            A Happy Evening
            Virtuoso and Artist
            Rossini's 'Stabat mater'.
            Concerning German Music.
            Performance of Der Freischütz in Paris.
            Halévy's 'La Reine de Chypre'.
            4 sketches: 'The Saracen Woman.'
                        'The Mines at Falun.'
                        'Wieland the Smith.'
                        'Jesus of Nazareth.'

*

Vol. II   – Oration at Weber's grave.
Programmes: III   9th Symphony. – Eroica. – Coriolanus. – Quartet in
                    C sharp minor. – Tannhäuser Overture, Flying Dutchman.
                    – Preludes to Lohengrin, Tristan, Mastersingers. –
            Agape of the Apostles.
            The Wibelungen – – The Nibelung myth. –
                Siegfried's Death (first draft) –

131

Poems: To King Friedr. Aug. – At Weber's grave. –

*

Vol. III   –   I(b) Art and Revolution.
                (c)
                (d) Art and Climate.
                     The Art-work of the future.

*

Vol. IV   –   Opera and Drama.

*

Vol. V   –   Sketch for Reorganization of Dresden Court Theatre. –
                     Address to Orchestra. –
              II(a) Letter to Liszt (concerning Goethe Foundation)
               I(a) Letter to Brendel (about music journal.)
              II(b) A Theatre in Zürich.
              II(c) The Viennese Court Opera Theatre.
                     Foreword to The Nibelung's Ring.
              II(d) Report on Munich Music School.
              II(e) German Art and German Politics.

*

Vol. VI   – III   From the Foreword to the 3 Opera poems.
                     Dedication of Lohengrin to Liszt.
              III(c) To Marie Wittgenstein about Liszt.
              III   Spontini's Death (Rossini) – Judaism in Music.
              III(d) The Overture to Gluck's Iphigenia in Aulis.
              III   Concerning the performance of Tannhäuser. –
                     Concerning the performance of Flying Dutchman.
              III(a) Letter to Berlioz
              III(b) 'Music of the Future' to Monsieur Villot.
                     Report of Paris Performance of Tannh:
                     (in Deutsche Allgemeine Zeitung.)

*

Vol. VII   –   Poem to King of Bavaria. –
                     Invitation to Performance of Tristan.
              (?III) Ludwig Schnorr. –
                     Poem. 'Above the Abyss'.
              (?)   Music (with reference to Schopenhauer.)
              (?)   On Conducting.

132

F. Hiller. – H. Riel. –
What is German?
On State and Religion. –

*

Vol. VIII   The Flying Dutchman.
Tannhäuser.
Lohengrin.
Tristan and Isolde.
The Mastersingers.

*

Vol. IX   The Nibelung's Ring.

*

Vol. X   Reminiscences from my Life. (From the Biography.)

26 April [*1868*]]]

Some indication of the extent of Wagner's shock at the early death of the tenor Ludwig Schnorr von Carolsfeld, his first Tristan, on 21 July 1865, is that it was not until almost three years later (end of April and beginning of May 1868) that he commemorated the singer in the recollections below. A copy for the King served as the original for publication in the Leipzig Neue Zeitschrift für Musik *for 5 and 12 June 1868.*

Recollections of Ludwig Schnorr

I first heard of the young singer Ludwig Schnorr von Carolsfeld through my old friend Tichatschek who visited me in Zürich in the summer of 1857 and directed my attention to this highly-gifted artistic disciple for the future. He had at that time commenced his theatrical career at the Karlsruhe Court Theatre under the direction of the excellent Eduard Devrient, well known to me from Dresden and a close friend; by the latter, who also visited me that summer, I was informed of Schnorr's special liking for my music and for my dramatic singing exercises. We agreed on this occasion that I might earmark my 'Tristan', the conception of which was at that time engaging me, for a first performance in Karlsruhe, in which connection it was to be hoped that the Grand Duke of Baden, who was very favourably disposed towards me, would be able to overcome the difficulties still making it impossible for me to return unmolested to German Federal territory. A little later I also received an agreeable letter from young Schnorr containing an almost impassioned assurance of his devotion to me.

For reasons, about which there remained much uncertainty, the plan for a performance in Karlsruhe in the summer of 1859 of my completed Tristan finally proved impossible. Of Schnorr himself it had been reported to me in this connection that, his great devotion to me notwithstanding, he did not think it feasible to overcome, in particular, the problem posed in the final act for the singer of the central role; apart from which, the state of his health was described to me as doubtful: he was suffering from a fatty degeneration which marred his youthful appearance. When, in the summer of 1861, I first visited Karlsruhe and new stimulus was given by the ever amicably disposed Grand Duke to the execution of the project previously decided on, I remained unfavourably inclined towards the management's offer to enter into negotiations with Schnorr, now engaged at the Dresden Theatre, for the part of 'Tristan': I declared myself reluctant to make the personal acquaintance of this singer, being afraid that his grotesque appearance might prejudice me to the point of insensitivity to his real artistic talents. When, after this, the projected Vienna performance of my new work proved impossible, I stayed for a while in the summer of 1862 at Biebrich on Rhine, attending from there at Karlsruhe a performance of 'Lohengrin' in which Schnorr was appearing as guest artist; I arrived in secret, intending to be seen by no one, so as to conceal my presence from Schnorr, and fearing to be so confirmed in my apprehensions concerning the repellent impression of his supposed deformity that, out of loyalty to my renunciation, I would wish to remain unacquainted with him. This timid attitude on my part was soon altered. If the sight of the Swan Knight landing in his tiny skiff at first created the somewhat astonishing impression of a youthful Hercules, the decided magic of the legendary, God-sent hero worked upon me the instant he appeared so that one did not ask oneself what he was like, but said to oneself: He is like that! This immediate and most heartfelt effect can only be likened to magic: I can remember experiencing it in earliest youth from the great Schröder-Devrient in a manner that was decisive for my whole life, and never again so peculiarly and powerfully thereafter as from Ludwig Schnorr's appearance in Lohengrin. Presently, as his performance proceeded, I detected much that was immature in his reading; but even this had for me the appeal of unmarred youthful purity, and the chaste capacity for most vigorous artistic development. The warmth and gentle enthusiasm that poured from the wonderfully affectionate eyes of this wholly boyish man, at once bore witness to me of the daemonic fire with which they were to blaze; quickly he became for me one for whom, on account of his infinite gifts, I felt apprehensive. At the end of Act I, I charged a friend sought out for the purpose, to bid Schnorr come and meet me after the performance. This was done; the young giant stepped unfatigued into my hotel room late that evening, and the bond was sealed; we had jocular things to say, but little else. A more protracted period together at Biebrich was agreed upon.

There by the Rhine we soon came together for several weeks to run through my Nibelung works and especially 'Tristan' to our hearts' content, accompanied on the piano by von Bülow who was visiting me at the same time. And here was said and done all that could bring us to the closest understanding regarding every artistic interest of concern to us. On the subject of his doubts about the performability of Act III of 'Tristan', he now confessed to me that these were to do not so much with the fear of exhausting voice and strength as with his failure to master the meaning of a single, but, it seemed to him, all important phrase, namely that of the love-curse and especially of the words 'aus Lachen und Weinen, Wonnen und Wunden' (from laughter and tears, from raptures and wounds). I showed him how I intended this and, indeed, what great expression I had tried to give this phrase. He swiftly understood, realized that he had mistaken the time, imagining it faster, and now saw that the resultant overhaste was to blame for the failure of expression, as well as for lack of comprehension. I ventured to observe that in the extended tempo of this passage I was making

135

certainly completely unusual, indeed perhaps enormous demands; this suggestion he declared to be of no importance, and immediately demonstrated his ability to extend this passage in performance to complete satisfaction. This one feature has remained as unforgettable as it has instructive: the greatest physical exertion ceased to be an effort once the singer was convinced of the correct expression of the phrase; the mental insight conferred the strength for material mastery. And from this delicate scruple the young man's artistic conscience had suffered for years, the to him seemingly dubious rendering of a single phrase prejudicing him against the possibility of employing his talent to solve the whole task: cutting, the method so swiftly invoked to their aid by opera singers of the greatest renown, would not of course have served, for he saw this very point to be the tip of the pyramid to which the tragic task of this Tristan towered. – Who will realize what hopes I allowed to animate me now that this wonderful singer had entered my life! – We parted and were not destined to be reunited for the final solution of our task for several years.

From now on, my efforts to secure a performance of 'Tristan' coincided with those to secure Schnorr's collaboration in it: they were not crowned with success until an exalted friend of my art, who had meantime appeared, made over the Munich Court Theatre to me for this purpose. At the beginning of March 1865, Schnorr arrived in Munich on a brief visit for the necessary discussion of the enterprise we were soon to tackle. His presence became the occasion for a performance of Tannhäuser in which, with one rehearsal, he took over the central role, but which was not otherwise prepared any further. To convey my ideas concerning the performance expected of him in this the most difficult of my dramatic singing roles, I was able to avail myself only of verbal discussion. I spoke generally of my sad experience in having, to date, found the theatrical success of my Tannhäuser unsatisfactory, and this by reason of the constant failure to resolve, indeed, to understand, the central role. As its basic feature I indicated extreme force of both ecstasy and remorse without any really comfortable in-between stage, but abrupt and determined in their alternation. To enable him to to grasp this feature of his performance, I referred him to the importance of Scene I with Venus. If the intended deeply moving effect of this misfires, the foundation is laid for the failure of the whole performance, which no vocal rejoicing in the first finale, and no rebelling and breaking out at the Papal ban in Act III is any longer capable of rendering properly effective. My new execution of this Venus scene which had been suggested by its subsequently recognized and, in the first draft, insufficiently clearly expressed importance, had not at that time been rehearsed at Munich, and Schnorr was obliged to make do still with the older version. So his concern should be to express all the more, through the force of his performance, the agonizing struggle in his heart, which

136

here is still left more to the singer solely, and he would, by following my advice, make this possible by interpreting all that preceded only as a powerful climax to the final cry 'Mein Heil ruht in Maria!' (My salvation lies in Mary!) This 'Maria!' I told him, must come with such force that the miracle that at once occurs, of release from the Venusberg enchantment and of rapture in his home valley, should be understood from it as the needful fulfilment of an irresistible demand by feelings driven to extreme decision. With this cry he adopts the attitude of one lost in the most exalted ecstasy and thus he is now to remain, motionless, his gaze rapturously directed towards heaven, indeed not changing this attitude until addressed by the knights who enter later. How he was to resolve this difficult task, rejected some years before by a highly renowned singer as impossible, I would specify to him direct, standing near him on stage in this scene at the rehearsal. I stood very close, and following the music beat by beat and the events going on about us, from shepherd's song to procession of pilgrims, whispered what was inwardly happening in the enraptured man's emotions, from sublimest total unconsciousness to gradually awakening consciousness of his present surroundings, and particularly by the animation of his hearing, whilst he, as if not to destroy the miracle, still resists apprehending again the old homely earthly world with the gaze of eyes enchanted by awareness of ethereal heaven; with gaze still riveted heavenwards, only the play of his expression, and finally the mild relaxing of the tension in the erect attitude betray the increasing emotion of re-birth until every spasm, produced by the divine overwhelming, eases, and at last crying out 'Allmächtiger, Dir sei Preis! Gross sind die Wunder Deiner Gnade!' (Almighty, to Thee be praise! Great are the wonders of Thy grace!) he sinks down in submission. With the quiet interest that he then takes in the singing of the pilgrims, his gaze, his head, his whole posture as he kneels, sink lower and lower until, choked by tears in a new, succouring swoon, he lies stretched prone and senseless on the ground. – Quietly advising him in the same spirit, I remained at Schnorr's side for the whole of the rehearsal. My very brief whispered suggestions and instructions were responded to by an equally quiet glance of inspired fervour on his part, which, while assuring me of a most wonderful harmony, itself in turn gave me new inspirations concerning my own work, and a certainly unprecedented example of the fruitful interaction that may come of a loving and direct communing of differently gifted artists when their gifts are perfectly complementary. –

After this rehearsal we said not another word about Tannhäuser. Even after the performance which took place the following evening, scarcely a word was said about it, and especially no word of praise and appreciation on my part: for on that evening I had, through the quite inexpressibly wonderful performance of my friend, had a sight into my own creative processes such as it has seldom, perhaps never before, been possible for an artist to have. This is the point at which an inviolable feeling of emotion enters, in face of which it is for us to maintain a most reverential silence. –

With that one – never repeated – performance of Tannhäuser, Schnorr had realized absolutely my most fervent artistic intention: the daemonic in rapture and pain was not lost for an instant: the decisively important passage in the second finale: 'Zum Heil des Sündigen zu führen', etc. (To lead the sinful man to his salvation), which I have so often longed for in vain, and which is so obstinately omitted by every singer by reason of its great difficulty, and by every conductor by reason of the usual cutting, was, for the first and only time, performed by Schnorr with affecting, and thus powerfully moving, expression, suddenly changing the hero from an object of abhorrence to the epitome of one deserving of compassion. His appearance as a madman in Act III, and, accordingly, his parting from Elisabeth, had been correctly prepared through the impassioned frenzy of remorse in the violently tempestuous finale of Act II; out of a state of numbness, emotion was all the more affectingly released until the renewed outburst of madness brought about the magical reappearance of Venus with the same daemonic force as the appeal to Mary in Act I summoned back, by a miracle, the Christian, homely, everyday world. Schnorr was truly horrifying in this final frenzy of despair, and I do not believe that Kean or L. Devrient can have risen to greater power in Lear.

The impression on the audience was most instructive to me: a great deal, such as the almost mute scene following release from the enchantment of the Venusberg was affecting in the true sense and occasioned stormy outbursts of undivided general emotion. On the whole, however, I observed more amazement and astonishment: in particular, that which was wholly new, like the otherwise always omitted Act II finale passage already discussed, produced, as a result of confusion regarding that which is customary, an effect bordering on alienation. I had straightaway to suffer myself to be instructed by an otherwise highly intelligent friend that I had no right to wish to have Tannhäuser performed my way, as the audience, like my friends who had everywhere received this work favourably, had obviously thereby stated that the more comfortable, more subdued interpretation of hitherto was basically the correct one, even if unsatisfactory to me. Objection that such assertions were foolish was accepted with a friendly and indulgent shrug in order that they might be persisted in. – And this quite general mollycoddling, indeed, beggaring, not only of public taste, but even of the views of our often interfering immediate circle was something that we now had jointly to hold out against: and this, in simple agreement concerning the right and the true, we did, creating and working in silence, undemonstrative save in artistic action.

And this too was now in the making with my fervent associate's return early the following April for full rehearsals of 'Tristan'. Never will the most incompetent of singers and musicians have been more ready to receive so much minute instruction as this leading singer at the very peak of mastery: the apparently highly pedantic pertinacity of my directions, since he immediately understood their sense, was greeted always with only the most joyous acceptance, so that I should really have appeared dishonest in my own eyes, had I, thinking to be found not sensitive by him, tried to suppress the slightest criticism. The reason for this lay, however, in my friend's having derived an ideal understanding of my work from within the work itself, and having made it truly his own. Not a single thread was there of this fabric of mind and heart that escaped him, or was not felt with the utmost sensitivity, and not a single suggestion, however faint, of the most obscure connection. All that now remained was to judge the technical means of singer, musician and actor most precisely in order everywhere to match personal gifts and their peculiarity with the ideal object of the performance. Any who attended these studies are unlikely to recall ever having experienced anything similar in terms of harmony between artists and friends.

Only concerning Act III of 'Tristan' did I say nothing to Schnorr ever apart from my earlier explanation of the one passage he did not understand. Having during the rehearsals of Acts I and II riveted both ear and eye on the tension in my actors, at the beginning of Act III I instinctively turned away from the sight of the mortally wounded hero on his bed of pain to sit motionless on my seat, eyes half closed, absorbing myself into myself. At the first rehearsal, the unusual duration of my apparent total apathy, my never once turning towards the singer throughout that immense scene, even at his most impassioned moments – indeed my doing no more than stir, seemed to have caused Schnorr inner embarrassment. For when finally, after the love-curse, I staggered to my feet quietly to tell my wonderful friend, bending to him still stretched on his couch, and in emotive embrace, that I had no judgement to pass on my ideal which, through him, had now been fulfilled, his dark eyes flashed like the star of love: a scarce audible sob, and never another solemn word from either of us concerning this Act III. But, as an indication of my feelings on this subject, I would permit myself jests such as: Writing a thing like this Act III was easy, but having now to listen to it from Schnorr – that was difficult, which was why, at first, I was not able to look. –

In truth, even now, three years later as I write these notes, I still find it impossible to express myself concerning this achievement of Schnorr's in that performance of 'Tristan' Act III, and perhaps for the reason that it defies comparison. At a total loss how to convey merely a rough idea of it, I can, I

139

believe, capture for future consideration so terribly fleeting a miracle of the art of musical and dramatic performance only by recommending friends genuinely disposed towards me and my works, always in future to take up the score of this Act III. They would have, to begin with, to submit only the orchestra to closer examination, and there, from the opening of the act, with 'Tristan' stretched out as if lifeless, to his actual dying, follow the musical motives that restlessly arise, evolve, combine, separate then merge anew, grow, diminish, and at last contend, intermingle and almost intertwine themselves. Then let be perceived that these motives which, for the sake of their significant utterance, have required the most detailed harmonization, as also independently agitated orchestral treatment, express a life of feeling that alternates violently between utter desire for bliss and a most determined yearning for death, the like of which could not, hitherto, have been dared with a comparable wealth of combination in a purely symphonic movement, and which, consequently, it has been possible to realize here only by virtue of an abundance of applied instrumental combinations such as hardly any purely instrumental composers have seen themselves obliged to bring so richly into play. Now let one tell oneself that this whole gigantic orchestra should relate to the vocal task of the singer lying stretched on the couch, merely as the accompaniment to a so-called aria, and accordingly draw one's own conclusions as to Schnorr's achievement when I invoke every true listener at those Munich performances to testify that from first beat to last all attention and all sympathy was directed towards the performer, towards the singer, and remained riveted upon him, and that never for an instant was there distraction or diversion vis-à-vis as much as a single word of the text, but rather that the orchestra disappeared completely vis-à-vis the singer, or, more correctly, seemed to be included in his performance. Certainly, to characterize the incomparable greatness of this artistic achievement on the part of my friend, all is said to him who has closely studied the score of this act, when I say that it was, on the other hand, by the dress rehearsals that impartial members of the audience were already predicting that this act would prove the most popular success.

As I attended the four performances we had of Tristan, what at first had been awestruck astonishment at the achievement of my friend became intensified within me to the point of veritable dismay. In the end it seemed to me an outrage to have to think of this feat made, say, a part of our repertoire, an achievement to be repeated on demand. And at the fourth performance, after Tristan's love-curse, I felt constrained to declare determinedly to those around that 'this was the last performance of Tristan; I would not allow another.' – It may well be difficult clearly to convey the sense of my feeling over this. Anxiety at the sacrifice of physical strength by my friend was no part of it, for that, as a result of experience, had been completely reduced to silence. On this point, the experienced singer

Anton Mitterwurzer, who, as Schnorr's colleague at the Dresden Theatre, and his companion, as Kurwenal, at the Munich production of Tristan, took the most profound and sympathetic interest in both the achievements and the fate of our friend, expressed himself very accurately and appositely: when his Dresden colleagues cried loudly that Schnorr had destroyed himself with 'Tristan', he very sensibly objected that anyone who, like Schnorr, was in the fullest sense master of his task, could never over-extend his physical powers, in which was included the application of those powers to the successful accomplishment of the task as a whole. Indeed, neither during nor after the performance was the slightest weakening of his voice observed or any other sign of physical exhaustion: on the contrary, if, before performances, he was kept in a constant state of excitement by his concern for success, so, following each fine new success a most cheerful and vigorous mood and bearing would immediately make its appearance. It was the results gained through such experiences and very accurately judged by Mitterwurzer which, on the contrary, caused us seriously to consider how these results might be exploited for the founding of a new style of musical and dramatic performance corresponding to the true spirit of German art. And here, out of my meeting with Schnorr, which had blossomed into such fervent association, an unexpectedly favourable prospect was opening for the results of combined work in the future.

The inexhaustibility of the gift of the true genius thus became very clear to us from our experience of Schnorr's voice. This it was, full, mellow and lustrous, which, the moment it had to serve as the direct instrument for resolving a task completely mastered mentally, produced upon us precisely that impression of genuine inexhaustibility. What no singing teacher in the world is able to teach we found it possible to learn solely from the example of the solving of such tasks. But what are these tasks for which our singers have not yet found the correct style? They present themselves firstly as an unusual demand on the physical stamina of their voices, and if the singing teacher tries to help with this, he believes – and from his point of view, with justice – that he has only to resort to material means for strengthening the voice, and in the sense of an absolute naturalizing of its functions. In this process, the voice is conceived, as in the fundamentals of its training, only as a human and animal organ; if now by further training the musical soul of this organ is at last to be developed, then for this purpose the given examples of the voice's application can still only serve as the norm, and, accordingly, the problems posed here are what is of importance for all else. But the singing voice has hitherto been trained solely after the model of Italian song: there has been no other kind. But Italian song was inspired by the whole spirit of Italian music: and at their best, it was the castrati who suited it to greatest perfection, this spirit being directed only towards sensual well-being without any

141

real anguish of soul, – the youthful male voice, the tenor, being at that time employed not at all, or, as was later the case, in a falsetto castrato role. But now the tendency of more modern music, under the inevitably acknowledged leadership of German musical art, has, particularly through Beethoven, elevated itself to heights of true artistic dignity by, for the first time, drawing into the domain of its incomparable expression not only the sensually pleasing but also the mentally vigorous and the profoundly passionate. How must the male voice, trained in accordance with the earlier musical tendency, relate now to the tasks offered by modern German music? Developed on a sense-appealing material basis it can see demands made on, in turn, purely material strength and power, and to train voices for these therefore appears to the singing teacher to be the important task. How erroneous this is it is easy to see, for any male voice trained only for material power will, in attempting to resolve the tasks of more modern German music such as are presented in my dramatic works, immediately succumb and wear itself out to no avail if the singer is not completely equal to the mental content of the task. The most convincing example of this was provided for us by Schnorr, and to show quite clearly the far-reaching and wholly disuniting distinction involved, I cite my experience of that passage in the adagio of the second finale of Tannhäuser: 'Zum Heil des Sündigen' (For the salvation of the sinful), etc. If nature has in our time produced a miracle in the shape of a masculinely beautiful natural male voice, then it is the tenor voice of Tichatschek which has endured now for forty years, ever powerful and sonorous. Any who, last year, heard the story of the Holy Grail performed in most noble and rich-sounding simplicity, were deeply moved and affected by a miracle experienced in reality. But some twenty-four years ago, after the first performance in Dresden, I had been obliged to delete that passage in Tannhäuser because Tichatschek, who at that time was in most brilliant and powerful possession of his voice, could not, after the bent of his dramatic talent, master its expression as that of ecstatic contrition, but, over some high notes, lapsed into purely physical exhaustion. If now I testify that Schnorr not only performed this passage with most moving expression but also produced the same dynamic high notes of anguish, I certainly do not wish to set Schnorr's voice above Tichatschek's as if it surpassed it in natural power, but precisely to vindicate the latter's uncommonly equipped natural voice vis-à-vis the inexhaustibility in the service of mental comprehension which we had experienced.

With the recognition of Schnorr's immense importance for my own artistic creation, a new spring of hope arrived in my life. Discovered now was the direct bond which should link my work fruitfully with the present. Here was something to learn and something to teach: what had been universally-doubted, mocked and calumniated was now to be turned into incontestable artistic achievement.

The founding of a German style in the performance and acting of works of the German Spirit – that became our watch-word. And making this hope for a great and gradual blossoming my own, I now declared myself opposed to any immediate repetition of Tristan: with this performance, as with the work itself, a too violent, almost desperate leap forward had been made, and over into ground that was new and to be won for the first time: gulfs and abysses yawned between, and had first carefully to be filled in to prepare for urgently needed associates a way across to that eminence where we stood alone. –

Now Schnorr was to belong to us: the founding of a Royal School for Music and Dramatic Art had been decided upon. The considerations imposed by the difficulty of freeing the artist from his Dresden engagements led us in turn to the particular character of the post for which we, from our side, had good things to offer the singer to make it a worthy one once and for all. Schnorr was to withdraw from the theatre completely, and, as a teacher at our school, be required to collaborate only in special theatrical productions that served to confirm out instructional aim. This too was to declare freed of the drudgery of the common opera repertoire an artist of the noblest mettle. And what it had meant to him to have to languish in this drudgery was something that I could feel and understand most clearly: indeed, throughout my own life, the most insoluble, tormenting and degrading burdens, worries and humiliations have proceeded from that one misunderstanding which, by virtue of the constraints of external position in life and the state of affairs, has presented me to the world and to all aesthetic and social relationships therein contained, simply as opera composer and opera conductor. If this strange quid pro quo has been the cause of placing me in a state of constant confusion concerning all my relationships with the world, and particularly my attitude to its demands on me, then the sufferings which that profoundly inspired, nobly and truly gifted young artist had to endure in the position of opera singer subject to a theatre code devised against recalcitrant stage heroes, and bound in obedience to uneducated and conceited professional managers, were not to be underestimated. Schnorr was intended by nature to be a musician and a poet; like me, he passed from a generally scholarly education to the special study of music; he learnt, apart from musical theory, to play the piano well, and seemed likely to be well on the way to following wholly in my footsteps when he developed the voice which, in its inexhaustibility, was to serve the fulfilment of my most ideal demands. And so no other expedient was offered by our modern culture than to accept theatrical engagements and become 'a tenor', rather as Liszt, in a similar way, became 'a pianist'. But now, under the patronage of a Sovereign high-mindedly inclined towards precisely my ideal of German Art, the scion was at last to be implanted in our culture, that, in growing and blossoming, would have prepared the ground for real German artistic existences, and indeed it was time for this deliverance to be offered to the oppressed spirits of my friend. Here it was that the secret worm lay concealed which was gnawing at the serene life force of this artistic being. And this was borne in ever more plainly upon me when I saw, to my amazement, the impassioned, indeed wrathful, violence with which, in his theatrical dealings, he confronted improprieties such as occur constantly in dealings which are a mixture of bureaucratic narrow-mindedness and professional lack of conscience, and yet are not perceived as such by those affected. Once he complained to me, 'Oh, it's not what I do and sing that affects me, but lying still on the ground after the great sweat-producing heat of my scene in the final act, that is fatal. For despite all my efforts I have not been able to get them to shut out the most awful draught that blows over me ice-cold as I lie there, motionless, giving me my death of a cold!' On our failing to perceive any sign of catarrhal cold, he observed darkly that such colds involved other, more dangerous consequences for him. His irritability during the final days of his stay in Munich assumed an ever darker hue. He appeared finally as 'Erik' in The Flying Dutchman, performing this difficult episodic role to our highest admiration, indeed, arousing real horror by the strange sombre violence which – entirely in accordance with my express wishes – he allowed to blaze up like dark consuming fire in the suffering of this unhappy lover. On this evening he gave only brief indications of a deep depression concerning all around him. Also doubts concerning the realization of our pleasing plans and projects seemed to assail him; he seemed unable to grasp how out of this matter-of-fact, wholly unfeeling, indeed, treacherously and hostilely lurking environment to our work, any seriously intended good could accrue. For the time being, all he could hear were urgent demands from Dresden to appear on a certain day to rehearse 'Trovatore' or 'Huguenots'.

From this sombre and disquieting depression of spirits, which I too began finally to share, we were rescued by the last glorious evening that we spent together. The King had commanded a private audition at the Residenz Theatre and the performance of excerpts from my various works. Out of Tannhäuser, Lohengrin, Tristan, Rhinegold, the Valkyrie, Siegfried and finally The Mastersingers, a characteristic piece was given by singers and full orchestra under my personal direction. Schnorr, hearing here for the first time much by me that was new to him, apart from singing, with ravishing power and beauty, Siegmund's love song, Siegfried's sword-forging songs, Loge in the Rhinegold excerpt, and finally Walther von Stolzing in a more lengthy extract from The Mastersingers, felt himself far removed from all the agony of existence. And then, returning from a half-hour interview to which the King, who had been listening entirely alone, most graciously invited him, he impetuously embraced me. 'God, how grateful I am for this evening!' he exclaimed. 'Yes, now I know what it is that strengthens your faith! Oh, between this godlike King and you, I too must still prosper and become something splendid!' – Now again it was an occasion for not another solemn word. Together with the Bülows we took tea in a hotel; quiet merriment, friendly faith, sure hope were expressed in our almost exclusively jocular conversation. 'Well, tomorrow it's back to the loathsome masquerade! Soon be free of it now, for ever.' So sure we were of seeing each other again very soon that we thought it almost superfluous and merely inappropriate to take leave. We parted in the street with a good-night in the normal way; next morning my friend left for Dresden. –

About a week after our scarcely-heeded farewell, I received a telegram announcing Schnorr's death. He had sung at a rehearsal, giving colleagues, who marvelled at his still having any voice, their answer. He was then affected by a dreadful rheumatism in the knee, which led in a few days to a fatal illness. His last lucid, and finally fading, moments of consciousness were occupied with our agreed plans, the acting of Siegfried, and anxiety lest over-exertion as a result of Tristan be blamed for his death. I was hoping to reach Dresden, with Bülow, by the hour for the burial of our jointly beloved friend. In vain. The body had had to be committed to the earth a few hours before the appointed time. We were too late. At that same hour, in bright July sunlight, Dresden was giving a joyous reception to the crowds arriving for the General German Choral Festival. My cabby, urged on violently by me to the house of death, said, whilst trying hard to make his way through the crowd, that nigh on 20,000 singers had gathered. 'Yes,' I said to myself, '*the* singer has just gone!'

In haste we turned away from Dresden. –

3 May. *[1868]*

The sketch opposite dates from the same period as the 'Recollections of Ludwig Schnorr von Carolsfeld', i.e. end of April to early May 1868. The entry is dated 7 May, but an earlier note is dated 21 April. This timing suggests that Wagner's grief at the premature death of his first Tristan originally had some bearing on the mourning theme. The title 'Romeo and Juliet' suggests as much, as well as a possible parallel with Tristan and Isolde. *Later, after the Franco-Prussian War of 1870–1, it was Wagner's intention to use the theme for a funeral symphony in memory of the fallen, but nothing came of it.*[150] *Cosima's biographer Du Moulin Eckart, presumably basing himself on an entry in Cosima's diaries which had been placed at his disposal, records for 1873 (Vol. 1, p. 660) that Wagner had promised her, Cosima, a composition of quite a special sort which should form the sombre counterpart to the 'Siegfried Idyll', the funeral march from 'Romeo and Juliet'. But nothing came of that either, so that the theme published here is all that remains.*[151]

ROMEO U. JULIE

[7. Mai 1868]

7 May
evening

In Zürich in the fifties, under the stimulus of Schopenhauer, Wagner had made acquaintance with the ideas of Buddhism, reading, for example, Eugène Burnouf's Introduction à l'Histoire du Bouddhisme indien. *On 16 May 1856 he wrote a prose sketch for a Buddhist drama 'The Victors'.[153] Under May 1868 he noted in his Annals (cf. p. 166 below) immediately after his 'Recollections of Schnorr': 'Buddism: Victors re-thought. Dhyana regions: music.' The result of this re-thinking was the entry below. It is undated, but definitely falls within May 1868 because in a letter to the King dated 31 May 1868, Wagner mentions 'The Victors' and sends Burnouf's book. Presumably this letter refers to a conversation that Wagner had with King Ludwig on 22 May 1868 at Schloss Berg. – The terms nirvana, brahman, samsara and dhyana are roughly equivalent to eternity, soul, life and paradise.*

[May 1868]

Truth = nirvana = night

*

Music = brahman = twilight

*

Poetry = samsara = day.

*

New world structure: out of dhyana and into the world again descend beings who, for former virtuous service, have received their reward in proper and now full measure, in order now to re-enter the cycle of births for the achievement of still greater perfection. From the earth gushes sweet juice; with this, longing refreshes itself until it has imbibed fresh love of life: then the juice runs dry; rice sprouts forth unsown, satiety to abundance; then it comes to an end. Now one has to do one's own planting, ploughing and sowing. Life's torment begins. Paradise is lost. The music of the brahman world recalls it to the memory: it leads to truth. Who understands it? The milk that has flowed from no cow? –

Brahman becomes desire, as music; the music which is turned towards samsara, poetry; which is the other, the side which is turned away from samsara? Nirvana – untroubled, pure harmony? –

Wahrheit = Nirvâna = Nacht

Musik = Bramâ = Dämmerung

Dichtkunst = Sansâra = Tag.

Neue Weltbildung : aus dem Dhyâna steigen die Wesen wieder in die Welt hinab, welche dort die Belohnung für frühe[re]n Tugend-dienst im richtigen, nun gefülltem Maasse empfangen haben, um sich von Neuem in die Reihe der felurten, zur Erreichung noch größerer Vollkommenheit, einzutreten. Ein süßer Saft entquillt der Erde; an dem lecht fühlbare Sehnsucht bis zum Einsaugen neuer Lebenslust = denen tsoitkuet die Saft; Reiz quillt ungestört empor Lätthgung bis zur Fülle — dann versiegt es. Nun Samen selbst erlangt gewählt u gesäet werden. Die Plage des Lebens —

Wagner had Ludwig II presented with a dedication copy of the etched score of The Mastersingers *for his twenty-third birthday on 25 August 1868. With it he enclosed a four-verse poem. The first three verses below were entered on 16 August, the fourth on 22 August (v. p. 156 below), the day on which he finished copying the whole poem for the King and sent it to Munich. The King's trust in Wagner as a person suffered a severe blow when, soon after the première of* The Mastersingers *on 21 June 1868, he learnt of the true relationship between him and Cosima. For the next eight years the King avoided personal contact with Wagner, and it was not until the opening of the Bayreuth Festival in 1876 that they saw each other again. But the performance of* The Ring[154] *worked a change in the King's mood. Evidence of this is provided by his letter to Wagner from Hohenschwangau on 12 August 1876 following his return from Bayreuth, which reads: 'Great, incomparable, dear above all, all, Friend! With what impressions I returned from attending the exceedingly blissful Stage Festival at Bayreuth and from my happy reunion with you, adored Friend, I find it impossible to convey ... Oh you know how to rock the foundations, how, by means of your conquering light, to melt away the crust of ice beginning to form around heart and mind as the result of so many sad experiences . . . You are a god incarnate, by God's grace the true artist who has brought the sacred fire of heaven to earth to purify, inspire and redeem it! The god incarnate, who in truth cannot fail or err! . . . Oh, how proud I am, Glorious One, by virtue of your friendship! And now truly for the first time having experienced such unutterably blissful things! . . . There is no bliss above this! And so I have experienced now the most exalted moment . . . Revelling in the sublime delight, I remain, to death, firm as a rock and eternally true, my sole true Friend's own Ludwig.'*

Considering Ludwig's highly sensitive disposition, one must admire his greatness in setting his sure recognition of Wagner's artistic significance above disappointment in him as a person, and in maintaining his oft-sworn loyalty to the end. But the King was able also finally to understand and appreciate the fate-decreed behaviour of Cosima. After Wagner's death, he wrote, on 16 February 1883, in his letter of condolence: 'How I love you for the proud love that you consecrated to Him, the Unforgettable One, with such unshakeable loyalty, thereby embellishing His life and making it a happy one!'

An den König. Zum 25 August.	To the King. For 25 August
Ein Werk versprach ich, scheelen Neid's Bezwinger, Der Misgunst finst're Wolken zu zerstreu'n; ein Werk, das, deutschen Geistes Preis-Bedinger, zeriss'ne edle Bünde sollt' erneu'n: wie Nürnberg's alt ehrsame Meister-singer sich selbst belächeind, doch dem Unwerth dräu'n, der zwischen alt und neuem Dichterwalten gern möcht' als Jeztzeit-Irrgelichter schalten.	A work I promised, envious ones' Subduer, the dark clouds of displeasure to disperse; a work, Prize-Determiner of the German Spirit, that should renew the sundered noble bonds: of how Nuremberg's old upright master-singers, self mocking, yet pose threat to lack of worth that, between old and new poetic rule, would gladly reign as modern will o'wisp.
Was ich versprach, ob ich das treu gehalten, ob ächt ich alte Schaffenskraft bewährt, ob mir gelang, das klärlich zu gestalten, was euch als Traum nur durch die Sinne fährt? Noch fühlt' ich nicht im Busen mir erkalten die warme Lust, die selber sich so werth: was sie entfacht zu freudig hellem Zünden, will wohlig mir des Werk's Gelingen künden.	What I promised, have I staunchly kept? Proved genuine my old creative power? Contrived clear shape and form for that which, passes but dream-like thro' your senses? Not yet do I feel cooling in my breast the warm delight worth so much in itself: what that fans joyously into bright fire, will tell me pleasantly the work succeeds.

Doch, den mein Stern im Chaos musste finden,	But him whom my star in chaos had to find,
der dort, wo mir nur Sand am Meer erscheint,	who, where I saw but sand beside the sea,
das Wirrsal meinem Blicke liess verschwinden,	made all confusion vanish from my gaze,
dass der nur säh' wer mit ihm lacht und weint, –	that it might see who laughed with it and wept, –
Er durfte um das Haupt das Reis mir winden;	His was the right to crown my head with green;
dem König sass der Dichter hehr vereint.	high and at one with King the poet sat.
Nicht log das Herz: der neid'schen Geister Zwinger,	The heart lied not: of envious minds Subduer,
Du kröntest selbst den kühnen Meistersinger.	you it was crowned the fearless Mastersinger.

16 Aug. *[1868]* Triebn.

After The Mastersingers *première under the musical direction of Hans von Bülow, Wagner left Munich never to return. The obligation to King Ludwig was maintained but henceforth restricted to correspondence. Taking leave of the King, Wagner had announced that they would 'now not be seeing each other again for a long time' (cf. Wagner's letter to the King of 12 June 1876). The direct cause of Wagner's remaining away from Munich was that in public his relationship with Cosima, and in private his troubled relationship with Hans von Bülow, made staying impossible. At the end of May 1868 Wagner writes in the Annals: 'Piano rehearsals: heavy oppressive feeling from Hans' deep hostility and estrangement' and again, at the beginning of June: 'Orchestral rehearsals: serious trouble with H'. A little later the 1868 Annals record: 'Profoundest lack of spirits for any kind of movement: reason for total incapacity of will seen in fate of relationship with Cos. and Hans. All futile; complete failure of Munich attempts. Thought imperative never to return there. (v. p. 167 below). A turning point came when, through Wagner's one-time friend Röckel, there was renewed intriguing against Cosima on account of her relationship with Wagner. The King informed Cosima of this in a letter of 12 July 1868, and she in turn told Wagner. In the Annals he noted: 'Letter to Cos. from K.: Röckel gossiping about my relationship with C. Letter to K. – Decision immediately taken for C. to leave M.' In his letter to the King of 16 July 1868 mentioned above, Wagner wrote: 'In a matter of days Frau v. B. will be leaving Munich and presumably not returning . . . For next winter she will probably choose Italy as the place to reside . . .' On 22 July 1868 Cosima betook herself to Tribschen, and from 14 September to 6 October 1868 toured Italy in company with Wagner. In the months of August and September 1868 what mattered to Wagner was to ensure that Cosima and his two children[155] remained permanently with him, and so to bring about Cosima's separation and divorce from Bülow. This involved considerable*

152

difficulties and at times even led to differences of opinion with Cosima. Her marriage to Bülow had been solemnized in the Catholic Church and was therefore not easy to dissolve. Moreover Cosima wished to show consideration to her father Liszt, especially as on 2 August 1865 he had been consecrated abbé, having received the four lower degrees of ordination on 25 April and 30 July 1865. An added difficulty was that Bülow was opposed to divorce, or at least did not consider it inevitable. For this there was a special reason, as Millenkovich-Morold reports on page 224 of his biography of Cosima: 'He [Bülow] was of Prussian nationality, and his marriage had been solemnized in Berlin and according to Prussian law. Under this, divorce by consent of both parties was not permitted; dissolution being possible only where the guilt of one party was proved. Against which, it was contrary to Bülow's inner nature publicly to condemn his wife and take legal proceedings against her. There were thus two decisive steps to be taken: Cosima had to ask for the divorce, and, in accordance with Wagner's desire, change her faith.[156] This was necessary to ensure the Protestant upbringing of the Wagners' children. Cosima knew that by both steps she would be injuring her father as well as Bülow, but there was no way out. The demand for a divorce may, in the end, have caused her less difficulty, for in her diary she says of her marriage with Bülow: 'Our dispositions being completely divergent, what joined us in marriage was a great misapprehension. From the very first years of my marriage I was in such despair over the confusions that I wanted to die.' Liszt was a different matter. Peter Raabe writes in his biography of Liszt (Vol. 1, p. 218): 'But when it came to the final break Liszt took his place at the side of the one who was suffering most. And that was Bülow. He did not fall out with Wagner completely, even though he did not see him again for years. . . . But he broke with his daughter completely, or she with him.' – All of which[157] was forming the subject of Wagner's and Cosima's thoughts, aspirations and sorrows in the months of August and September 1868. Wagner translated his thinking into an artistic parallel, an expression of which is the brief outline for a play dated 19 and 22 August 1868. Its theme is Luther's marriage to the nun Catharina von Bora. Emil Heckel refers to Wagner's having, apart from the Luther outline, also conceived a play 'Hans Sachs' Second Marriage'. No outline of this exists and there is no other reference to it. Heckel supplies neither details nor date, but if he, basing himself on Cosima, is correct, 'Hans Sachs' Second Marriage' might be placed near the Luther outline chronologically.[158] On the same day as the second part of the Luther outline, 22 August, Wagner entered his previously unpublished meditations on loving and being loved (p. 155 below), and his thoughts here no doubt have a direct bearing on the altercations between him and Cosima on how to proceed in the matter of the divorce. That there were differences of opinion we know from the Annals for the second half of

153

1868. Immediately after Cosima's arrival at Tribschen on 22 July 1868[159] we find: 'Difficult communications re decision: Plutonic and Neptunian solutions! – Agreed about main thing' [Cosima's remaining with Wagner]. Plutonic and Neptunian are here used in Goethe's sense: 'Plutonic' meaning sudden, violent formation (of mountains in geology), and 'Neptunian' – gradual development. Over the question of divorce, Wagner was in favour of an immediate, violent solution, whereas Cosima favoured gradual, amicable clarification. She asserted herself against Wagner, and in the end she was right. – The Annals for August state: 'Sad and impassioned days' and, immediately after, 'Comedy'. This refers to the peculiar 'Comedy in 1 Act', at the end of the previously unpublished sketch of which, dated 1 September 1868 (p. 158 below), Wagner has written 'To counter grave ill humour', arising, it may be supposed, from the disharmony between himself and Cosima.

Luther (in the Wartburg) after fearful turmoils, at open window, rapidly transformed, softened, gaining in vigour, as result of a mild current of air, sight of greenery, song of a bird, – and another time, by a good swig of Einbeck beer, sings again 'Ein' feste Burg'. –

This – the enigmatic effect of a woman's eyes with the peace of ignorance in them, a cooling gentleness, the certainty of narrow mindedness: this, suddenly confronting the unbridled imagination of his contentiously-craving man's heart, has a shaming, confusing, subduing effect. What? The man in whom the whole world is fermenting, who a thousand times disregards this woman with all his reason? Is it not humiliating? A devil's frolic? And yet is it not more than that current of air, that birdsong, and especially too, that pot of Einbeck beer? Is it not first related to you, and what you must then first say to yourself, if, again, it does not speak out for itself? 'Brother, forget and be mindful!' And the hand that gives you drink, the lip that blesses it? – But Catharina's blonde plait descending to your bed pillow, won't it do the same to your work table too? – Yes! It would seem worth a try. –

19 Aug. [1868]

Where shall I get with my eagerness! Still the monkish lust? Shall not your work stand surety for men? And what men? I know them only as a monk does! There, in priestly pride, lurks the devil: him I must ban! – I shall take a wife and Catharina it shall be.

Wedding: Lukas Kranach, (Melancht) – guests. – Music. 'Who loves not wine, women and song'. –

Jovial tendency towards aims of German 'Renaissance' through philosophy, poetry and music – foreshadowed in the development of Protestantism and popularly expressed through Luther's marriage. –

22 Aug. [1868]

*

[[Two who are truly in love have only one religion, the knowledge of their being in love. Upsets can only occur when this faith falters in some respect: but the least faltering has, for the moment, the effect of total collapse, precisely because here all is of ecstatic tenderness. Only by virtue of this voluptuous tenderness of the awareness is the extravagance of love's ecstasy possible. The very least estrangement through distraction, taciturnity, ill-humour, the least harshness of expression, a minor rebuke, indeed, hidden indisposition even, or the tiniest untruth such as with any other being scarce attracts notice, immediately, for the afflicted one, puts in question the whole dogma of being in love. As now the most destructive outbursts and terrible conflicts spring from the most trivial causes, they must, by reason of their very violence, soon blow over again completely because each of those involved becomes in turn quickly aware of the immeasurable loss; for never could just part of the love, that is, part of the faith of being in love, be lost – such part, let us say, as could be deemed proportionate to the trivial cause of the upset – but always at once the whole. As a lasting and long-nurtured loving relationship of such a perfect nature must quite essentially be often exposed to those occasions because being constantly in the other's company must of necessity show and discover more sharply to the lover the poverty and state of affliction of the human individuality, and because here, in loving trust, all caution vanishes which good sense and experience of life impose upon us when we associate with anyone else, so there is only one relief for those deep and violent agitations, and this would seem to be supplied only by the religion of love in the manner in which the Christian has learnt to keep himself in balance by means of his faith in the inexhaustible forbearance of the Redeemer. In every deep-lying, often-recurring and long-lasting hostile conception of the loved one, the lover can do no more, and absolutely no more, than recognize the doubt of his being in love. The most painful thing that can now befall him from this delusion on the part of the loved one, is never to be regarded as emanating from faltering love, but merely from faltering faith in his being in love. Now let him consult with himself and recognize that that which is occurring within his own self, the very thing which is for those reasons tormenting him, and which he is now minded to have to reciprocate, is that very same faith which has begun to falter; but this faltering (which, of course, represents the complete loss), is, in its effect, all the more violent and destructive, as one's own love is violent and

155

ineradicable. Indeed, perhaps only in recognizing this do we become clearly aware of the love itself which previously was manifest only as joy in being in love. May relief against the upsets of faith now be gained out of this recognition: let it be roughly expressed in that constantly observed commandment: 'Whatever you encounter from your loved one, be certain that you are loved just as much as you love!' – (Of this there would seem much still to be said.)

22 Aug 1868]]

Nachtrag zur Widmung der MS	Addendum to Dedication of MS[160]

Nun lasse demuthvoll das Glück mich büssen
dass ich so herrlich hoch Dir nahe stand:
hat ferne Dir der Meister weichen müssen,
drückt' er zum Abschied Dir die
    Freundeshand,
nun lieg' sein Werk zu seines Königs Füssen,
dort wo es Schutz und höchste Gnade fand.
Und durft' ihm wonnig eine Weise glücken,
die mög' an 's Herz nun hold der Freund sich
    drücken!
	Let Fortune now make me humbly atone
	for standing near to you so grandly high:
	far had the Master to withdraw from you,
	when in farewell he pressed your friendly
	    hand.
	Now at his Monarch's feet his labour lies,
	where it found patronage and highest favour.
	And should his music prove a sweet success,
	may my friend now press it sweetly to his
	    heart.

22 Aug [1868]

The previously unpublished sketch for a comedy that follows is astonishing for its unpretentiousness, crudity and foolishness. It may be that in descending to this level, Wagner is simply letting off steam. Cosima, in her diaries,[161] hands down his remark: 'It is the saving of me to have been granted the ability to turn the most serious thing instantly into nonsense, and thus I have been able to preserve myself on the edge of the abyss.' At moments of relaxation Wagner was readily disposed for fun and mischief. We are told of capers and headstands performed at such times. And he would sometimes, if annoyed, respond with tomfoolery rather than sarcasm. His occasional verses and poems, the sonnets to David Strauss and Heinrich Laube (p. 125 above and p. 161 below) for instance, provide examples. But what appears to us today to some extent foolish, was for Wagner funny or amusing. His wit too is in some measure subject to fashion, and this was the case even in the seventies. Glasenapp (Vol. VI, p. 247) records: 'Thus he [Wagner] spoke once . . . of the lack of freedom now so grievously prevalent that, for example, his jest in the manner of Aristophanes, "The Capitulation", had been understood by no one. Aristophanes, were he to return, would not be understood at all. He had a fancy to write a comedy for the "Bayreuther Blätter" in which he would make everyone appear under their own names: Porges, Rubinstein, Wolzogen, Liszt, Lothar Bucher — all innocent, "But full of nonsense" . . .' Wagner's reference to Aristophanes is significant: he knew the nature of Aristophanes' situation comedy, of which we know next to nothing any more, for which reason we are scarcely able to understand his reanimation of it. The sketch of 'The Capitulation' is explicitly subheaded 'Comedy by Aristop Hanes'.[162] All of which is to be borne in mind when reading the outline which follows, and that for the comedy 'The Capitulation' on p. 182. As regards the 'Comedy in 1 Act', the possibility is not excluded (v. end of note, p. 154) of Wagner's wishing to extricate himself from a disagreement with Cosima. Zdenko von Kraft is of similar opinion.[163] He mentions that the crisis of Wagner's life concerning final possession of Cosima was being forced towards a decision at precisely the time when the sketch was written, and observes: '. . . it is perhaps just here that the key lies: . . . Thus in the very tension of these fateful weeks for Wagner there may have been a need to withdraw into the crude and unproblematical and to don a sort of fool's cap freeing him from all standards involving obligations.' No other point of reference, such as to his annoyance with Heinrich Laube (v. three sonnets, pp. 161–163 below), is contained in the sketch.

Undoubtedly apt, however, is Curt von Westernhagen's remark: 'Here, in the setting of a ham theatre vividly reminiscent of Bethmann's troupe at Lauchstädt,[164] *Wagner is for once burlesqueing the wretchedness of the theatre with which he had to deal throughout his life.'*

[[A Comedy
in 1 Act

Dramatis personae: Barnabas Coolwind, prompter
                       Hermine, his daughter
                       Caspar Scribely, student gone to seed
                       and novice actor
                       Lorenz Pimper, stage doorman
                       David Bubes, stage manager
                       Napoleon Baldachin, lead actor

*

Room at Coolwind's. Alcove at rear with bed. Morning. Coolwind in bed asleep and dreaming restlessly. Hermine concerned about her father. Scribely sticks his head in: Hermine draws bed curtain. It is new year's day: the new year's eve performance was ruinous for the old prompter; in spite of all warnings he again took a great deal of snuff and had a sneezing fit just as Baldachin, playing the hero, needed him most: Coolwind came on, irreparable misunderstanding accompanied by audience's laughter which, in consequence of Coolwind's resounding sneezes, grew into uproar. Actor's fury: C.'s dismissal imminent. Great despondency. – Conversation frequently interrupted by sleeping man's snores. – Fresh sneezing fits. – Stage doorman Pimper comes about the new year's booklet, wanting the latest theatre anecdote slipped in. Scribely promises to deliver. – Dreadful explosion of sneezing from bed, whereupon Coolwind collapses through it. Help from all sides to free him. They extricate him. Minimum of dressing behind bed curtain: during which, editing of sneeze-anecdote which Scribely sets up for Pimper. – Then breakfast coffee. Consultation how to avert impending misfortune. Coolwind very downcast: his grievances. Scribely, looking forward to his own great future, seeks to comfort: if C. will only give him Hermine to be his wife, he will take care of the family. C. does not prophesy well for S.; he has no talent as an actor. His memory, certainly, is remarkable: wonders in this respect – anything he has read he remembers by heart. But that is the ruin of him: for in speaking lines he makes absolutely no pauses, says it all in one go. Only through pauses is the actor effective: what is said, be it by Schiller, Goethe or Shakespeare, not a soul heeds or understands, but pauses, meaningful hesitation – those are what excite attention. Application of maxims to recent events. Ingratitude of this Baldachin whom Coolwind, as scrupulous prompter, has helped to many a profound effect. But now, occasionally, there were also cases, etc. (Frequent interruption.) Pimper with proof of anecdote. Reports of movement against Coolwind – accompanied by coffee: snuff; no smoking! – Growing concern about how this day will be decided: fear of dismissal. Imminent family penury. Scribely's past. (All mixed up.) Hermine resolves to go and see secretary of Court Theatre who is on friendly terms with Cabinet Secretary. All she hopes for is a good pension for her father.) Main dialogue between Scribely and Coolwind continues. Pimper announces stage manager Bubes. Extraordinarily solemn behaviour. Dismissal inevitable: argument about it. Scribely inquires about being given an engagement. Prospects poor. Baldachin said to be threatening to resign: he, it seems, is afraid of Scribely's being engaged on account of the latter's absurd memory which enables him to learn any part between morning and evening, and consequently whenever Baldachin is not yet ready, will, by swiftly stepping in, make it possible for the management to put on the desired plays and by-pass the real lead-actor completely. Discussions about Baldachin. Yesterday evening he is said to have been urging Coolwind's dismissal. – Pimper announces aside to Scribely that Baldachin is prowling around the house and seems to be awaiting Bubes' return. Scribely calls down to Baldachin out of the window and invites him to a conference. The latter appears unwillingly and out of countenance. Extraordinarily tense meeting with Scribely: incomprehensible discussions, with Baldachin solemnly reticent. Question of finding out what's wanted by powers-that-be. Baldachin scheming to make Scribely prompter, thereby diverting him from acting career he has opted for. – Pimper interrupts, bringing revised proof of anecdote as booklet now has to be published. Letter from Secretary to Coolwind: latter is kindly to apply for release. Scribely left by Bubes and Baldachin to consider whether he ought not to take the post of prompter. They go. – Deliberation between Coolwind and Scribely. (Enter note of pathos). Underground revenge vowed against Baldachin and whole hollow business of theatrical leads. – Hermine comes from Cabinet Secretary himself. Full pension for father against Scribely's pledge to take over position as prompter for which he enjoys general confidence of cast – growing pathos. Added to efficient prompting, success of a theatrical journal: reviewer, even writer, poet – Scribely's real vocation. Henceforth he will regard the prompt box as the position required by Archimedes for lifting the earth from its axis. A bottle of new year's wine is brought by Pimper for the anecdote: booklet rapidly bought up at street corners. Even Coolwind tries to enthuse: in clinking glasses to the enormous

159

success of the future activity of the new prompter, he, in consequence of too much snuff, is forced to sneeze so violently that he spills his glass: this praised by Scribely as auspicious omen for his future plans. On top of which – a betrothal.

(To counter grave depression) 1 September. *[1868]*]]

Heinrich Laube, author, dramatist and producer (1806–84) to whom the three sonnets that follow are dedicated, was from 1833 editor of the Zeitung für die elegante Welt *(Journal for the Elegant World) in Leipzig and friendly with Wagner. The years 1850 to 1867 saw him Director of the Vienna Burgtheater. Subsequently he sought to take over management of the Munich Court Theatre and asked Wagner to recommend him. His application being unsuccessful, he believed it to be Wagner's fault,*[165] *went over to the Wagner opposition, and in 1833 wrote a venomous review of* The Mastersingers. *Following the non-fulfilment of his Munich hopes he accepted appointment as Director of the Leipzig Municipal Theatre in 1868, and was its manager from 1869 onwards. The three sonnets are Wagner's answer to Laube's review of* The Mastersingers.

An Heinrich Laube.

I.

Kein Dichter zwar, kein selig blond
    gelockter,
die Welt doch möchtest gerne Du beluchsen,
dass, was Du theatralisch liebst zu drucksen
zur Abwehr Göth'- und Schiller'scher
    Verstockter,

des Titels werth sei, den Du führst als
    Dokter;
und wagte Einer gegen Dich zu mucksen,
als Jäger lerntest Du vom schlauen Fuchsen,
wie man dem Gegner tüchtig aufpasst, bockt
    er.

Du hieltest klug Dir des Theaters Sperling
zu Hand, statt auf des Tempel's Dach die
    Taube;
die Politik auch liessest Du Herrn Schmerling;

Nun pensionirt mit Wiener Pfunden
    Sterling,
schmäh'st sauer Du des Dichters süsse Traube;
entpupp'st als Rezensent Dich, Heinrich
    Laube!

To Heinrich Laube.

I.

No poet, true, or happy curled blond
    head,
you would like to make the world believe
that what you care theatrically to print,
to ward off Goethe–Schiller
    obdurates,

is worthy of the doctorate you
    bear;
and if any breathe a word against you,
you have learnt, as hunter, from sly fox,
if you lie well hid, your foe will
    sulk.

Smartly you have held theatre's sparrow
in hand while temple pigeon sat on
    roof;
politics you've left to Schmerling[166] too;

now, pensioned off with money from
    Vienna,
the poet's sweet grape sourly you berate;
emerging as a critic, Heinrich
    Laube!

161

II.

Jetzt sei gepriesen Leipzig's Stadttheater!
Wer um die Kunst nun heulte noch und flennte,
da, wo einst herrschte Präsident von
    Ente[167],
der Rath Dich wählt zum Komödianten-
    Vater?

Bald pack'st Du nun der Presse Attentater,
Du kirr'st sie durch Tantièmen und Prozente;
Dir fängt den Speck der kühnste Rezensente,
und Katz' und Mäuse hält in Zucht der Kater.

Nur dort, wo traulich Wissenschaft und
    Handel,
zu eins gepresst durch des Buchdrucker's
    Schraube,
sich conserviren trotz der Zeiten Wandel,

nicht da, wo stets die Kunst nur bleibt
    Getandel,
und an was Recht's Dir nie erwuchs der
    Glaube,
sei noch einmal Director, Heinrich Laube!

II.

Praise now be Leipzig's Town Theatre!
Whoever'd now still howl and blub for Art
when, where von Ende[168] one time ruled the
    roost,
the Council chooses you comedians'
    father?

Soon now the press assassins you will seize,
and tame by means of royalty and percentage;
the boldest critic brings you home the bacon,
the tom cat keeping cat and mice in check.

Only there, where snugly trade and
    learning,
pressed by printer's screw-bar into
    one,
preserve themselves despite the changing times,

and not where Art is just a constant
    toying,
and where for nothing proper you found
    faith,
Director once again be, Heinrich Laube!

III.

O, Welt! Nun wende Deinem Blick nach
    Sachsen,
vertrauensvoll lass' ihn nach Leipsig schielen:
auf jenem Feld, wo Deutschland's Krieger
    fielen,
dort hörst Du bald das Gras der Kunst nun
    wachsen.

Jetzt merke auf, wie des Theaters Faxen
sich wandeln zu verteufelt ernsten Spielen;
des Dichter's Hand bedeckt sich bald mit
    Schwielen,
von ihren Schlägen soll die Bühne knacksen.

Dann hörst Du unerhörten Lobes
    Kracher:
für Deutschland's Vortheil kämpft mit
    Wuthgeschnaube
der associirte einst'ge Widersacher:

III.

O World, turn now to Saxony, your
    gaze,
and, trusting, toward Leipzig let it peer:
upon that field where German warriors
    fell,
there soon you'll hear the grass of Art
    a-growing.

Note now how theatrical tomfoolery
is made into a devilish serious game;
swiftly calloused grows the poet's
    hand,
and from its hammering shall the stage resound.

Then of praise unheard-of hear the
    crash:
for Germany's advantage, snorting
    rage,
the associate one-time adversary's struggling:

und Alles eint sich dann in sanftem
  Schacher,
bringst unter Leipzig's Stadttheater-Haube
Du mit der Kunst Dich, grosser Heinrich
  Laube.

and all will one become in gentle
  haggle,
if, 'neath the wing of Leipzig Town Theatre,
with Art you take yourself, great Heinrich
  Laube.

10 September *[1868]*

163

Details concerning Wagner's Annals are given in the note on p. 93. With the continuation below for the year 1868 Wagner's notes end. This is because from 16 November 1868, the day of her final and permanent removal to Wagner at Tribschen, until his death on 13 February 1883, Cosima kept a regular diary,[169] and in so doing assumed the task of recording everything of interest in Wagner's life. According to Wagner's Will, Cosima was eventually to continue alone the autobiography which ends with his coming to King Ludwig in Munich on 4 May 1864. On 22 July 1865, while dictating My Life to Cosima, he wrote to Ludwig: 'We have decided to continue dictating to the point of my association with you, dear Glorious One: from there Cosima is to continue the biography alone, and, it is hoped, one day complete it. She is best able to do this and will accomplish it splendidly.' Up to 4 May 1864 the biography was completed according to plan, but the continuation by Cosima was not undertaken. The material, however, remains available: in the Annals and, from 1868 until Wagner's death, in Cosima's diaries. These she protected scrupulously at least for the period of her own and her children's lifetime, because also committed to their pages were highly personal matters that she wished kept secret. At the age of seventy-one, she gave the 21 volumes of the diary into the custody of her daughter Eva. This came about as emerges from Eva's letter of 4 October 1935 (quoted p. 17 above) to Cosima's biographer Max Millenkovich-Morold, in the form of a gift by way of dowry on the occasion of Eva's marriage to H. S. Chamberlain on 25 December 1908.

In view of some contradictions in connection with this gift, it is appropriate to examine the circumstances more closely. There is no reason to doubt the truth of Eva's statement to Millenkovich-Morold. Apart from which, there is, in the Richard-Wagner-Gedenkstätte at Bayreuth, a letter from Eva to the Oberbürgermeister of the Town of Bayreuth dated 20 January 1935, in which she affirms that the Cosima diaries, as also her other gifts to the Town of Bayreuth (amongst them the Brown Book) were 'made over' to her by her mother 'to be her property'. Now Cosima could not have physically 'made over' the diaries because they at this time were not in Bayreuth, Glasenapp having, at Cosima's suggestion, removed them from the Wahnfried Archive to his home in Riga for use in his Wagner biography. He did not return them to the Wahnfried Archive until two years later, in March 1909. Cosima may, however, on 25 December 1908, have promised her daughter the title to the diaries. Eva then did not remove the diaries from the Wahnfried Archive and into her own safe-

164

keeping until 22 October 1911, the 100th anniversary of the birth of her grandfather, Liszt. Out of regard presumably for Cosima's not being able, or allowed, to write on account of her eye trouble, Eva herself entered in the manuscript catalogue of the Wahnfried Archive under 'Cosima's Diaries': 'The complete Diaries were presented by her mother to her daughter Eva on 22 October 1911 and entrusted to her own safe-keeping.' This entry is misleading, the gift having already been made on 25 December 1908. Correct would have been: '. . . presented by her mother to her daughter Eva [on 25 December 1908] and on 22 October 1911 entrusted to her own safe-keeping.' Why that did not happen in 1909 after the return of the diaries from Riga, is explained by the fact that the newly-weds, Eva and Houston Stewart Chamberlain, had taken up residence at Wahnfried 'until the house could be built across the way where Chamberlain was setting up his observatory . . . He lived at Wahnfried and had merely a kind of tusculum where he did his writing and where virtually only his wife came, in order to participate in his work while still supervising the nursing of her mother at Wahnfried across the road . . .' (Du Moulin-Eckart, Vol. II, p. 838). For this reason the diaries remained, to begin with, in the Wahnfried Archive, and Eva did not take them into her own custody until 1911, which, given the trust between mother and daughter, cannot have happened without Cosima's knowledge. Hence the statement in Eva's letter to Millenkovich-Morold of 4 October 1935, expressly intended to be forwarded to Wahnfried: 'My mother's diaries . . . were taken by her personally from the iron safe with the words "They belong to you – with you I know them to be safe."' That can only have been in 1911, and not, however, in 1908 for the reason stated.

When herself approaching seventy, Eva, in turn, gifted the diaries, on 20 January 1935, to the Town of Bayreuth for its Richard-Wagner-Gedenkstätte with, however, the provision in her 'Last Will' of 28 April 1939 that on her death (which was in 1942) they were to be preserved in the vault of the Bavarian State Bank, Munich, for 30 years, and then handed back to the Town of Bayreuth for its Richard-Wagner-Gedenkstätte where they had lain for the four years prior to her death. After protracted difficulties raised by Dr Bandorf-München, the successor of Eva's Executor, the diaries were received by the Town of Bayreuth on 12 March 1974. A publisher's agreement concerning their publication in three volumes, commencing 1976, was entered into by the Town of Bayreuth on 15 July 1975.

Annals continued

1868

First hour of the year. Omens. C.'s ring lost and found again. Great apprehension. – Hans back. His birthday (8 Jan.) at Queroy's. Toast: 'joyless successes!' Lonely walk through the town. Good spirits. – Perfall: (speaks when I speak.) – Draeseke. (doesn't listen.) – Concert programmes. (Schumann:) Manfred. – Lachner's farewell (Armide.) – Tenor Bachmann. (Chorus for 'Die Stumme'.) Mastersingers fixed for March. (Beck- and Betz-confusion.) Much that is hard and full of suffering. – Very often unwell. (Schanzenbach.) Also Prince Hohenlohe. Temporary return to Tribschen decided on: week's postponement. Low spirits. (also Grandma B.[170]) Second week February leave by night train. – Eva. – 17 Feb.: 1st birthday. – Annals. – March: – 'David Strauss'. Publication of Art and Politics, with Foreword, attended to. (Schiller. Goethe.) Buddha. Letter from King in the old language. My refusal. Enthusiastic answer on his part. C. warns against re-visiting Munich. About 20 March: travel to Munich. Confused, uncertain memories. (My arrival seems to take K. by surprise. Allows nothing to be seen or heard of him.) Heart heavily overcast. Children-mornings: three with Loldi (Franz and Anna!), 'Water Carrier'. (Lachner's cordiality.) Arrest-visit: Lawyer Simmerl. (Old Klepperbein debt.) Düffl. – Soon after: Schauss about Semper; about to travel to Zürich to bring S. round. Talks with Schauss. (Lawyer: he, too, Swabian!) and Düfflipp. King's break with Semper. Theatre scrapped. – Mastersingers, baritone Stägemann from Hannover. (Concert.) Not even a seat at concert. (Also Overture to Vestal.) Perfall to Dresden (needlessly for tenor Bachmann). Necessary to postpone to mid-June. (Betz. Nachbaur.) Richter to Gotha (for tenor: – Wurst.) Hans rushes out of room one evening because of photograph on title page of draft manuscript of Mastersinger imprints. – Conservatoire (Freischütz rehearsal: Christen. – Perfall's behaviour. My uncertainty.) Lohengrin (Prince of Prussia!) (Stayed at home.) – C Lila. – Gloomy: half-light. Impossibility of Munich attempt already clearly recognized. Result: wait and see what comes of Mastersingers. – Negotiations with J. J. Weber.) Return to Tribschen repeatedly resolved upon and mid-April carried out. (King not seen.) Night train: Augsburg; Town Hall. 3 Moors. – Eva! – 26 April: preface to second edition of 'Opera and Drama' sent to C. Frantz. – Arrange complete edition of my works in 10 volumes. May: 'My Recollections of Schnorr.' – Buddhism: Victors re-thought. Dhyana regions: music. Mournfully tender mood. – Mérimée: Alfr. Musset.) Liszt's letter to Cotta!) Violence: confusion. Most impassioned misunderstandings. Extreme tension. – Mid-May Cos arrives evening with children and mother-in-law: cannot receive; they take tea alone in dining-room. Great confusion of feelings:

all the time fresh difficulties. Unspeakable love-torment. Inclined to run away and disappear. Harz. Frigid existence! – All the time rapid change: most sublime appeasements. Deliverance needed. – On 20th C. back to Munich. (Previously: Jacob as bringer of horror!) Myself follow on 21 May. Good arrival. C. steps out from door-curtain. 22nd. Birthday morning: ('not 10 horses!'), Presents: Mother's picture! A great, deep source of happiness! – Mastersingers coming on. (Perfall already found to be complete backslider. All recognized.) – Lunch (Birthday) with King on Roseninsel. (Tristan journey.) – Betz, Nachbaur. (Richter's miracle) Hölzel. Piano rehearsals: heavy, oppressive feeling from Hans' deep hostility and estrangement. Direction, all restrained. Singers good: Schlosser (David.) – Costume designer Seitz. Perfall's anxiety-chicanery: rehearsal on Corpus Christi! In between: Beck's guest performance with Fly. Dutch. (wretched. – Pecht.) Richter in glory. Drives with Cos. – Weissheimer: Körner trouble; his estrangement. Cornelius still foolish and in depths of soul ill at ease. – June: Orchestral rehearsals: serious trouble with H. – Perfall chicaning wherever possible. Apparent rebellion by orchestra. (Horn-player Strauss![171]) Stage-Manager Hallwachs. My arrangement of rehearsals. – Esser from Vienna. Growing number of people arriving. – Malw. Meysenbug with Fräulein Herzen from Florence. Invitation of sister Clara with daughter. – Good rehearsals with Esser and Cos. – Pleased with Betz. – Many visitors: also Cläre. Frau Laussot: spectacles; no one else does it like me; K. and P. write to her from their hearts. Fränzi Ritter. Math. Maier (reserved!) Cosima likes Mastersingers. – Dress rehearsal: again anger at – everything. No pleasure any more. (Final words to company.) 21 June: 1st performance (Hofbräuhaus!) Secretly join C. in box. During prelude summoned to King: obliged to listen to Mastersingers at his side in public. Very weary and exhausted. C. unhappy at my not remaining at her side. Take leave of Parz. after performance. – French: Pasdeloup, Leroy, Chandon etc. Schott. Cläre. (Dinner before at Hotel Bellevue.) ('Ami de Weissheimer'.) C. promises to follow in a week. 24th return to Triebschen early. Children alone. Vreneli pregnant. – Gloomy depressed mood. – Few days later, cold: ill. Doctor every day: nerves, sweats, weakness. Great clarity dawning as to my condition and the state of things. Profoundest lack of spirits for any kind of movement: reason for total incapacity of will seen in fate of relationship with Cos. and Hans. Everything futile; complete failure of Munich attempts. Thought imperative never ever to return there. – Dealings with Schott. With Dresden and Vienna re mutilations of Mastersingers. Powerless against them. Give way. Appalling reviews: must, on account of my needs, be glad to salvage Mastersingers as vulgar theatrical success. After ten days' debility, slow recovery. (Children no pleasure without mother.) Surrender to most wretched fate seems inevitable: really foreseen by Cos. since our last year's separation:

believing in nothing, she consequently could not help doubting me. – King's letter to Cos.: Röckel gossiping about my relationship with C. – Letter to the K. – Decision immediately taken for C. to leave M. Her delayed arrival. Tension. Comes on 20 July.[172] Children's reception. Difficult communications re decision: Plutonic and Neptunian solutions! – Agreed about main thing. – Cornelius for five days in August. (Gunlöd: also Suttung!) Lucerne society to dinner. Eva – Loldi. Sad and impassioned days. (Mirror frame; also Fugger chair.) Bath. Robber-park. – Comedy. Much correspondence. Lucca. (Giovanna!) Sale of my operas to him for Italy. In between Pasdeloup: Paris contract for Rienzi. Much Paris confusion: Truinet, Perrin. (Also Eckert.) Trip to Interlaken: Jungfrau. (3 days.) Sept.: trip to upper Italy. Depart 14th. Twilight of gods on Gotthard. (Piroscafo.) Stresa and Borromean Islands.[173] (Cablasatoni!) 17th Genoa. Much joy. Cos. full of life. 'I mille palazzi'. Van Dyck. Pianella. Angelo peccatore. (Maria Stuart: Duke of Lerma.) Liphort junior and senior: annoying. (Café and market.) Lake trip. Villa Pallavicini. (Mi. Vannenes.) To Milan. (Coupé trouble for journey back.) Luccas, (Mme. Chaillot) cirque. 28 Sept. leave via Como. News of floods: stay Lugano. 29 Bellinzona. Wait or turn back? Thursday 1st to Biasca. Thence on foot (Bodio, Ciornico etc.) to Faido. (March out from Ciornico, dreadful thunderstorm: one hour of most terrifying sort: Cos keeps jumping from her seat. Lavorno – muddy marsh. Lantern! Bridge broken: by waters. Faido – Hôtel de Poste! With C. in one room. Flood continues: impossible to proceed by carriage. Three bad but deep days. 3 Oct.: (Saturday): lowest spirits. Cos. writes. Nearness of death. Jacob wanting to return home for wife's confinement. Sunday: 4 Oct. all the time pouring rain. (Deceptive stars: dars (as Loldi would say.)) Indecision: increased difficulties concerning route. Post caravan. Midday, decision to depart. 1.30 off. Cos. in oilskin coat. Pouring rain. Dreadful march: four post miles in four hours. Arrive Airolo. (Coupé!) Spend night. 5th by early post via Gotthard (with difficulty). Andermatt, Amsteg. – to Flüelen. 6th (Tuesday) home again. What did fate desire! – Vreneli gives birth. Children good. 7th morning Cos. into cold bath! Packing: to Munich. Great anguish. Bad night. – 8th calmer. 9th Understanding and agreement. Sad, vitally important days. C.'s promise. 14th C. leaves for Munich with 4 children: accompany them to Augsburg, whence at midday on 15th return to Tribschen alone. – Fearful expectations. – Only letters. (Aladdin. Luther. Derniers abbés.) C.'s report: promise to change faith. (Goethe and Knebel.) To Rome? – Confusion and burning sorrow: write to Cl. Charnacé – to Munich. C. beside herself. Great depression: decide to make trip calling at Arcostrasse. C. calmer. 1 Nov. to Munich: (moonlight on Lake Constance). C. at Mrazeck's: Eva. (2nd Nov.:) Afternoon to Leipzig. (3rd Nov.) Clemens. Herm. and Ottil, (– Anna and Doris). Write to King about interview. (Family?) Marbach. (Portrait of

Schiller.) Dr Nietzsche. Dr Ritschel with wife. Empress of Russia impeding requested interview: write to Düfflip). 9 Nov. to Augsburg: railway hold-up: obliged to wait; telegraph. 3 Moors. Evening 3 children from Munich (Loldi fourth Moor!) 9 p.m. on Lindau train: jump off again; children delayed by obstruction on railway. Back to hotel: all to bed. – 10 Nov. up early: children to Munich five minutes before me. Late to Tribschen. (Much misfortune in world: railway deaths, floods, blizzards on St Gotthard. Earthquakes everywhere!) C.'s letter (reminiscences of Liszt through Nohl: sketch book). Anxiety about Hans. (Lower appartment moved into permanently. – Fate?) French enthusiasts: German vileness. (Geibel. Heyse catastrophe.) Awaiting C. – 16 Nov. Cos. arrives with Loldi and Eva alone. (Delayed decision explained.) My part of the house occupied by C. and the children. – Little from without. Within: dictation of biography, Siegfried score. Beginning December, Swabian parlour maid: nursery furnished. (Judith Mendès.) Write to Porges about book he is to write. (Nohl: trouble over sketches.) Many deaths: start register. 'Reminiscences of Rossini'. Hans writes. Negotiations with Vienna. (Dingelstedt.) Berlin – Mimi Buch:[174] Eckert engaged. (Caviar and herring: Leipzig.) Marbach: Medea evening.[175] Otherwise much Körner and some Schiller. Finish fair copy of Siegfried Act I. Consider Judaism again. Claire Charnacé: something Mathilda-ish. – Abdominal trouble with serenity of heart. Cos: suffering mostly. Genelli†. His Outlines to Homer. 1 black and 4 white songs from old times: birthday Christmas, children as butterfly angels. 25 Dec.: 'Schiller and Chaillot'. Dictation up to Schopenhauer. Nothing external: great regularity; work machinery. Piece of Düfflipp: Munich University Treasurer and daughter (reportedly made pregnant by King through my agency![176]) Fresh confirmation of decision to have nothing more to do with Munich. Good Christmas under Büchi's agency in Zürich. Sulzer. Gentle, somewhat relaxed New Year's Eve. Up and down: triple-tiered happiness!

With the moving in of Cosima, Isolde and Eva for good, happiness came to Tribschen.[177] The time of uncertainty and torment was at an end. Wagner took great pleasure in his two children, Isolde (three-and-a-half) and Eva (almost two), and was looking forward to the birth of his third child (to be a son, Siegfried, born 6 June 1869). At fifty-five and for the first time in his life, Wagner had found a real home. His family happiness and his children filled him with delight. Evidence of this is the cradle song 'Sleep, baby, sleep' (v. also Annals for New Year 1868). Two years later, Wagner employed the theme in the 'Siegfried Idyll' in which he expressed his gratitude to Cosima on her thirty-third birthday, Christmas 1870.

New Year's Eve 68–69

Schlaf, Kindchen, schlafe;
im Garten geh'n zwei Schafe:
ein schwarzes und ein weisses,
und wenn das Kind nicht schlafen will,
so kommt das schwarz' und beisst es!

Sleep, baby, sleep;
in the garden are two sheep:
a black one and a white,
and if baby will not sleep,
the black will come and bite!

170

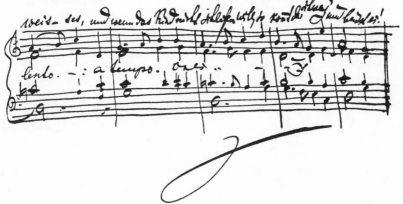

22 Aug. 1869

Siegfried: III Akt an den König | Siegfried Act III to the King[178]

[1.]

Sie ist erweckt, die lang in Schlaf verloren,
erfüllt ist nun des Gottes stummer Rath:
den sie geliebt, noch ehe er geboren,
den sie geschirmt, noch eh' an's Licht er trat,
um den sie Straf' und Göttergrimm
        erkoren,
der nun als kühner Wecker ihr genaht:
zu ihr ward auf den Fels er hingetrieben,
der nur erwuchs, weil sie ihn sollte lieben.

[1.]

She is awake who long was lost in sleep,
fulfilled is the mute counsel of the god:
he whom she loved ere he was ever born,
whom she protected ere he saw the sun,
for whose sake she chose punishment, gods'
        wrath,
who now as bold awakener has come:
to her upon her rock he was impelled,
who grew up only to be loved by her.

171

2.

Ein Wunder! doch kaum wunderbar zu
nennen,
dass hier ein Knab' zu Jünglingskraft gereift;
der mochte muthig durch die Wälder rennen,
ihm nützt' es wenn der Jahre Rad sich
schweift:
als gröss'res Wunder muss ich dies erkennen,
wenn Mannes Vollkraft schon das Rad
bestreift,
dass dem die Jahre dann die Kräfte stärken
zu seiner Jugend unerfüllten Werken.

A miracle, though scarce wondrous to be
named.
that here a boy matured to youthful strength;
he who boldly loved to run the woods,
knew profit when the wheel of years was
shaped:
this I must see a greater miracle
that when man's full vigour feels the
wheel,
his powers then are strengthened by the years
for labours not completed in his youth.

3.

Und diese That ist Deinem Freund gelungen:
was eilf der Jahr' in stummen Schlaf er schloss,
das hat er nun zum Leben wach gesungen,
der hold Erweckten eint sich der
Genoss.
Und doch, wie wär' diess Wecklied je
erklungen,
wenn Deiner Jugend Blüthe mir nicht
spross?
Mich mahnt der Tag, an dem ich Dir es sende,
dass gänzlich sich zu Dir das Wunder wende.

And in this your Friend has won success:
what for eleven years he locked in silent sleep,
that has he now sung and roused to life,
the sweetly wakened one is joined by her
companion.
And yet how had that rousing song e'er
sounded
if your youth's blossom had not bloomed for
me?
The day on which I send you it reminds me
toward you should the miracle be all directed.

Wagner's annoyance at the Munich performance of The Rhinegold, *which took place on 22 September 1869 against his wishes, is reflected in the 'Rhinegold' lines of 25 September. As early as 1864, the King had promised to pay Wagner 30,000 gulden for the musical composition of the Nibelung poem,[179] and was therefore owner of the three works before their completion. He had, however, promised to allow Wagner to stage the completed* Ring Cycle *himself and in accordance with his own intentions. And although he had had the* Rhinegold *score in his hands for four years already and* The Valkyrie *for three, he stood by this promise until 1869. But after the upset of 1868 and the abandonment of the plans for building a Munich theatre, the command was given for the production of* The Rhinegold *and the enormous sum of 60,000 gulden – double the total payment – was made available. Moreover, the King sent the producer and the stage designer to Tribschen to see Wagner in order to acquire an authentic grasp of detail. But Intendant Perfall failed to comply with Wagner's wishes, and his rendering threatened to expose the work to ridicule. This was the opinion not only of those involved, including, above all, the conductor, Hans Richter, but also of Liszt, who attended the rehearsals. Wagner sought therefore to prevent the production by every means, but without success. The King was inexorable, and Wagner had to give way. But the experience of this botched production, which in milder form, was repeated in the same place a year later with* The Valkyrie, *now determined Wagner to strive for his own production of* The Ring. *This was the beginning of Bayreuth.*

Rheingold

Spielt nur, ihr Nebelzwerge, mit dem Ringe,
wohl dien' er euch zu eurer Thorheit Sold;
doch habet Acht: euch wird der Reif zur
    Schlinge;
ihr kennt den Fluch: seht, ob er Schächern
    hold!
Der Fluch, er will dass nie das Werk gelinge,
als dem der furchtlos wahrt des Rheines Gold.
Doch euer ängstlich Spiel aus Leim und Pappe
bedeckt gar bald des Niblungs
    Nebelkappe.

Rhinegold

Just play with The Ring, you dwarfs of mist,
well may it serve as wages for your folly;
but have a care: for you The Ring's a
    noose;
you know the curse: see if it's kind to
    thieves!
Never, the curse wills, shall the work succeed,
save for him who, fearless, keeps the gold.
But your timid game of cardboard and of glue
will soon be covered by the Nibelung's
    Tarnhelm.

25 Sept. 69.

The lines below were written as a dedication on a picture of himself which Wagner sent to Dr Ludewig, theatre physician at Brunswick, after the première there of Lohengrin. *Ludewig had himself laboured to bring about the* Lohengrin *production, and reported on its reception to Wagner in Lucerne. (Oesterlein-Katalog, Vol. III, pp. 7, 42–43.)*

Braunschweigt Wurst für Lohengrin

Zu Worms ein Krug Einbecker Bier,
der labte Luther's Durst;
Held Lohengrin nach dem Tournier
zu Braunschweig stärkt' ihn Wurst.

Daraus nehm' Jeder sich die Lehr':
Und wenn die Welt voll Teufel wär',
hilft ihm das Bier vom Durst,
dem Deutschen ist Alles dann Wurst!

Brunswick Sausage for Lohengrin

At Worms a mug of Einbeck beer
slaked Martin Luther's thirst;
Brave Lohengrin, the tourney o'er,
was refreshed by Brunswick sausage.

Of which for each the lesson is:
though the world be full of devils,
beer helps to take the thirst away,
then no German cares a sausage!

6 March 70

A copy of the poem below dated 13 April 1870, was sent by Wagner to the King headed 'At the approach of 3 May' but without the 'dernier effort' added in the Brown Book. *The 3 May referred to, is the date of Wagner's first meeting with the King in 1864.*[180] *'Dernier effort' indicates a last effort by Wagner to deter Ludwig II from producing* The Valkyrie *in 1870 without his collaboration. In a letter to the King dated 12 January 1870, he had offered, if there was no other way, to stage* The Valkyrie *in Munich himself, subject to definite preconditions. But Ludwig did not reply, and in his effusive letter of thanks for the poem, on 2 May 1870, simply included the sentence: 'Forgive my youthful impetuosity that cannot wait till next year for a production of* The Valkyrie.' *The 1870 Munich production of* The Valkyrie *could not therefore be stopped and took place on 26 June 1870, against Wagner's wishes, but was at least less of a failure than* The Rhinegold *the previous year. – Cf. note pp. 172–173.*

An den König (dernier effort!)

Noch einmal mögest Du die Stimme hören
die einstens aus Dir selber zu mir sprach;
noch einmal lass' den Zauber mich
    beschwören,
durch den Dein Herz einst meine Sorge brach:
wie sollte jetzt mich scheue Furcht bethören,
ruf' ich Dir Stimm' und Zauber wieder wach,
die einst aus Dir sich über mich ergossen,
als Deiner Liebe Lenz sich mir
    erschlossen?

Er naht, im hehren Wonnekleid des
    Maien,
des Königslenzes holder Jubeltag:
da wolltest Du mir neuen Muth verleihen
durch Deiner Liebe edlen Ritterschlag,
mit Deines Segens Huld das Werk da weihen,
das, wie sein Schöpfer, Dir am Herzen lag:
und meines Königs herrliche Verheissung,
nun ward sie meines Glaubens' sich're
    Weisung.

Dem Genius ergrollen die Dämonen,
und die Gespenster scheu'n den reinen Geist:
will oft mit ihnen sich der Kampf nicht lohnen,
wenn uns're Sendung uns zur Stille weis't,
so schmückten edle Häupter sich mit Kronen,
um ihre Kraft man Fürstenscepter
    preisst:
ich setzt' in eines König's Macht Vertrauen,
wob still mein Werk, frei von
    Gespenstergrauen.

To the King (dernier effort!)

May you once more give ear to the voice
that from within you once did speak to me;
let me once more conjure forth the
    magic
by which once my sorrow broke your heart:
how should timid fear delude me now
if I can reawaken voice and magic
which poured forth upon me once from you
when the spring-time of your love unfolded
    to me?

In May-time's noble, blissful robe draws
    near
that sweetly joyous day of Kingly spring,
when you desired to give me new courage
through your affection's noble accolade,
and with your blessing consecrate the work
as close to your heart as to its creator's:
and my Sovereign's glorious command
became now a sure guidance to my
    faith.

The daemons are not well disposed to genius,
and spectres shun the spirit that is pure:
if oft with them the struggle naught availeth,
whene'er our mission tells us to be still,
noble heads have become adorned by crowns,
and for their power are princely sceptres
    praised:
my trust I placed in a King's authority,
and wove my work in silence, phantom
    free.

So war ich treu, und blieb was ich gewesen,
was neu ich ward durch meines König's
  Wort:
es wuchs das Werk, zu dem ich auserlesen,
am Seil der Nornen spann ich kundig fort;
von Grau'n und Sorge mocht' ich frei
  genesen, –
ein Königsherz war meines Heiles Hort.
Nun wieder naht des Maien Jubelwonne:
wie bängen mir Gespenster seine Sonne?

Wie sollten jetzt Dämonen frei am Tage
des holden Bundesfestes sich mir nah'n?
Von Hex' und Kobold hört' ich wohl die Sage,
dass sie im Mai zum Blocksberg ziehn hinan,
doch nimmer ward mir kund die graus'ge Plage
geleitet sie zu seh'n vom heil'gen Schwan!
Fort mit dem Spuck! Zur Hölle die
  Verhexten! –
Bald fei're ich der Jubeltage
  sechsten! –

O Holder! Hör' denn Deine eig'ne
  Stimme,
wie sie mein Herz Dir heute wiederhallt,
dass nie das edle Feuer Dir verglimme,
Dein Heerd in meinem Herzen nie erkalt'!
Wenn ich geduldig meine Höh' erklimme,
dem jähen Drange biet' auch Du Gewalt!
Und diese Höhe werde ich ersteigen:
da führe Du dann Deinen Göttereigen.

So I was true, remaining what I was,
and newly had become through my King's
  word:
the work for which I was elected, thrived,
and at the Norn rope skilfully I worked;
from sorrow, fear, I wished, free, to
  recover, –
a Kingly heart was shield of my salvation.
Now again May's joyous bliss draws near:
how fearful will the spectres make its sun?

How should now daemons freely on the day
of this sweet bond-festival draw near to me?
Of witch and goblin I have heard the tale
that they to the Blocksberg do proceed in May,
yet ne'er the gruesome torment have I known
of seeing Sacred Swan escort them there!
Begone that apparition! To hell with the
  bewitched!
Soon shall I celebrate the sixth[181] of joyous
  days! –

O Sweet One, give then ear to your own
  voice
as my heart echoes it to you today,
that ne'er for you the noble fire shall die,
nor your hearth in my heart grow ever cold!
And while, in patience, I ascend my height,
oppose to rash impulse your authority!
And this eminence I shall ascend:
then lead off your godly round dance there.

Tribschen, 13 April 1870

In 1870 the musical world was commemorating the centenary of Beethoven's birth (16[182] December 1770), for which reason Wagner published his essay in honour of his great predecessor in September of that year. It served also as a counter-blast to his most resolute opponent, the Viennese critic Eduard Hanslick, and in particular to his essay 'Vom Musikalisch-Schönem, ein Beitrag zur Revision der Ästhetik der Tonkunst' (Of the Musically Beautiful; Material for the Revision of the Aesthetics of Music), 1854. In this, Hanslick objects that music is not able to express feelings, and claims that it is no more than an ingenious game of tone combinations – a thesis contrary not only to Wagner's conception but also to Beethoven's art, so that the memorial essay was a suitable place for Wagner to oppose it. – The following previously unpublished notes under the later abandoned title 'Beethoven and the German Nation', already contain crucial points for his memorial essay. It is undated but post 13 April 1870, and probably not pre 3 July 1870, Wagner being until 2 July engaged with the composition and orchestral sketch for The Twilight of the Gods, Act I.[183] His Beethoven essay was begun on 20 July, so that the notes may be assigned to the period 3 to 19 July. – The final paragraph of the notes on page 177 refers to Eduard Hanslick personally. Wagner did not use it in the finished essay, just as in the 'Mastersingers' poem he did not, as originally intended, give Beckmesser the name Hans Lick. Whether Hanslick knew of this is not known. He did, however, on attending a reading by Wagner of the 'Mastersingers' poem, take the portrayal of Beckmesser personally. From then on he became wholly hostile to Wagner, which, in fundamentals, he had long been already. The 'higher academic degree' reference is to the fact that Hanslick, an associate Professor of Vienna University since 1861, had been appointed Professor in ordinary in 1870.

[[[Between 3 and 19 July 1870]

Beethoven and the German Nation

Relationship? – to German spirit only? How latter relates to 'beauty'? – Concept of beauty – peculiar to Greek spirit; as concept, borrowed from latter. – To visual art uniquely too peculiar. To poetry – in so far as it feeds on conceptions which devolve upon visual art: the most essential ingredients of poetry come, however, from music. – In what way is music beautiful? –

176

More detailed examination. Starting point: Schopenhauer: 'World as Will and Conception', II p. 415. Vague background in consciousness for idea. – On this: p. 418. Distinction in inwardly and in outwardly directed consciousness.

This second is what music creates from. Great diversity, dream theory. (Day-side – Goethe. Night-side – Beethoven.) Interpretation of dreams. Music the direct dream image. The innermost power on which our poets unconsciously fed, whose presence they divined and sought to explain. In Beethoven directly creative. In accordance with what laws? Own cry – external sound. Indiv: – nature. – Plastic art only as direct life act in dance. Folk song. – Further – ideal reality. – (French – Italians.)

Confusion in conceiving of music. Lack of clarity and of taste. Unwareness of self. Sculptors and poets give nation what it would like to seem, – the musician – what it really is. – Terror of inner world basis of sublime. Sublimity. Effect of music always that of sublime: form, however, that of beauty, i.e., in first instance, liberation of individual from conception of any causality. – Musical beauty form in which musician plays with sublime. Beeth. = Schopenhauer: his music, translated into concepts, would produce that philosophy. Similarity – to both, German nation. –

Life of musician. Production of genius – delight: meaning of this delight. Life itself pain throughout: physiognomy. – Banality of world, wishing without sacrifice to enjoy what delighted him whenever he extracted himself from life. – Saintliness. Church.

The objectively beautiful? – Effect of what is beautiful only condition for onset of true effect of work of art, that is to say, the sublime one. In music first effect immediately and universally achieved through its form precisely because it is pure form. – If it does not lead to sublime effect, then that which is beautiful is mere play. Hence aequivoca of word which can be used in any frivolous sense, which not conceivable with sublime.

Not through Helen is Faust redeemed but through Gretchen. –

But what is to be thought of a nation in which he who blathers such miserable stuff, is, having been suitably admonished, immediately, as consolation for this mortification, promoted to a higher academic degree. Does Beethoven belong to these?]]

177

For the King's twenty-fifth birthday on 25 August 1870, Wagner presented him with the complete orchestral sketch for the Prelude and Act I of The Twilight of the Gods *in a copy by Hans Richter. The title page and, on the second page, the copy of the poem below, were in Wagner's own hand. Wagner sent the score, together with the poem, to Court Secretary von Düfflipp who was to hand the present to the King. In the accompanying letter of 21 August 1870, however, Düfflip was given another important task, that of informing the King that (following the dissolution of the Bülow's marriage on 18 July 1870 in Berlin) Wagner's marriage to Cosima would be taking place in the Protestant Church at Lucerne,*[184] *and moreover at 7 a.m. on the King's birthday. Wagner writes: 'Will you also intimate to our Most Gracious Lord how deeply moved we both are at being able to let our wedding proceed on the very day of the birthday celebration of our Gracious, Exalted Friend.' The King conveyed thanks in a telegram saying: '. . . Need I assure you that, on this present, and for you and for the Friend so momentous day, more than ever am I with you in spirit!' Wagner's poem, entered at the latest on 19 July, the day the King's copy was sent to Munich, struck a political as well as a personal note. On 19 July France had declared war on Prussia. Shaken internally, and to solve its difficulties, the Empire needed a popular war and certain victory. The French were expecting – vainly, as it turned out – the support of Austria and Italy, as well as the neutrality of the South German states. And of especial importance in this was that King Ludwig II had ordered mobilization on 16 July, and, at the declaration of war, placed the Bavarian troops at the disposal of the Prussian High Command. This was the 'Kingly word' whereby it became possible for Germany to 'resurge'. It is in this sense that Wagner pays 'homage' to the King in the following poem.*

Zu des König's Geburtstag. 25 Aug. 1870.	For the King's Birthday, 25 August 1870
Gesprochen ist das Königswort,	Spoken has been the Kingly word
dem Deutschland neu erstanden,	wherefrom Germany anew is risen,
der Völker edler Ruhmeshort,	the nations' noble bastion of glory,
befreit aus schmähl'chen Banden;	released from ignominious bands;
was nie gelang der Klugen Rath,	what wise counsel never could effect
das schuf ein Königswort zur That:	a Kingly word has transformed into deed:
in allen deutschen Landen	in all the German lands
das Wort nun tönet fort und fort.	that word now sounds forth and resounds.

Und ich verstand den tiefen Sinn	And its deep sense I did understand
wie keiner ihn ermessen;	as no other person understood it;
Schuf es dem Volke Siegsgewinn.	if for the people it meant victory,
mir gab das Wort Vergessen;	for me that word brought a forgetting;
vergraben durft' ich manchen Schmerz,	and I could inter many a grief
der lange mir genagt das Herz,	that had long been gnawing at my heart,
das Leid, das mich besessen,	and the suffering that had possessed me
blickt' ich auf Deutschland's Schmach dahin.	as often as I gazed on Germany's shame.
Der Sinn, der in dem Worte lag,	And the meaning that lay in that word
war Dir auch unverborgen:	also did not stay concealed from you:
der treu des edlen Hortes pflag,	he who staunchly kept the noble hoard,
er theilte meine Sorgen.	was participator in my sorrows.
Von Wotan bangend ausgesandt,	By Wotan, in anxiety, sent forth,
sein Rabe gute Kund' ihm fand:	tidings his raven found him that were good:
es strahlt der Menschheit Morgen;	the dawn of humanity sends out its beams;
nun dämm're auf, du Göttertag.	shine now brightly forth, you Godly Day.

What Wagner understands by journalism in the following important previously unpublished entry, presumably prompted by his earlier work on the Beethoven essay, is obviously not general daily journalism, but any author, not himself creative, who writes interpretatively, thereby so confusing or ruining the audience that it is no longer in the position to accept the work of art that proceeds from the naïve and attempts to work directly, in the same spirit, unhampered by other people's usually imported interpretations, directly and naïvely. – Important at the same time is how Wagner confesses to employing all his art towards achieving the greatest precision of direct, naïvely-working effect, and to counting upon that solely. In other words, Wagner did not wish to be understood by the audience in any way beyond what the work itself directly states. With this Cosima too is in agreement in her own, but certainly subsequently Wagner-influenced, understanding of the effect of art. Her last letter to Nietzsche, dated 22 October 1877, states that she does not ask what the poet meant by this or that since she accepts what he says, literally and symbolically. Thus she had grown to know and love the poetry of The Ring *without having an inkling of Germanic mythology. All interpretations of Wagner's works were welcome retrospectively but were not necessary to her own understanding.*[185]

[[21 Sept *[1870]*

Concerning journalism. – This has rendered man (vulgo: the audience) so incapable of allowing the effect of an event – or ultimately of a work of art – to work on him directly and naïvely, that now even I who count solely on this direct impression and employ all my art towards achieving the greatest precision of the same, find myself after all obliged to 'write' in order again simply to prepare the audience's power of comprehension for this impression. –

*

Delicacy of the kind of art – according to locality and auditorium. – Cothurnus. – (Instrumentation.)]]

Wagner's comedy 'A Capitulation', set in besieged Paris at the end of 1870, has been described in France as a gibe at the French as losers in the war. The play was published in 1873 in Vol. IX of Complete Prose and Poetry. Wagner declares in the Foreword: 'If I now give my friends the text of this farce, it is quite certainly not to ridicule the Parisians in retrospect. My subject brings to light no facet of the French other than that, in the reflected light of whose illumination, we Germans cut indeed figures more ridiculous than those who, in all their acts of folly, show themselves ever original, whereas we, in disgusting emulation of the same, sink far below being ridiculous even.' In fact the play is not about the capitulation of the French to the German troops either, but about the capitulation of the Germans to the French theatre. Wagner lets Gambetta put it into words: '[The Germans] have capitulated and are overjoyed at being able to go to our theatres again!' (Complete Prose and Poetry, Vol. IX, p. 27). Towards the end of the play Jacques Offenbach appears, the inventor of modern operetta in France, but of German origin, born in Cologne. The sketch (p. 185 below) reads: 'The Prussians have discovered the underground ways: Offenbach sent as negotiator. – Agreeable effect of this. . . . These Germans one doesn't mind.' At the end of the play, however, Victor Hugo, depicted by Wagner as 'Génie de la France', announces:

'Wir haben euch alle geschlagen,
nun lasst auch raison euch sagen!
Als Feinde nicht nehmt ihr Paris,
doch schenken wir's euch als amis.
    Was klopft ihr am Fort?
    Wir öffnen das Tor,
    was ihr alle begehrt,
    's ist hier euch beschert:
. . .
    Chignons und Pomaden,
    Theater, Promenaden,
. . .
concert populaire, –
was wollt ihr noch mehr!'

'We have beaten the lot of you,
now let raison tell you too!
You'll not, as foes, take Paris,
we'll give it to you as amis.
    Why knock on the outside?
    The gate we'll open wide,
    what all of you desire,
    is here to acquire:
. . .
    Chignons and pomades
    theatres, promenades,
. . .
concert populaire, –
all you want is there!'

Before the curtain falls, the attachés of the European and non-European embassies crawl on stage from the prompt box, to the accompaniment of a ballet to Offenbach's music, followed by the Intendant of the Great German Court

181

Theatre! No one who reads Wagner's farce, as he calls it, can misunderstand it, which is not always the case with German writers. The sketch below has not previously been published. It is entitled 'The Capitulation' whereas the completed play was called 'A Capitulation', with the obvious intention of making the figurative sense clear. But while the comedy was, of course, prompted by the events of the war, Wagner pursues no political or hostile aim in it, as the text unequivocally shows. Moreover, the capitulation of Paris did not take place until 28 January 1871, more than two months after this comedy came into being. – Cf. note p. 157.

[[*[Mid November 1870]*

The Capitulation

Comedy by Aristop. Hanes

Classical stage. Orchestra (Square in front of Hotel de ville). The thymele representing an altar to the Republic, at the same time serving as prompter's box, stands over an opening to the égouts. The classical steps leading from two sides of the orchestra up to the stage represent a grand balcony of the town hall, the rest of the building has been removed, this balcony alone being sufficient for the government. Directly above it, just air; all that is to be perceived of Paris are the spires of the Pantheon and Notre Dame. On either side of the foreground on the orchestra level stand statues of Strasbourg and Metz. – Daybreak. – Head of Victor Hugo ascending from depths of thymele (prompter's box). He is sweating and groaning. By wandering all the égouts of Paris he has found the way in under the besiegers. He greets his sacred city after his long banishment and describes the thrill of bliss that has just affected him on this way to his home. But before making his public entry he is just going to take another look at some most dreadful sewers because he thinks he has heard wonderful voices, like the grunting of pigs; feeling deeply and sympathetically drawn to them, he believes he might there light on the real inner voices of the sacred city which interest him both as writer and as patriot. Hearing military music approaching in the distance, he shrinks back, listening hard.

Chorus of National Guard marches on, headed by band: singing in 6/8 march time. 'Only the Republic: Republic for ever; Republic – blic – blic: Rerepubul – pub – pubbulreplic!' etc. They dance around the altar to the Republic gesturing as in the cancan (muskets in their arms, bear-skin caps on their heads). Hugo

182

sobs with bliss and emotion. – March to the two statues. The bouquets which the guards carry on their musket barrels are laid before the statues. Songs of homage for Elsace etc. Hugo beside himself with enthusiasm, tries to emerge but, to his alarm, is held fast from below: 'Who is holding me!' Answer through speaking tube: 'The true spirits de la France.' Hugo 'Ha! As I anticipated!' Disappears. – The chorus gathers again around the thymele: complaining that, hearing no sound of cannon, they smell treachery. They confess to being in need of courage, and the cannonading outside the forts never fails to fill them with it. (/*Margin note by Wagner:*/ An old deaf chorus leader always misunderstands.) Call for the government. – Finally J. Favre and J. Ferry appear on the balcony. They embrace. General jubilation. 'Oh, if only there were now a proper cannonade!' Why isn't there? Ferry forgives Favre for not being able to speak for emotion; apart from which he has sobbed himself completely hoarse in his parley with Bismarck, added to which there had been the great indignation at his impudent demands. He was really quite done for! – Tumult and general rage at Bismarck's impudence. 'What, would he have Strasbourg.' Renewed hymn to tune 'Strasbourg, oh thou beauteous city.' Ha, the insolent one. – Forward, to Strasbourg. – Let us send them encouragement, but above all, encourage ourselves: therefore let there be a cannonade. – Ferry: 'But how are we to get to Strasbourg? – We can't fly through the air, can we?' – Nadar's voice: 'Why not?' He appears on the balcony with an enormous wrapping around him, at first filling all with terror. He reassures them: he is the protective spirit of the air of the French; he will save France if he is made government councillor. <u>Gambetta</u> springs out from behind the balcony. 'None of that! I alone am the saviour.' Both come to an understanding. Nadar reveals himself to be a balloon; after having previously asked the chorus to blow him up; bellows are distributed: cheerful chorus during blowing up of balloon. Nadar, as inner voice of balloon, calls upon Gambetta to climb in. He climbs in. The two Jules embrace. 'Oh, for a cannonade now!' They watch the flight of the balloon: it becomes trapped on Notre Dame. Gambetta reports what he sees. 'The Prussians are completely and utterly defeated; the Strasbourg garrison is chasing them over the Rhine!' – 'Oh, for a cannonade now!' – The balloon frees itself again: Nadar's voice quarrelling with Gambetta; they get caught on the Pantheon. The chorus demand to know what can be seen. What about Metz? – <u>Gambetta</u> furious with Nadar; what's he to say now? – Ah! Yes. – There, Metz! All the Prussians killed! Jubilation of Bazaine; they're now slaughtering 5000 oxen and are in good heart. – Chorus: Oh, glorious, fifty-fold hecatomb! How sweet to the tutelary gods of the Republic must be the savour of that! Would that we only had something of it; if only the aroma which here is becoming ever more unusual. 'Can you smell anything, Gambetta?' – Gambetta: 'Delicious!' – Chorus: Let us into the balloon: Nadar!

Nadar! – <u>Gambetta</u> 'Citizens, that can't be done – Just a little more renunciation! Republicans, be virtuous! (Balloon swinging this way and that.) Chorus 'Tell us, what do you see now! Don't you see any oxen for us too? – <u>Gambetta</u>: poised above the thymele: 'Oh, more than that! Cattle for slaughter by the hundred thousand; right around the whole holy city!' – Chorus: 'Well, drive them in here.' Gambetta: – 'Just be patient! The slaughterers are after them already! Coming from south, west and north.' He depicts the approaching people's armies taking the Prussians in the rear and causing dreadful carnage amongst them. Exhortations to virtue, renunciation! Prophecy of immeasurable happiness. – Chorus: 'But why no cannonade then? The balloon continues to travel around. General delight. The Jules embrace. –

Hugo, followed by Flourens and Ledru-Rollin etc., climbs up from below. With fearful cries of woe they interrupt the chorus's joy. 'Citizens, you are betrayed!' Treachery! Treachery! You are being told lies out of the air; we have come the right way, through the vitals of the city: my poetic wonder-gaze has enabled me to find the égouts through the whole of France to Strasbourg and Metz! Treachery! Strasbourg has surrendered! – Dreadful consternation and rage! – Imprecations. Statue of Strasbourg smashed. – Hugo emerges and seats himself on the thymele. – Flourens climbs out after him: 'That is not yet all! Metz has capitulated!' – Dreadful outburst. 'Bazaine! Ha! Judas! Blackguard!' – Metz gets smashed. 'Where is Gambetta?' – The balloon has slipped away towards the rear. – Ledru-Rollin: ' – The army of the Loire defeated, Garibaldi – gout. All betrayed! Bonaparte! Tropmann!' – Rising anger! Chorus: 'Ha! And still no cannonade! – Cannonade! Cannonade!' – Hugo: in the highest ecstasy, prophesying and carrying all with him. There sits the enemy! Favre has collapsed in a faint; Ferry guards him. 'Up! Storm the Capitol!' Cannon! Cannon! – In the distance a fearful cannonade! <u>Chorus</u> terrified: 'God! The Prussians!' Hugo: 'Prussians nothing! I – I gave the order: they're firing from Mont Valérien, into the blue! – Balcony stormed: Hugo and companions appointed government. Ferry and unconscious Favre are dragged down and stuffed into prompter's box. – Constant cannonade. Enormous joy? Red Republic! – That is not enough for Flourens: Black Republic! – No state at all! No society – that would be something! – Voice from air: all the better for the church! We're with you! – 'Who spoke?' Hugo: I don't know, but certainly a genius of France, inspired by me.' – Great clamour in the air. Nadar's voice: 'That damned cannonade! I'm burst!' The balloon drops uncertainly to earth. Gambetta grabs a rope and swings to the spire of the Pantheon. From there, through a megaphone, he surrenders. He warns people to take care. Out there they are surrendering to the Prussians. Thiers is there! – Shouts of rage! Ferry and Favre climb up out of the égout. They embrace, having found the means for

184

deliverance. Ferry: 'Citizens, to red we would not object: but black? Do you know what that means!' He describes the horrors of a fight to the death: everything in Paris would then be ruined, and never more would one be able to go to a theatre. Powerful response! Hugo played out and soft! – 'France, rescue your writer!' It's these whom I found down there, they have led me too far astray. – Ferry takes courage: the Chorus agrees with him: Hugo faints. Nadar, again recovered, rapidly inflates himself and floats towards the Pantheon to pick up Gambetta. – General cry. 'We want theatres again! – Yes! Also little suppers' etc. – Flourens etc. are seized. – As Ferry and Favre are carried back to the balcony, an Offenbach melody is heard from below. Offenbach appears by the prompt box as trumpeter. The Prussians have discovered the underground ways: Offenbach sent as negotiator. – Agreeable effect of this. Offenb. declared international, one who belongs to the world: these Germans one doesn't mind. To him they surrender: Gazing deeply, Hugo recognizes in him the bond of civilization-fraternity and recommends his proposals. Gambetta, floating in air, opposes. But soon Offenb. is followed from the depths by the ladies of the ballet with Frau Thérèse. General amusement. Unhappy ones! It was you who banished civilization. We are bringing it back to you! – Surrender! Surrender! – General fraternization.]]

*

[[On behalf of what, of whom are these battles supposed to have been fought? Possibly on your behalf, journalists and literati. Let us first begin to realize what wretched people we are, and whether it would be worth the trouble of wasting one shot of powder on behalf of, say, the protégé of the Allgemeine Zeitung. For the present these victories still belong quite solely to those who won them, quite definitely neither to the Jacobys nor to the H. Linggs[186] etc.

10 Dec *[1870]*

German aristocracy. Excellent as lieutenants in the field, only dreadful as theatre intendants at home.

*

Hector is not (alone) recognizable by virtue of the fact of being (as an individual) a Trojan prince, but by virtue of the fact of being, apart from all that, as he is.]]

Moved by the successes of the German troops in the 1870–1 war and by the crowning of Wilhelm, King of Prussia, as German Emperor on 18 January 1871, Wagner dedicated the poem below to the German Army, but did not publish it straightaway. As a demonstration of personal respect, he sent it to Bismarck. Bismarck's letter of thanks of 21 February 1871 reads: 'Much as I feel honoured that you should, as I am told,[187] intend this patriotic poem for me alone, I should be very glad to see it published.' But it was not published until 1873, and then under the title of 'The German Army before Paris' in Wagner's Collected Prose and Poetry, *Vol. IX. – For the troops' return to Berlin, Wagner intended to write a march for military band, the finale of which should form an imperial hymn to be sung by the troops or by a soldiers' choir, a rough draft for which he entered on 16 March 1871 (v. p. 188). When Berlin showed no interest in this, Wagner wrote his 'Imperial March' for the concert hall, scoring it for large orchestra. The national song appended to the finale of this march is to be performed only when, through suitable arrangement, it is possible for the audience to participate. The rehearsed singers must therefore not appear as a choir apart on stage or concert platform, but be suitably distributed amongst the audience, who in turn would be furnished with the music. But in any case, performance in the manner indicated could only be considered for special festive occasions. The*

Berlin première of the march was conducted by Wagner on 5 May 1871 at a concert in the presence of Emperor Wilhelm I.[188]

Dem deutschen Heer	To the German Army
	January 1871

Was schweigt es doch im deutschen
  Dichterwald?
Versang «Hurrah, Germania!» sich so bald?
Schlief bei der Liedertafel – Wacht am Rhein
beruhigt sanft «lieb Vaterland» schon ein?
    die deutsche Wacht,
da steht sie nun in Frankreich's eitlem Herzen;
    von Schlacht zu Schlacht
vergiesst ihr Blut sie unter heissen Schmerzen:
    mit stiller Wucht
    in frommer Zucht
  vollbringt sie nie geahnte Thaten,
zu gross für euch, nur ihren Sinn zu rathen.

Why is the grove of German poets
  silent?
Is 'Germany, hurra' so quickly sung to death?
Has, at the sign to strike up 'Watch on Rhine',
'dear Fatherland', lulled sweetly, fallen asleep?
    That German watch
now stands in France's empty heart;
    in battle after battle
sheds blood in searing agony:
    with quiet weight
    and pious discipline
  performs undreamt-of deeds,
too great for you to guess but their import.

*

Das eitle Wort, das wusste freilich Rath,
da im Geleis' es sich gemüthlich trat;
der deutschen Lieder-Klang und Singe-Sang,
man wähnte selbst Franzosen macht' er bang.
    Du treues Heer,
hast Du's mit deinen Siegen nun verbrochen,
    dass jetzt nur mehr
in Kammerreden wird von Dir gesprochen?
    Das hohe Lied
    dem Siege-Fried
  jetzt singen ängstlich Diplomaten,
vereint mit ärgerlichen Demokraten!

Plain words, they were at no loss
as feelingly they marched on in the rut;
the noise and singing of the German songs
would, one fancied, scare even the French.
    Faithful Army,
have you by your victories done some crime
    to be now more spoken of
in Chamber speeches only?
    The song of praise
    to victory's peace
  sing timidly now diplomats
at one with angry democrats!

*

«Zu viel des Sieg's! Mög't ihr bescheid'ner
  sein:
begnügt euch friedlich mit der Wacht am
  Rhein!
Lasst uns Paris, wo sich's so hübsch
  verschwört,
und seid zufrieden mit der Schlacht bei
  Wörth!»
    doch unbethört
in ernstem Schweigen schläg'st du deine
  Schlachten;
    was unerhört,

'Too much of victory! May you be more
  modest:
be satisfied to watch the Rhine in
  peace!
Leave us Paris where such sweet plotting's
  done,
and make do with the battle fought at
  Wörth!'
    But unbeguiled,
you fight your fights in solemn
  silence;
    the unheard-of deed,

187

das zu gewinnen ist dein männlich Trachten.
   Dein eig'nes Lied
   in Krieg und Fried',
  wirst Du, mein herrlich Volk, Dir
    finden,
mög' drob auch mancher Dichterruhm
   verschwinden!

*

Das Lied, blick' ich auf Deine Thaten hin,
aus ihrem Werthe ahn' ich seinen Sinn:
Fast klingt's wie: «Muth zeigt auch der
   Mameluck».
Dem folgt: «Gehorsam ist des Christen
   Schmuck». –
    Es ruft der Herr:
und ihn versteht ein ganzes Volk in Waffen,
   dem Ruhmgeplärr'
des Übermuth's ein Ende da zu schaffen.
    Es rafft im Krampf
    zu wildem Kampf
   sich auf des eitlen Wahn's Bekenner;
der Welt doch züchtet Deutschland nur noch
   Männer.

*

Drum soll ein Deutscher nur noch Kaiser
   sein;
im welschen Lande solltet ihr ihn weih'n:
der treuen Muth's sein Werbeamt
   erfüllt,
dem sei nun seiner Thaten Werth enthüllt.
    Die uns geraubt,
die würdevollste aller Erdenkronen,
   auf seinem Haupt
soll sie der Treue heil'ge Thaten lohnen.
    So heisst das Lied,
    vom Siege-Fried,
   von deutschen Heeres That gedichtet:
Der Kaiser naht: in Frieden sei
   gerichtet!

Kaiserlied.
(für das Heer.)

Heil! Heil dem Kaiser!
   König Wilhelm!
Aller Deutschen Hort und Freiheitswehr!
   Höchste der Kronen,

---

that is your manly striving to achieve.
   Your own song
   in war and peace
  you'll find, my glorious soldiers, for
    yourselves,
for which may, too, fade much poetic
   fame!

*

Of that song, as I gaze upon your feats,
I am able, from their worth, to guess the sense:
'Mameluke's too are brave,' it almost
   is.
Then: 'Obedience is the Christian's
   ornament.' –
    The Lord's call comes:
and a whole armèd people understands:
   to vaunting, vociferous
arrogance put an end.
    Convulsed, they rise
    for savage fight
   the followers of vain delusion;
but Germany breeds the world still only
   men.

*

Therefore shall a German only still be
   Emperor;
on foreign soil you were to consecrate him:
to him who with true courage laboured as
   recruiter,
be now revealed the value of his feats.
    Once stolen from us,
the worthiest of earthly crowns
   upon his head,
it shall reward the sacred deeds of faith.
    That is the song
    of victory's peace,
   as set down by the German Army's deeds:
The Emperor draws near: in peace be
   judgement done!

Imperial Song
(for the Army.)

Hail! Hail to the Emperor!
   King Wilhelm!
Shield and bulwark of all Germans' freedom!
   Loftiest of crowns,

188

Wie ziert Dein Haupt sie hehr!	how augustly it adorns your brow!
Ruhmreich gewonnen	Gloriously won,
soll Frieden Dir lohnen!	peace shall be your reward.
Der neu ergrünten Eiche gleich	Like the newly verdant oak,
erstand durch Dich das deutsche Reich:	through you has risen up the German Reich:
Heil seinen Ahnen,	Hail to its forebears,
seinen Fahnen,	to its banners
die Dich führten, die wir trugen,	bearing your device, which we carried
als mit Dir wir Frankreich schlugen!	when with you we defeated France!
Trutz dem Feind,	Defiance to the foe,
Schutz dem Freund	protection for the friend,
allem Volk das deutsche Reich	the German Reich for all peoples'
zu Heil u. Nutz!	advantage and salvation!

16 March. 1871

The following notes, undated but apparently written in 1871, are isolated thoughts and ideas which occurred to Wagner in reading or in conversation, and which he recorded in order to make occasional use of in articles or essays planned at the time or for later.

[[The Jesuit general (after Carl Wittgenstein) against Bismarck. Romanic-Jesuitical: frivolous pessimism. – Germanic-Protestant: discreetly concerned belief in the development of good tendencies.

Romanic – – as nothing remains finally of aristocracy but arrogance and with it, perfidy, so with the Romance person who has finally lost his gifts.

C.W.[189]]]

Mixed nations fortunate for political development but not for mental productivity. – Originality. Naïvety – etc. Whilst mixed nations are active and make history, new formations of states (Normans), the unmixed nation retains a natural view of things – writes creatively. (Saxons – Shakespeare.)

[[Originality of language: difference between English prose and poetry.]]

For the King's twenty-seventh birthday on 25 August 1872, Wagner sent him a copyist's copy of the orchestral sketch of Act III of The Twilight of the Gods. *For his twenty-fifth birthday he had received Hans Richter's copies of the orchestral sketch for the Prelude and Act I of the same work, also with a poem by Wagner (v. p. 178). Act II in a copy by the Zürich music teacher Spiegel[190] reached the King on 4 December 1871, accompanied by a letter in which Wagner wrote: 'A fair copy of the composition [i.e. orchestral sketch] of Act II of* The Twilight of the Gods *has just been completed, which I now hasten to lay at your feet. On the sublime festive day of last August it pained me still to be in arrears.' But for the King's twenty-sixth birthday on 25 August 1871 no poem or letter of congratulation is to be found either in the* Brown Book *or in correspondence with the King. — The year 1871 was one of the most critical in Wagner's dramatic career. It was a question first of all of preventing the King from staging, after* Rhinegold *1869 and* The Valkyrie *1870, a performance of* Siegfried *in 1871 (cf. notes p. 172 and p. 174). On 2 February, however, Court Secretary Düfflipp informed Wagner that he had been commanded by the King to inquire of him concerning the performance of* Siegfried. *Wagner had in fact completed the score of* Siegfried *Act III on 5 February, but was forced to conceal as much from the King lest he demand the score and have it performed. To a letter on 18 February, in which the King said he failed to understand Wagner's lack of interest in the performance of his musical creations (i.e.* The Rhinegold *and* The Valkyrie *at Munich), Wagner, on 1 March, wrote an extremely candid, even strong reply. In this he speaks of the 'unutterable pain' occasioned him by the production of* The Rhinegold *and later of* The Valkyrie *'as opera performances contrary to his wishes', and complains of 'feeling as the father whose child is torn from him and delivered into prostitution'. He rounds off this passage by exclaiming 'What to me are those works now? . . . What to me can they be now other than defiled caricatures?' The King did not react. He loved Wagner but felt himself to be his King and master absolutely, looked upon him as a piece of property, and felt entitled to make any demand, be it of a mental, emotional or artistic nature — as he very soon showed. On 15 April, Düfflipp informed Wagner at a meeting in Augsburg that the King now wished to have the first two Acts of* Siegfried *performed. Wagner, knowing no compromise where his works were concerned, said that he would rather burn* Siegfried *and go begging than deliver it up in this way.*[191] *But this meeting served the purpose of informing the King via Düfflipp of Wagner's plan to give his own performances of the entire* Ring *at Bayreuth. The King was therefore supposed not only to forgo* Siegfried *but also to waive his rights over* The Twilight of the Gods, *and to give his agreement to Bayreuth. In this Wagner was risking a break with the King and grave consequences for himself, for his vague hope of help from Berlin and the new German Reich soon proved false. On 11 May, following a report from Düfflipp, Wagner went so far as to write to him that the King's reaction had 'the painfulness of an estrangement about it'. Düfflipp, who, in difficult negotiations with the King, had constantly proved himself Wagner's friend and a skilled diplomat, showed his letter to the King. The latter, concerned at the possibility of losing Wagner, and perhaps fearful of his receiving aid from Berlin, wrote on 26 May: 'Your last letter to Düfflipp, in which you declare yourself forced to believe in an estrangement on my part, has really pained me . . . Oh may you never allow such doubts to arise! . . . Your plan concerning your Nibelung work to be performed at Bayreuth is divine . . . We shall remain true; true to death.'* But that was still not a declaration to waive the Munich performances of Siegfried *and* later, if occasion arose, of The Twilight of the Gods. *If these were to take place, the Bayreuth plan would become meaningless, since its aim was to provide the authentic model for all future productions of* The Ring, *including those in Munich. And barely a year later, in March 1872, in spite of having welcomed the 'divine plan', the King requested Wagner, through Düfflipp, to hand over the* Siegfried *score, even calling attention to the fact that by the terms of agreement of 18 October 1864, he was owner of the work (cf. note p. 172). Wagner's reply to Düfflipp of 27 March states however: 'A contract of sale in respect of these scores was duly [1864] proposed to me by Court Secretary Hofman, and only, as he put it, as a formality to reassure public opinion if need be, for which reason also, as it would otherwise have appeared unseemly, this contract of sale was concluded. I sincerely regret that it should have occurred to anyone . . . to return to this contract of sale, and may I, on the other hand, kindly be allowed . . . to continue to adhere to the first assurance expressed to me by His Majesty, that His Majesty entertained no other wish or desire in my regard than to remove me by His Favour from all worries of life, and know me preserved for the free practice of my art.' From this it is clear how seriously endangered at that time the Bayreuth plan was, and how ominously close to a break the King's friendship for Wagner had moved.*

Unable to send the as yet uncompleted Act II of The Twilight of the Gods *for the King's twenty-sixth birthday, Wagner presented him with Karl Klindworth's newly printed piano score of* Siegfried *in a special de luxe edition on vellum. The King was thus to have* Siegfried *but not in a form that could be staged. In a letter*[192] *of 22 August 1871 to Court Secretary von Düfflipp Wagner wrote: 'I feel doubtfully placed with you as your obdurate silence in face of my inquiry concerning the possibility of a visit to us should, I suppose, give me cause for concern. To break this silence I have today, for my part, noble cause in notifying you of the dispatch to your address of a parcel whose contents, a grand piano score [of Siegfried], copies in my wife's hand,*[193] *and a letter from me, I cordially request you to be so good as to deliver to His Majesty in time for His Majesty's birthday.' This commission was performed by Düfflipp, but this time the King took no pleasure in Wagner's present, and must instead have been annoyed at not receiving the full score he so longed for. Wagner's accompanying letter is no longer available, having, it may be assumed, fallen victim to the King's anger. The King kept Wagner waiting for four months before thanking him. It was not until 3 January 1872 that he wrote: 'How am I to stammer thanks for three such exceedingly kind, inestimable letters [of 13 July, 4 and 27 December 1871] and the splendid birthday present and Christmas present (Act II of* The Twilight of the Gods*), that allowed me to breathe heaven's delights and forget all earthly sorrows. Oh may you now also indeed sojourn in my land for ever and never incline your ear to offers from others!' The final sentence establishes the accuracy of the comment above concerning the King's fear of Wagner's establishing a connection with Prussia, which, from 25 August until 5 May 1871, was in fact the case in Berlin.*

[For 25 August 1872]

Bei Übersendung des III Aktes der Götterdämmerung an den König Ludwig II	On dispatching Act III of Twilight of the Gods to King Ludwig II
'Vollendet das ewige Werk! Wie im Traum ich es trug, Wie mein Wille es wies, – Was bange Jahre barg des reifenden Mannes Brust, aus winternächtigen Wehen der Lieb und des Lenzes Gewalten Trieben dem Tag' es zu: dort steh' es stolz zur Schau, als kühner Königsbau Prang' es prächtig der Welt!	'The immortal work is complete! Borne by me as in a dream, as my will did direct, – what for years of anxiety, the maturing breast has concealed, out of winter-night woes the forces of love and of spring have impelled toward light of day: proudly on view may it stand, like a bold edifice of the King's its splendour show to the world!'

The death of Karl Tausig on 27 May 1871, aged barely thirty, affected Wagner as deeply as the early death of Ludwig Schnorr von Carolsfeld six years earlier. Tausig was a master-pupil of Liszt and, in spite of his youth, one of the most distinguished pianists of his time. Hans von Bülow praised his playing as 'the most ideal he had ever heard'. The first piano score of The Mastersingers *is Tausig's work, and three months before his death he had been appointed by Wagner to be manager of the planned Bayreuth Festival Undertaking.[194] In 1872 when the gravestone was raised to him at the Halle Gate Cemetery in Berlin, Wagner wrote the following lines which were inscribed on a marble tablet to be a fitting memorial.*

Grabschrift für Karl Tausig	Epitaph for Karl Tausig
Reif sein zum Sterben, des Lebens zögernd spriessende Frucht, früh reif sie erwerben in Lenzes jäh erblühender Flucht, – war es Dein Loos, war es Dein Wagen, – Wir müssen Dein Loos wie Dein Wagen beklagen.	To be mature for death, life's slowly thriving fruit, to win it early ripe in sudden blossoming flight of spring – that was your fate, and that your daring, – your fate we must lament, so too your daring.

7 Sept. 72

*

[[Professors: = apes climbing about on the tree of knowledge.]]

Wagner had been closely acquainted with Georg Herwegh (1817–75) since the first years of his stay in Zürich (1849–58). Highly-gifted and in his youth a successful lyric poet of liberal inclination, he had, since being expelled from Prussia, lived in Switzerland. As a result of repeated disappointments his creative powers flagged and he became more and more embittered, without ever abandoning his revolutionary views. If it was their liberal views that originally brought the two men together, it was Wagner's friendship with King Ludwig II of Bavaria which led Herwegh to drop him in 1864, seeing it as treachery to his one-time republican ideals. In 1866 he gave vent to his resentment against Wagner in two ironical poems. His annoyance grew even greater on Wagner's becoming associated with the imperial family in Berlin. A concert conducted by Wagner on 4 February 1873 in Berlin in the presence of the royal couple, prompted him to a new satirical poem dated 8 February 1873, of which the second verse runs:

'Viel Gnade gefunden hat Dein Spiel *beim gnädigen Landesvater,* *nur läßt ihm der Bau des Reichs nicht viel* *mehr übrig für Dein Theater.'*	*'Much favour has your playing found* *with the Nation's Gracious Pater,* *but his building of the Reich won't leave* *much over for your theatre.'*

The lines below are Wagner's also ironic, but not malicious, reply to his opponent in whom, before as after, he esteemed the one-time friend (v. Glasenapp, Vol. IV, pp. 367–8). Wagner's republican ideals, which derived originally from his artistic idealism and led to the Utopian idea of a union of monarchy and republic, certainly differed fundamentally from those of the

193

uncompromising revolutionary and, by nature, obviously controversial, Georg Herwegh. Cf. here Bernhard Prince von Bülow (1849–1929): Denkwürdigkeiten *(Memoirs) Berlin 1931, Vol. IV, p. 671.*

An Georg Herwegh	To Georg Herwegh
Ja, lieber Herwegh, man wird alt;	Yes, dear Herwegh, one grows old;
doch stets noch aus dem Wald es schalt	but still the wood re-echoes bold
wenn spielt der kühne Rattenfänger;	to the tune of brave Rat-Catcher;
und Du, ob Politik Du treibst,	and you, whether politics your game,
Ob Poesie, Physik, Du bleibst	or poetry, physics, still stay the same
der demokrat'sche Bänkelsänger.	democratic ballad basher.

24 Febr: 73

The two entries which follow are connected with a visit by Nietzsche and his friend Rohde to Bayreuth from 7 to 12 April 1873. Nietzsche read from the manuscript of his work Philosophy in the Tragic Age of the Greeks, *and attention was given to the anti-Wagnerite David Strauss's* Der alte und der neue Glaube *(The Old Faith and the New), published 1872, of which Cosima said that it liberated us 'from redemption, prayer and Beethoven's music'. Nietzsche decided to write a refutation, which he brought out in the same year, 1873, as the first part of his* Untimely Meditations. *Here, too, are to be found comments on ideas recorded by Wagner in the entries below: the question of a German culture (p. 184 in the* Complete Nietzsche, *Leipzig, 1905, Vol. I), Greece and Barbarism (p. 194), Beethoven (p. 209). In his ironic criticism of Strauss's Beethoven interpretations in particular, Nietzsche concurred with Wagner's antipathy to Strauss. Cf. here note p. 125.*

[[*[April 1873]*

On: What is German?[195]

We must understand a thing in <u>our</u> language if we want to understand it properly. (barbaros – un-German. Luther.) That is the sense of a *German* culture. What we cannot ever or in any language understand about the Greek way, is what wholly separates us from it, e.g. their love – in – paederasty.]]

*

Plain evidence of the musician's not characterizing his creations in accordance with conscious didactic and poetic reflection and guided by the

194

same, but from a deeper seated, directly impelling perception, is provided by the final movement of the Pastoral Symphony: here, in accordance with the scheme of the external plan, he[196] again depicts the cheerful feelings of the country folk; only how completely all the motives and treatments differ from those of the movements preceding the thunderstorm! – The change of mood resulting from this powerful natural impression leads to a sublimity of feeling. This great dramatic 'catharsis' has escaped Dr D. Strauss who finds the symphony dull because the powerful thunderstorm is not in agreement with the previous peasant merriment!! –

[[/Between May and August 1873[197]]

]]

For his twenty-eighth birthday on 25 August 1873, Wagner sent the king the just-printed ninth and, for the time being, final volume of his Collected Prose and Poetry *in a special de luxe edition. According to the original plan of 26 April 1868 (v. p. 133), Volume X was to contain reminiscences from Wagner's life, that is, the autobiography at which he was still working (until 1880). The first nine volumes appeared between 1871 and 1873, the tenth did not appear until ten years later, in 1883, after Wagner's death, but in accordance with his provisions and containing, apart from* Parsifal, Bayreuth *and other writings. An eleventh volume and a twelfth were published posthumously in 1911. Still later, within the compass of* Collected Prose and Poetry *(Popular edition), in Volumes XIII–XV, came the autobiography* My Life. *The sixteenth, and final, volume contains addenda and an index.*

Bei Zusendung des 9ten Bandes der gesammelten Schrift. u. Dicht. an den König.	On forwarding to the King Volume IX of the Collected Prose and Poetry (25 Aug. 1873)
Ein neues Werk nicht, was ich heut' Dir sende.	No new work this I send to you today
Zu grüssen Dich am hohen Festes-Tage:	as greeting on the Exalted Celebration:
mein Wirken selbst leg' ich in Deine Hände,	my work itself I give into your hands,
wie mir bestimmt im Schicksalsschooss es lag:	as it reposed, marked for me, in Fate's lap:

was ich gewirkt, dass ich mein Werk vollende,	how I have laboured to complete my work,
was hier gesammelt, Dir es sagen mag:	what here is gathered may convey to you:
Neun Bücher bot dem König Rom's Sibylle;	the King was offered nine books by Rome's Sibyl;
Neun biet' ich Dir: erfülle sie Dein Wille!	nine I offer: may your Will fulfil them!

Du war'st es, der zuerst mich dess' gemahnet,	You it was who first admonished me
zu wahren, was ich sinnend einst gedacht,	I should preserve my thoughts and cogitations,
die Wege, die ich selber einst gebahnet,	the ways I pioneered once for myself
die ich beschritt durch Dämmerung und Nacht,	and which I walked in half-light and in dark
den Tag zu grüssen, den ich je geahnet,	to hail the day which always I foresaw,
der nun im Sonnenlichte hell erwacht.	which now has woken in the sun's bright light.
Weissagte einst dem König die Sibylle,	The Sibyl prophesied once to the King,
was klar er weiss, sagt Dir des Freundes Wille.	your friend's will tells you what he clearly knows.

Du weisst es, Herr der königlichen Hulden,	You are aware, Lord of Royal Favours,
Du kennst mit mir des Lebens schwere Bahn;	you know with me the onerous way of life;
verschlossen nicht blieb Dir der Welt Verschulden,	not hidden from you is the world's indebting,
bekannt ist Dir misgestalter Wahn:	well known to you is its misshapen folly:
doch eines König's göttlichem Gedulden	yet for the Godly Indulgence of a King
bricht endlich wohl des Glauben's Tag auch an:	there also dawns at last the day of faith:
was neunfach sie geweissagt, die Sibylle,	what she ninefold prophesied, the Sibyl.
vor aller Welt ein Königswort erfülle!	may a King's word for all the world fulfil!

Wagner made entries in the Brown Book *from 1865 to 1873, albeit with numerous minor and some major breaks resulting from his circumstances and his creative work. The entry dated 28 December 1873 below was followed by a break of six-and-a-half years until 2 August 1880, after which entries continue until 1882. The long break coincides with the building of the Festival Theatre, the completing of the composition of Acts II and III of* The Twilight of the Gods, *and the preparations for the first festival in 1876. From 1877, Wagner was occupied with the writing and composition of* Parsifal. *By all of which Wagner, now seventy, was taxed to the uttermost, and he could hardly have succeeded in it without the help of Cosima, who by Christmas 1877, was celebrating her fortieth birthday and at her efficient best. And this should, in fairness, be remembered against the disparagement to which her activities are only too often and gladly subjected.*

To the best of her ability also, Cosima filled the gap in Wagner's Brown Book *from 1874 to 1880 by recording numerous remarks of his in her own diaries. A selection of these, undertaken by Eva Chamberlain, was published in the* Bayreuther Blätter, *1936–7, and may be regarded as supplementing the missing years in the* Brown Book.

When Toscanini was at Bayreuth conducting performances of Tannhäuser
(1930–31), Tristan *(1930) and* Parsifal *(1931), Eva wrote out for him some of
Wagner's unpublished remarks as recorded by Cosima in her diaries. Her
selection was then published by Hans von Wolzogen in the* Bayreuther Blätter *in
eight numbers between January 1936 and December 1937.*[198] *On 24 December
1937 Eva presented the 130 quarto-sheets to the Richard-Wagner-Gedenkstätte,
where they now are.*

*The remarks selected by Eva are concerned mainly with music and musicians,
his own creative method, and his works, especially the writing and composition
of* Parsifal *between 1874 and 1882. At the same time it is of interest that, apart
from Beethoven, it was Bach who claimed his constant attention. He would often
get a young devotee of his, the young pianist Joseph Rubinstein, or Liszt, to play
to him from 'Das wohltemperierte Klavier', and he would also play the preludes
and fugues himself. Bach figured most prominently in the* Parsifal *period, while
Beethoven remained as important as ever, the symphonies, the quartets and the
piano sonatas, op. 106 and op. 111 especially. There is evidence of interest not
only in a variety of composers, writers and philosophers, but also in religion,
politics, the Germans, socialism, the workers, the Jews, and vivisection, and some
part of this interest is reflected in the entries below.*

It is no small thing to peruse world history and be supposed in so doing, to
preserve love for the human race. The sole thing that can enter here to retie the
thread that has been rent through viewing the whole, is the indestructible feeling
of kinship with the people, with the stock from which we have sprung in the first
instance. The effect of that here is what we ourselves feel, we have compassion
and are anxious to be able to hope, as we do for the fate of our own family. On the
other hand, he who is torn away from his stock – that futile phantom, the
cosmopolitan – where will he get love of humanity from?

28 Dec. 73

The final entries from the years 1880 to 1882, contain thoughts which had long occupied Wagner. His active engagement in the May unrests of 1849 – albeit prompted by the artist's protest at the state of cultural enterprise at that time – had its deeper reason in his seeing in the purely human the supreme maxim of his view of art and of the world, the danger to which through prevailing political circumstances he recognized. Thus the first thing he undertook following his flight to Switzerland, was his essay 'Art and the Revolution', with which he opened his series of Zürich artistic writings of the years 1849–51. There we read: 'Out of its state of civilized barbarism, true art can, to its dignity, raise itself up only on the shoulders of our great social movement: . . . [The] aim is the strong and beautiful human being: may the revolution give him the strength, and art – the beauty! (Collected Prose and Poetry, *Vol. III, p. 32). But such philosophizing had soon to stand down in face of the creative tasks imposed by fate upon the musician and dramatist. Not until 1867 do we again encounter anything similar. Meanwhile the revolutionary idea had transformed itself into one of regeneration. It is found, allusively to begin with, in the essay on 'German Art and German Politics'. Wagner's ideas concerning a regeneration of humanity and of culture did not take concrete shape until ten years later, during the writing of the 'Parsifal' poem at the beginning of 1877, and during the subsequent work on the composition and orchestral sketches of it up to the beginning of 1879: the idea of regeneration is directly connected with Parsifal. From 1879 to 1881, largely before the completion of the* Parsifal *score, the essays and papers followed which are gathered under the term of Regeneration writings: 'Shall we hope?', May 1879; 'Religion and Art', July 1880; 'What use is this knowledge?' October 1880; 'Know yourself', January 1881; 'Heroism and Christianity', September 1881. – The première of* Parsifal *in 1882 marked the end of Wagner's artistic creation. He did, it is true, brood on the idea of completing 'The Victors' as another music drama, but abandoned the plan in 1882. What still engaged him were ideological and political problems that had been near to his heart since 1849. What about our social order is not good? How could it be improved, and the social life and culture of people regenerated? Strangers as we may be to his system of thinking, and Utopian as we may regard many of his ideas, we can still see in Wagner something of the[199] advanced thinker. In 'Religion and Art' of July 1880, Wagner speaks of 'the great unions of workers . . . whose rights must not be overlooked by benevolent friends of humanity' and goes on to say that one might be able 'to regard even today's socialism as much deserving of notice on the*

198

part of our state society once it entered a true and fervent union with . . . the
vegetarian, animal protection and temperance societies'. In which we see the
mode of thought of the idealist which is not consistent with political reality.
Following his paper on 'Heroism and Christianity' of September 1881 Wagner
had planned another on the subject of regeneration, for the notes below, still,
with the exception of the first (23 October 1881), for the greater part
*unpublished,*²⁰⁰ *were made when the essay on 'Heroism and Christianity' had*
already been finished. This further paper was never written, and the fragmentary
thoughts which follow here must suffice. The two essays 'On Male and Female in
Culture and Art', 1882, failed, like 'On the Feminine in the Human', 1883, to
progress beyond their beginnings. In this there may well be no cause for regret,
for what Wagner had to communicate in the way of thought has entered his
music dramas in artistic form and is the more plainly to be seen there than
Wagner might have expressed it as author.

[Thoughts on the regeneration of mankind and of culture]

[[Fear of over-population of earth – war seen as necessary to prevent it. – War
carries off – proportionately – only a small part, but this the most vigorous; thus
war serves not as a remedy for over-population, but as a means of weakening the
human race and causing its degeneration; it has, for example, swallowed up the
great tribes of the Goths, and in return left us the lesser – unfortunately still
recognizable today. –

[Naples] Villa d'Angri 2 Aug. 80]]

Strictly speaking, we all come disinherited into the world: possession is
chance; no one has a right to it, except land-owning aristocracy – from conquest;
but even this has become blurred, and what the Jew covets, he can have, – he
has only to pass the appropriate laws, which, as we see of course, he manages to
do so easily, especially in the German Reichstag.

What kind of greater intellectual equality amongst people is to be hoped for, is
uncertain: genius will always be rare. Against that, greater moral equality is to be
expected, and – this is what matters, even if to ease the genius's work for him. –

Any enrichment of our means of perception via instruments and special
sciences merely proves the decay of our natural powers of perception; certainly

199

antiquity (Brahmans etc.) had fewer instruments but clearer senses. – Thus spectacles show that we have ruined our eyes.

[[Negro-slave-owners etc. as extreme consequence of the conqueror's becoming far more savage than the animals, – against which, in the older countries, the consequences of the stratified subjugation periods revealed themselves more chronically than acutely, as decay of the lower strata.]]

Questions as to how this or that shall be altered or eliminated, e.g. what to do with animals, how to distribute property, order sexual unions etc. are not to be answered in advance by speculative guidance; they answer themselves of their own accord through the consequences of the act, when this proceeds out of a great religious awareness.

Recurrence of natural efficiency (instinct) in the various national roots.

Latin poetry (Renaissance.) Ovid's Metamorphoses as example of poetic trifling with religious allegories, – as outlet for degeneration of religion. Ariosto toyed thus with the sagas of the Middle Ages.

The questions are what is metaphysical, the answers can be only allegorical, i.e. in accord with the natural conception.

[[The strength of moral exertion for regeneration would have to equal that of the physical revolution caused by the degeneration of the human race.]]

[[Aestheticizing on the basis of an immoral world. – 'per gli veneni del signor Duca!' – (Renaissance.) – Beautiful beasts of prey: tigers, panthers!]]

[[Our human race has really completely and utterly forfeited the right to be shown the way to salvation: Just see how things look in that respect!]]

[[With us, any science is infected with the taint and therefore with the suspicion of the dishonesty and untruthfulness of the masses, so that fantastic dilettantism is summoned forth as a reaction against it. (Medicine!)]]

[[Prayer: diversion from volition.]]

[[Not the light which illumines the world from without is God, but the light which we cast upon it from within us: i.e. perception through sympathy.]]

200

[[Jesus could foresee nothing but the end of this world: we no less. Materially and empirically composed, we await the destructive forces which, even for the Roman world, did not fail to appear.]]

[[If property and its inviolable possession is to be reckoned the condition for the continuance of a moral society, then it becomes obvious that this can only be the case if no one is excluded from and everyone included in possessing it. Conquerors have understood it this way too in distributing property amongst themselves, only they have excluded the original owners. Our state theories accept the situation which has arisen from this as of necessity a given fact, and now all together tell lies for all they're worth!]]

[['The other world has no where-and-when'. v. Schopenhauer. (Realm of God. v. Schop.)]]

[[Hamlet – 'Hamlet' – we, as perceiving and not-able.]]

[[Sonata (111) Samsara – and nirvana. The latter as affirmati.]]

[[One might wish to refuse to recognize decline on grounds 1) of the impossibility of foretelling how it might be prevented, 2) of a complete decline being a very slow process, as may be seen from the centuries-long delayed downfall of the Roman World. To apply the latter phenomenon correctly to our own time could, however, only succeed if the immense difference between ancient and modern culture were correctly evalued.]]

[[(1) Schopenhauer – Providence. – Answer to question of what use this knowledge of decline is if the decline is past remedying. –]]

[[That possession even claimed solely by virtue of manifest authority, by, e.g. a family, has been regarded and preserved as inviolable through all other vicissitudes of fortune, would seem explicable only by the fact that the same quality has been granted to property acquired by authority as to that originally appropriated by cultivation of the soil, from which the true force of the concept of property might be concluded to be that of a sacred right. – Great misrepresentation – gradually introduced through habit.]]

[[If people cannot understand how to guard against the old (barbaric) abuses – such as unequal possession etc., history will have to begin from the beginning again in order to teach us anew and still more forcibly.]]

201

[[Abrogation of law (Ten Commandments) v. Sch. a. G.[201] – But we now commence our Christian instruction with the implanting of the Ten Comm. – Luther may not have been able to arrange his catechism otherwise – etc. But what guidance do we now provide with it? Any who, in observing and judging the modern world, take a penetrating look, see that all these commandments get circumvented and broken, and that they therefore probably cannot be divine but profane: whilst Jesus' one commandment: love your neighbour as yourself, surely abrogates all those commandments? – But, – that goes on and on in such Jewishly-stupid fashion. – What we need is another quite different catechism!]]

[[If Christ for us is in the end even still merely a most noble poetic fiction, then it is at the same time more realizable than any other poetic ideal, – in the daily communion with wine and bread.]]

[[Criticism: – 'so that is how you do it: what do you hope to achieve by it?' Consequently always the practical question? (Ideal)]]

[[In the mingling of races the blood of the nobler males is ruined by the baser feminine element: the masculine element suffers, character founders, whilst the women gain as much as to take the men's place. (Renaissance). The feminine thus remains owing deliverance: here art – as there in religion; the immaculate Virgin gives birth to the Saviour.

[Bayreuth] 23 Oct. 81.]]

[[The oddity of the genius in this world can be very well judged of from the stupid questions he is asked.

[November/December 1881?] Palermo]]

The first form of Christianity did not worry about the improvement of society as the philosophically instructed jurists of Roman rule did, and as nowadays seems incumbent on wise rulers: it believed in the complete destruction of this whole civilization as founded on unkindness and injustice, which, on the other hand, every law-giver, however wise, must leave intact in its original stock. Anyone to whom it suddenly occurs how all that came about, can also have nothing more to do with this which has come about: he is obliged wholly to abandon seeking out on the way of improvement that which may lead to a new genesis.

26 Jan. 82]]

[[Renan: 'La funeste terreur répandue sur toute la société du moyen âge par le prétendu crime d'usure fut l'obstacle qui s'opposa, durant plus de dix siècles, au progrès de la civilisation.' – That really is naïve![202] –]]

[[The difference between you and us is that you for your knowledge of the world are determined only by physiological interest, and we – by moral. The poet is presented with the moral world order, the scientist with the mechanical.

4 March 82]]

The following essay fragment 'On Male and Female in Culture and Art' of the spring of 1882 concludes Wagner's entries in the Brown Book. *A year later, in the last three days of his life, from 11 to 13 February 1883, Wagner was again occupied with a similar subject: 'On the Feminine in the Human.'*

Arthur Comte de Gobineau referred to in the final paragraph of the fragment was a French diplomat also active as a writer, enthnologist and historian. After a brief encounter in Rome, Wagner became closer acquainted with this author 'so divergent from him in many respects' (v. Glasenapp, Vol. VI, p. 431) in 1880 in Venice, and was prompted to study his works. He read first the historical scenes La Renaissance, *and, taking particular pleasure in the original presentation, the* Nouvelles Asiatiques, *which won Gobineau posthumous literary fame in France. Gobineau's early work 'Essai sur l'inégalité des races humaines' (1853) Wagner read in February and March 1881, being moved to agreement and also to opposition. In May 1881 Gobineau attended Angelo Neumann's production of* The Ring *in Berlin with the Wagner family. Subsequently he stayed at Wahnfried, also May–June 1882.*

Wagner's idea of regeneration is – as indicated by Curt von Westernhagen in Richard Wagner, sein Werk, sein Wesen, seine Welt *(Zürich 1956, pp. 284f.) – not Gobineau's but Darwin's: sexual love as natural selection for refinement of the races; Wagner, according to Westernhagen, 'formally rebelled' against the rigidity of Gobineau's conception of race; the theme of Wagner's unfinished essay 'On the Feminine in the Human' was also sexual love as 'moulder of noble races'. Of interest in this connection is the fact that in Wagner's Bayreuth library there are no fewer than five books by Charles Darwin (1809–82):* The Origin of Species *(in German and French),* The Descent of Man, The Variation of Animals and Plants, *and* The Expression of Emotion in Man and Animals.

[[Acireale. 1882 *[Between 21 March and 9 April]*

On Male and Female
in Culture and Art

The inadequacy of the causal form of perception of the nature of things may become thoroughly apparent to us on examination of the priority in space and, particularly, time, of male and female considered together. – Is man 'earlier', or woman? An idle question, conception without procreation, like procreation without conception, being inconceivable; according to which we have before us merely a division of the genus, again conceivable only as a unity, which through the act of the suspension of this division gains its reality as well as ideal dignity.

So long as for the judgement of natural and human things the division of sex is discernible to us solely in its dissimilar efficacy, the genus remains far removed from the ideal. Culture and art, too, could only be perfect if a product of the act of that suspension of the divided unity of male and female.

Act: – the perfectly matching marriage. – Plato: – his state defective and impossible. – However, the bad experience of historically propagated humanity stands as a constant warning to us as racial decline through wrong marriage: physical decline combined with moral. Plato's fall into error must not deter us from the problem he saw so clearly; accordingly it is our task to recognize as infallibly certain that marriage without mutual affection for the human race has been more pernicious than anything else.

Gobineau: definition of the reasons for the superiority of the white race: trend towards beneficial through recognition of the pernicious in unbridledness of will. To be precise: cautious exploitation of power of violence for enjoyment of possession. (Male). Apparently: correction of – again only apparently – purposelessly formative nature; at same time, however, incomprehension of nature's true purpose which aims at deliverance from within itself: (Feminine.)]]

NOTES

The abbreviation: Strobel: KLIIURW, B = *König Ludwig II und Richard Wagner/Briefwechsel* (King Ludwig II and Richard Wagner, Correspondence)

1 For which the reasons will be stated in the notes.
2 Eliza Wille: *Fünfzehn Briefe von Richard Wagner* (Fifteen Letters), Berlin 1894, p. 154.
3 This assertion by Eva is incorrect. *Entwürfe, Gedanken, Fragmente* (Sketches, Thoughts, Fragments) did appear in 1885 but it contains nothing from the *Brown Book*. The Parzival sketch was first published in 1907 by Hans von Wolzogen.
4 The civil marriage was performed at Wahnfried, Bayreuth, on 27 December 1908 by Oberbürgermeister Preu. The religious ceremony took place on 27 December 1908 in the Reformed Kreuzkirche at Zürich, the Bayreuth Consistory having refused the Church's blessing. The papers concerning Chamberlain's divorce from his first wife had failed to satisfy the provisions of Bavarian Church Law (cf. Millenkovich-Morold, p. 452).
5 The designation of 1931 as a Year of Remembrance obviously refers to the deaths, a year before, of Cosima (1 April 1930) and of Siegfried Wagner (4 August 1930).
6 That Cosima had herself already started inking in might be inferred from the pasting over of inked-in pages. This fact is not, however, conclusive, for Eva may have decided later to paste over pages already inked in. In any case, the destruction of the seven pages, as also the pasting over of five sides, was done not by Cosima but by Eva. See in this connection the two following paragraphs.
7 All ten letters published by Joachim Bergfeld in *Maske und Kothurn/Vierteljahrsschrift für Theaterwissenschaft* (Mask and Buskin/Theatrical Quarterly), Graz/Cologne 1964, vol. 3/4, and in *Archiv für Musikwissenschaft* (Archive for Musicology), Wiesbaden 1970, vol. 3.
8 A selection of the letters of Peter Cornelius (d. 1874) appeared in 1904–5 containing, in letters to various people, a number of disapproving comments concerning Wagner and Cosima. Presumably it was that which prompted the step taken by Cosima 'in accordance with the principle and custom of Wahnfried', as she wrote to Elisabeth Förster-Nietzsche on 15 November 1900 in similar circumstances.
9 A copy of this in Eva's hand is in the Richard-Wagner-Gedenkstätte.
10 This dedicatory note is in the Richard-Wagner-Gedenkstätte.
11 cf. Millenkovich-Morold, p. 448.
12 cf. with the above, Du Moulin-Eckart II, pp. 806–9.
13 cf. Eva's letter of 4 October 1935 to Millenkovich-Morold, and note pp. 164–5.
14 Du Moulin-Eckart, with Cosima's diaries at his disposal, writes in Vol. 1 of his biography, p. 422: 'From the moment of arriving at Triebschen [16 November 1868] she kept a diary which she opened with some words to her children: "You shall know every hour of my life so that in days to come you will be able to know me . . ."' Against which Otto Strobel, as early as 1936, states that Cosima's . . . 'diary' . . . 'comprising 21 quarto note books,' . . . 'extends from January 1869 to 12 February 1883' . . . (Strobel: KLIIURW, B., vol. III, p. 164. fn. 3). The opening of the diaries on 4 June 1974 confirmed the date of Cosima's first entry as 1 January 1869.
15 The composition of which was not begun until February 1877, twelve years later.
16 v. Curt von Westernhagen: *Richard Wagner, sein Werk, sein Wesen, seine Welt* (Richard Wagner, his Work, his Personality and his World), Zürich 1956, the illustration following p. 56.

17 Wagner in a letter to Mitterwurzer dated 17 August 1865. – In his first entries in the *Brown Book* Wagner repeatedly uses the name 'Tristan' for Ludwig Schnorr von Carolsfeld.

18 In connection with Bülow's arrival in Munich on 7 July 1864, Wagner speaks of the 'tragic marriage' of Cosima and Bülow (Glasenapp, Vol. IV, p. 16).

19 Concerning the spelling of the name Wesendonck: Otto and Mathilde Wesendonck always wrote their ancient Lower-Rhine name with 'ck'. This spelling was also used by Wagner. Their son, Karl Wesendonck, ennobled in 1900, thereafter wrote Wesendonk with 'k' only. Wolfgang Golther, who, at roughly the same time, received from Karl the task of publishing Wagner's letters to his parents, naturally adopted this innovation, but made no alteration to the original spelling in the letters themselves, and so let the 'ck' stand. Others did not follow Golther's example, and especially the grandson, Friedrich Wilhelm von Bissing, who in his *Mathilde Wesendonck, die Frau und die Dichterin* (Mathilde Wesendonck, the Woman and the Poetess) adhered to the 'ck' spelling, as also Max Fehr in his *Richard Wagners Schweizer Zeit* (Richard Wagner's Swiss Period). On Otto and Mathilde's common gravestone in the Old Cemetery at Bonn, Wesendonck is both times spelt with the 'ck'. For all of which reasons it seems right to preserve the 'ck'.

20 The German shows, as the English cannot, that both Cosima and Hans are addressed or that Hans is included – *Translator*.

21 Quoted from the original in the Richard-Wagner-Gedenkstätte, Bayreuth.

22 Cf. note, p. 35, paras. 4f.

23 On 10 April 1865 Cosima gave birth to Wagner's first child, Isolde.

24 Wagner's manservant Franz Mrazeck.

25 The just-completed pianoforte arrangement of *The Valkyrie* which Wagner had sent to the King on 8 August 1865.

26 According to Wagner in the Annals for 1865 under *mid-August*, Hugo's *Les Misérables* was the novel in question.

27 This reference is as yet unclarified.

28 In the Viennese suburb of Penzing, Cosima had wanted to view the house in which Wagner had lived from 1863 to 1864.

29 Written diagonally across the page on the same day as the entries above and below. It can only refer to the final sentence above: . . . 'that we found each other', and to memories that Wagner did not wish to entrust to his pen.

30 Violinist of the Karlsruhe Court Orchestra who died suddenly and at an early age.

31 Peter Cornelius.

32 Indian national epic of third or fourth century B.C., translated into German by A. Holtzmann.

33 die *angeleckte* Krone – *Translator*.

34 Written diagonally across the page.

35 First draft score of Act II (according to Glasenapp) or, more probably, fair copy of score of Act I (according to Strobel).

36 At the Villa Pellet, Kempfenhausen, which Ludwig II had leased for him.

37 See note, pp. 25f.

38 The friendly relationship was maintained. After the first festivals at Bayreuth, Cosima's diaries contain, for 9 September, the statement: 'Good-bye to Mathilde Maier, the last lady-friend'. Yet on 25 January 1878 Wagner was writing to Mathilde on a postcard – his last preserved written communication to her – requesting the return of the private printing of the autobiography: 'Dearest Darling, you must send me that book at once otherwise My Life will be angry with you.' – Mathilde Maier was, the bourgeois narrowness of her familiar environment notwithstanding, and as her letter to Nietzsche concerning his *Menschliches, Allzumenschliches* (Human, All-Too-Human) 1876–8 shows, mentally a woman of decided distinction. Cf. the letter on p. 271 of the Appendix of *Richard Wagner an Mathilde Maier* (Richard Wagner, Letters to Mathilde Maier), Leipzig 1930, 3rd edition.

206

39 The name Parzival was used by Wagner within a most intimate circle for King Ludwig II, who also occasionally, e.g. in a letter to Wagner dated 2 June 1868, signed himself thus.

40 The original score which Wagner had requested Otto Wesendonck, its previous owner, to return for the King.

41 Cosima had herself embroidered the King a cushion for his birthday depicting motives from *The Dutchman, Tannhäuser, Lohengrin, Siegfried* and *Tristan*.

42 Leipzig publisher married to Wagner's sister Luise.

43 Where Liszt's *St Elisabeth* had been performed.

44 This poem by Cosima is not preserved, she having presumably destroyed it together with her letters to Wagner (cf. Introduction, p. 16). In the Annals for mid-August 1865, Wagner notes: *Poem (Siegfried – Tristan)*. As the *Brown Book* entry (22 August 1865) practically agrees with the Annals note, it can be assumed that the reference is to Cosima's poem which, accordingly, would have had as subject arguments or comparisons concerning Siegfried and Tristan.

45 Pet name for Blandine von Bülow, Cosima's second daughter.

46 Reference to Liszt's paper *Die Zigeuner und ihre Musik in Ungarn* (The Gypsies and their Music in Hungary).

47 Poem for the King's twentieth birthday.

48 Written obliquely across the whole page.

49 The words bracketed have been struck through by Wagner.

50 The lance with which Longinus once pierced the Saviour's thigh, and which Klingsor had possessed himself of as a most valuable means of magic – *Wagner's footnote*.

51 Originally the wording from this point was: 'hangs helmet, shield and sword on it, then kneels and gives himself up to silent prayer'. These words were deleted by Wagner and replaced by the present.

52 This sentence is written obliquely across the page at the end.

53 Szegzárd, estate of the Hungarian Baron Anton von Augusz with whom Liszt was acquainted. (Concerning the spelling of the name, *v. Briefe hervorragender Zeitgenossen an Franz Liszt* – Letters to Franz Liszt from Prominent Contemporaries – Leipzig 1904, p. 246.)

54 The journey to Venice did not take place. On 16 September 1865, Hans von Bülow writes to Bernhard Cossmann: '. . . the excursion to Venice which we had agreed on, had, for various reasons, to be foregone . . .' (Hans von Bülow, *Briefe* – Letters – Vol. IV, p. 59, Leipzig 1900).

55 cf. Peter Raabe: *Franz Liszt*, Stuttgart 1931, Vol. 1, pp. 202 and 301, also Millenkovich-Morold, p. 142.

56 cf. Millenkovich-Morold, p. 142.

57 cf. Millenkovich-Morold, p. 153.

58 Later, from 1867, when Wagner was already living at Tribschen, the Bülows were at 11, Arcostrasse where they kept two rooms constantly ready for Wagner which, on his visits to Munich, he used as a pied-à-terre (Millenkovich-Morold, p. 194).

59 cf. note p. 27.

60 In which connection it should be borne in mind that Liszt was under the influence of the bigoted Princess Wittgenstein, and, as a cleric (*v.* note 66), was himself obliged also to disapprove of his daughter's behaviour, the more so as later, in 1872, she turned Protestant.

61 Szegzárd. *v.* note 53.

62 Liszt had lived in Rome since 21 October 1861 (and continued to live there until the end of 1868).

63 On 2 August 1865 in Rome, Liszt had acquired clerical status as an *abbé*.

64 Wagner decided in favour of the first version.

65 These words are written in English – *Translator*.

66 Wife of the late Ludwig von Carolsfeld, the tenor.

67 Mathilde Maier in Mainz with whom Wagner had had a close relationship since his stay in Mainz and Biebrich (1862). cf. note, pp. 34ff.

68 *v.* Strobel: KLIIURW, B., Vol. I, p. 96. Cf. here and further, also Heinrich Habel: *Die Idee eines Festspielhauses* (The Idea of a Festival Theatre), in D. and M. Petzet's: *Die Richard Wagner-Bühne König Ludwigs II* (The Richard Wagner Theatre of King Ludwig II), Munich 1970, pp. 298ff., and Manfred Semper: *Das Münchener Festspielhaus* (The Munich Festival Theatre), Hamburg 1906.

69 *v.* Hans Scholz (Ed.) *Richard Wagner an Mathilde Maier* (Richard Wagner's Letters to Mathilde Maier), Leipzig 1930, 2nd edition, p. 194.

70 The politically-motivated attacks on Wagner were obviously also played up in order to bring about the downfall of the theatre plan and the Music School and so protect the political and financial interests of the court officials. Glasenapp (Vol. IV, p. 129) writes: 'Had he [Wagner] allowed himself to be used as a willing tool of political intrigue and declared himself ready to bring his influence as "favourite" to bear on the young ruler and bend him to the Cabinet's way of thinking, the artificially fomented and organized campaign against him, would have been checked instantly, and he [who had no desire at all to do so] could have built as many new theatres in Munich as he wished!'

71 Source: Strobel: KLIIURW, B., Vol. II, p. 124.

72 *v.* pp. 62–3 together with preceding note.

73 Wagner's manservant Franz Mrazeck.

74 *v.* notes, pp. 63 and 73.

75 St Mark's in Venice where Wagner supposed Cosima to be on this day together with Liszt and Bülow. Cf. footnote 57.

76 Jules Ferry, Paris acquaintance of Wagner's from the year 1859. *Mein Leben* – My Life – (1911, Vol. II, p. 709) states . . . 'nevertheless I struck up a lasting, very friendly' . . . 'relationship, with Jules Ferry.' Wagner also brings Ferry (as a minister) into his comedy *Die Capitulation* – (The Capitulation' – (*v.* p. 182 below).

77 Refers to Wagner's opinion of Liszt's character. Cf. entry of 10 September 1865 on p. 72. This opinion, predominantly concerned with the externals of Liszt's life, does not exhaust Wagner's conception of Liszt's character, and above all of his character as friend and artist which he always rated highly. It is prompted here by Wagner's annoyance at Liszt's keeping his daughter away from him in order to put 'different thoughts' into her head.

78 Continuation missing.

79 An interesting remark confirming that Cosima did not think much of Wagner's literary activity and had admonished him to compose instead.

80 Cf. Otto Strobel. *Über einen unbekannten Brief Richard Wagners an Mathilde Wesendonk und seine Geschichte* (Concerning an Unknown Letter of Richard Wagner's to Mathilde Wesendonk and its History), in *Bayreuther Festspielführer* (Bayreuth Festival Guide), 1937, p. 152.

81 In October 1865 attacks on Wagner from those close to the King mounted. The Cabinet officials and those subordinate to them regarded their personal financial interests, i.e. their percentage share in the moneys saved from the Civil List, as threatened by the King's disbursements from that source in favour of Wagner, the projected Festival Theatre and the Music School that was to be built (Glasenapp, Vol. IV, p. 38). Above all, the allocation to Wagner of 40,000 florins in cash on 18 October 1865 had occasioned displeasure which, on 26 November 1865, turned into a press campaign against Wagner and led finally to his forced departure from Munich on 10 December 1865. Cf. also on p. 79 in the entry of 28 October 1865 Wagner's: 'Parzival is again wrapped round in a web: but I believe in him and do not budge. He will come or I shall go.'

82 Refers to the position adopted by Bavaria in the conflict between Austria and Prussia. For further details see Curt von Westernhagen: *Wagner*, pp. 341–3.

83 Hohenschwangau, where the King was staying.

84 Dr Josef Standhartner, Wagner's doctor and friend in Vienna.

85 Presumably the Viennese banker Anselm Salomon Rothschild (1803–74); further details concerning the visit are lacking.

86 From 11 to 18 November 1865 Wagner was the guest of Ludwig II at Hohenschwangau. The music is the motive from *Lohengrin* mentioned in the text.

87 On 17 July 1865, Wagner had begun dictating his autobiography *My Life* to Cosima.

88 *v.* note 86.

89 Toulon.

90 Roland's horn.

91 Wagner's dog, Pohl, had died in Geneva at the end of January 1866.

92 Minna Wagner who died at Dresden on 25 January 1866.

93 The spelling of Triebschen with an 'e' is an invention of Wagner's. Glasenapp, Vol. IV, p. 169, writes: 'Liking to find the etymological derivation of any name, he explained Triebschen as a piece of land that had, since time immemorial, been "driven ashore" ' (angetrieben) . . . The Swiss Max Fehr in his book *Richard Wagner's Schweizer Zeit* (Richard Wagner's Swiss Period), Vol. 2, Aarau 1953, writes the name without 'e', and on p. 223 calls attention to the fact that the spit of land was called originally *die Tripschen*. For this reason, the correct spelling, without 'e', is adopted in the notes, while the Wagnerian spelling in the original text has not been corrected.

94 Song composed by Wagner in 1840 in Paris.

95 Cosima's name day.

96 The Popular Edition, Munich 1914 (2nd edition 1915), particularly commends itself on account of the improved Index of Names as compared with the first, 1911, edition.

97 Wagner is one day out in the dating of events between 29 April and 5 May 1864. For correction, *v.* Strobel: KLIIURW, B., Vol. I, p. 3.

98 First violin.

99 Vereine – *Translator*.

100 Two revolutionaries.

101 Editor of Viennese journal *Der Botschafter*.

102 In Wagner's Dresden library, much underlined.

103 Reference to text of choral finale of Beethoven's Ninth Symphony – *Translator*.

104 Proudhon.

105 Auch Abendstern besorgt – *Translator*.

106 Fluntern.

107 As written by Wagner – *Translator*.

108 To Schopenhauer.

109 Fairy story by E. T. A. Hoffmann.

110 *Träume* (Dreams) the orchestrated Lied performed as a birthday serenade for Mathilde Wesendonck.

111 Pierre Antoine, Comte Daru (1767–1829): *Histoire de la république de Venise*, German translation 1854.

112 Possibly General Baron de Wimpffen.

113 Cosima. *v.* Millenkovich-Morold, p. 103.

114 Fips and Peps – Wagner's little dogs.

115 Illegible.

116 Wagner's name for his friend Standhartner's niece, the pretty Seraphine Mauro who looked after him in Vienna.

117 Possibly: (*du*-terms of address). The significance of the (*Du:*) between Puppe and Cornelius who was himself in love with her, is uncertain.

118 By Calderón.

119 Portrait of Wagner by Cäsar Willich executed for Otto Wesendonck.
120 Querzug mit Friedr. – Friedr. stands for Friederike Meyer. – *Translator*.
121 Luise Wagner, a friend of Mathilde Maier's.
122 Alexander Ritter, married since 1854.
123 *v.* note 121.
124 Blandine, second daughter of Cosima and Hans Bülow, born 20 March 1863.
125 Peter Cornelius's fall while descending from omnibus – *Translator*.
126 Ottilie, daughter of Wagner's sister, Luise Brockhaus.
127 Chateaubriand: La vie de Rancé.
128 Hier liegt Wagner, der gar nichts geworden,
nicht einmal Ritter vom lumpigsten Orden;
Keinen Hund hinter'm Ofen entlockt er,
keiner Universität selbst'nen Dokter.

Here lies Wagner who never made good,
or got so much as a beggar's knighthood;
not even a look from a dog could get he,
or from college as much as a doctor's degree.

129 This note has not been expanded in *My Life*. The reference is to Johann Joseph Abert (1832–1915), a composer, who from 1853 was contrabass, and from 1867 conductor, of the Court Orchestra at Stuttgart. To the courtesy of Curt von Westernhagen and Frau Professor Anna Amalie Abert of Kiel, Abert's granddaughter, we are indebted for the following: J. J. Abert stayed in Paris from 1860 until 1861, attended the performance of *Tannhäuser* on 13 March 1861, and was often in Wagner's company. He reported on the events in Paris in the *Staatsanzeiger für Württemberg* (Stuttgart), expressing himself very critically about Wagner who was immediately told of this. Wagner never forgot Abert's adverse criticism and alluded to it again at their meeting in Stuttgart at the beginning of May 1864. He behaved very affably nevertheless, but a more intimate relationship did not develop. Cf. Hermann Abert's biography of his father (Leipzig 1916). The significance of the letters 'h.a.w.' remains obscure.
130 cf. note, p. 76.
131 cf. note, p. 34.
132 Dr Eduard Liszt, lawyer and uncle of Franz Liszt.
133 cf. note, pp. 63f.
134 Obscure – *Translator*.
135 Wagner's name for Schnorrs.
136 Inept remark of Bülow's which gave offence to all Munich theatregoers; *v.* Millenkovich-Morold, p. 157.
137 Also Wagner's name for Schnorrs.
138 Second Cabinet Secretary, later Minister.
139 Prince Thurn and Taxis, Adjutant to the King.
140 Wagner's dog was ill and had to go about wrapped in blankets.
141 Pet name for Daniela.
142 Abbreviation for Frau von Bissing – *Translator*.
143 Italian order conferred on Wagner.
144 Wagner's name for his living-room at Tribschen.
145 Wagner's little dog.
146 According to Emil Heckel, who cites Cosima, Wagner at that time is supposed to have conceived a play *Duke Bernhard of Weimar*.
147 Not decipherable with certainty.
148 Play is possible on 'Strauss' in the meanings of 'duel' or of 'ostrich'. Strauss detested Wagner

whom he likened to a cat, regarding his work as destructive of the 'beautiful' in music such as he saw preserved in Lachner's compositions, particularly his opera in the grand Meyerbeer-Auber-and-Halévy tradition, *Katharina Cornaro* which, he judged, would 'live for ever'.

149 *v.* Strobel: KLIIURW, B., Vol. I, pp. 281f. And cf. Curt von Westernhagen: *Wagner*, Zürich/Freiburg 1968, pp. 333f. and 496.

150 Berlin declined his proposal, not wishing for any 'additional arrangement of unwelcome impressions'. But Wagner returned repeatedly to his 'previously nurtured but Berlin-frustrated intention'. In her diaries Cosima reports him as saying on 15 December 1878, 'I am still going to write the funeral music for the fallen'. Glasenapp (Vol. VI, p. 413) reports a similar remark from 1880.

151 First publication was by Otto Strobel in *Neue Wagner-Forschungen* (New Wagner Research), Karlsruhe 1943, pp. 54–5. Curt von Westernhagen also published the theme in *Richard Wagner, sein Werk, sein Wesen, seine Welt*, Zürich 1956, between pages 56 and 57, supplemented by a facsimile first copy of Wagner's first note of it dated 21 April 1868.

152 At the repeat in bar 10, Wagner writes an A-flat as last quaver. The title is given here as 'Romeo und Julie', but elsewhere always as 'Romeo und Julia' (Juliet).

153 In this context he conceived a musical theme later used as the World Inheritance motive in *Siegfried* Act III. See Curt von Westernhagen: *Die Entstehung des Ring* (The Genesis of The Ring), Zürich/Freiburg 1973, p. 192, note 25.

154 i.e. the dress rehearsals from 6 to 9 August 1876. The King then attended the third performance of *The Ring* from 27 to 30 August.

155 Wagner's son Siegfried was not born until 6 June 1869.

156 In the Annals for mid-October 1868, there is a note of Cosima's 'promise to change faith'.

157 Cf. also the notes on pp. 88, 89 and 91.

158 Cf. Otto Strobel: *Richard Wagner: Gedanken zu einem 'Luther'-Drama* (Ideas for a Luther drama) in the *Bayreuther Festspielführer* 1937, p. 158.

159 Wagner writes 20 July in error.

160 Cf. note, p. 150.

161 6 August 1878.

162 The title of the play as performed is *Comedy in the Classical Manner* (*Collected Prose and Poetry*, Vol. IX, p. 5). Cf. also Curt von Westernhagen: *Richard Wagner, sein Werk, sein Wesen, seine Welt*, Zürich 1956, pp. 156f.

163 Cf. *Bayreuther Festspiel-Nachrichten* (Bayreuth Festival News), 1965, No. 6, p. 8.

164 Curt von Westernhagen: *Wagner*, Zürich/Freiburg 1968, p. 367.

165 In fact, the King did not wish to have a commoner in the post of Intendant.

166 Von Schmerling, Austrian minister at time of Laube's directorship at Vienna.

167 For von Ende.

168 Harsh Chief of Leipzig Police in thirties.

169 *v.* note 14.

170 Bülow.

171 Father of Richard Strauss.

172 In fact, 22 July.

173 The first two letters of the next word cannot be read with certainty.

174 Marie von Buch, later Baroness von Schleinitz and Countess Wolkenstein.

175 Professor Dr Oswald Marbach, married to Wagner's sister Rosalie (d. 1837); in 1858 he wrote a play *Medea*.

176 Fanny Vollmann.

177 Cosima's daughters of her marriage to Bülow – Daniela, eight, and Blandine, nearly six – did not come to Tribschen and into Cosima's custody until 6 April 1869.

178 For the King's twenty-fourth birthday on 25 August 1869, Wagner presented him with a copy in his own hand of *Siegfried* Act III accompanied by this poem.

211

179 On signing the agreement on 18 October 1864, Wagner at once received 16,500 gulden in cash, thereafter, and up to 31 October 1867, a further 7,500 gulden. The balance of the payment, 6,000 gulden, was included in the cash present of 40,000 gulden made to him by the King on 20 October 1865. *v.* Otto Strobel: *Richard Wagner und die Königlich Bayerische Kabinettskasse* (Richard Wagner and the Royal Bavarian Privy Purse) in *Neue Wagner-Forschungen*, Karlsruhe 1943, pp. 107–13.

180 More accurately: 4 May, for it was then that the first meeting took place.

181 Six years had passed since Wagner's first meeting with King Ludwig.

182 Beethoven was christened at Bonn on 17 December 1770, having supposedly been born on 16 December 1770 (v. *Riemann-Musiklexikon*, Mainz 1959, Vol. 1).

183 Cf. Curt von Westernhagen: *Die Entstehung des Ring*, Zürich/Freiburg 1973, p. 237.

184 Cosima's conversion to Protestantism did not take place until 31 October 1872 at Bayreuth following a visit by Liszt from 15 to 21 October.

185 Quoted from Curt von Westernhagen: *Vom Holländer zum Parsifal* (From Dutchman to Parsifal), Zürich 1962, pp. 95–6. Wording of letter from Erhart Thierbach: *Die Briefe Cosima Wagners an Friedrich Nietzsche* (Cosima Wagner's Letters to Friedrich Nietzsche), Weimar 1940, Part II, pp. 78f.

186 Johann Jacoby (1805–77), Prussian politician, committed republican, publisher of magazine *Die Zukunft* (The Future), described the unification of Germany as the grave of freedom and declared himself against the annexation of Alsace-Lorraine. Hermann Lingg (1820–1905), lyric and epic poet as well as writer of plays (amongst them, *The Valkyrie*, 1865). His dramatic works were lacking in inner concentration and showed little dramatic impact and no truly dramatic style.

187 By Lothar Bucher, Reporting Councillor in the Prussian Foreign Ministry who was close to Bismarck; it was he who handed Bismarck the poem.

188 According to Glasenapp, Vol. IV, pp. 349–50, the première took place on 23 April 1871.

189 The C.W. may mean that the preceding sentence or paragraph records an idea of Cosima Wagner's.

190 The first three pages were written by Wagner himself.

191 Quoted from Du Moulin Eckart, Vol. 1, p. 557.

192 Published in D. and M. Petzet's *Die Richard-Wagner Bühne König Ludwigs II* (The Richard-Wagner Theatre of Ludwig II), Munich 1970, p. 810.

193 Presumably of passages from the autobiography at which Wagner was working with Cosima.

194 Karl Tausig, like Josef Rubinstein, the arranger of the piano score to *Parsifal*, was a Jew. Towards both Wagner felt a strong attachment that can be described as love. Hermann Levi, the conductor of the Bayreuth première of *Parsifal*, and also a Jew, writes to his father of Tausig 'whom he [Wagner] loved tenderly'.

195 This subject had long occupied Wagner, and especially since September 1865 when he made precise notes for the King, of which he published the greater part in 1878 in the *Bayreuther Blätter*. More on the subject is found in his essay *Deutsche Kunst und deutsche Politik* (German Art and German Politics), 1867/1868.

196 Beethoven.

197 This hitherto unpublished motive was noted down by Wagner during the scoring of *The Twilight of the Gods* which he began on 3 May 1873.

198 Comparison of this publication with Cosima's original text, following the opening of the Cosima diaries, has shown Eva's copies not always to have been accurate.

199 Cf. here Henri Lichtenberger: *Richard Wagner der Dichter und Denker* (Richard Wagner, the Poet and Thinker), Leipzig 1899, also Arthur Drews: *Der Ideengehalt von Richard Wagners dramatischen Dichtungen im Zusammenhang mit seinem Leben und seiner Weltanschauung* (The Ideas in Richard Wagner's Dramatic Poems in the Context of his Life and Outlook), Leipzig 1931.

200 Only seven of the total of twenty-nine entries are printed in the *Bayreuther Blätter*, 1931, p. 144.

201 In the original: S: Sch. a. G. – *Translator*.

202 Quotation from *Marcus Aurelius* (1880) by Joseph Ernest Renan (1823–92, French orientalist and scholar of religion) with Wagner's criticism added. Translation: The pernicious terror spread throughout medieval society by the alleged crime of usury, was the obstacle opposing the progress of civilization for ten centuries. – Glasenapp (Vol. VI, p. 568) comments: 'He was struck by the passage concerning usury, according to which Christianity, by forbidding the levying of interest, delayed civilization by so many centuries.'

INDEX

Abert, Anna Amalie 118 n129
– Hermann 118 n129
– Johann Joseph 118 n129
Aristophanes 94, 157, 182
Augusz, Anton Baron 62 n53, 66, 117

Bach 72, 75, 197
Balzac 79
Bayreuth 14, 15, 19 n14, 37 n38, 70, 150,
    164, 165, 173, 191, 192, 197
Beethoven 20, 72, 142, 176, 176 n182, 177,
    179, 194, 195 n196, 197
Bergfeld, Joachim 15 n7
Bismarck 17, 183, 186, 186 n187, 189
von Bissing, Friedrich Wilhelm 26 n19
Bodmer, Daniel 21
Brockhaus, Friedrich 40
Bucher, Lothar 157, 186 n187
Buddhism 20, 148
von Bülow, Blandine 43 n45, 63, 74, 88, 92,
    170 n177
– Cosima (v. Wagner, Cosima)
– Daniela 16, 17, 63, 74, 88, 92, 121 n141,
    170 n177
– Hans 13, 19, 25, 26, 32, 36, 38, 39, 41, 42,
    62, 62 n54, 63, 64, 70, 71, 72 n75, 84, 89, 90,
    91, 92, 120, 121, 135, 145, 152, 153
– Isolde (v. Wagner, Isolde)
– Marie 89
Burnouf, Eugène 148

Chamberlain, Eva (v. Wagner, Eva)
– Houston Stewart 14 n4, 164, 165
Cornelius, Peter 15, 26, 33 n31

Darwin 203
Drews, Arthur 198 n199
von Düfflipp, Lorenz 178, 190, 191
Du Moulin-Eckart, Richard, Count 19 n14,
    146

Eger, Manfred 21

Fehr, Max 26 n19, 88 n93
Ferry, Jules 72, 183, 184, 185
Förster-Nietzsche, Elisabeth 15 n8
Frantz, Constantin 128

Fröbel, Julius 75, 76

Glasenapp, Carl Friedrich 15, 18, 64, 70
    n70, 88 n93, 146 n150, 157, 164, 187 n188,
    203 n202, 203
Gobineau, Arthur, Count 203
Goethe 154, 177
Golther, Wolfgang 26 n19
Görres, Josef 46

Habel, Heinrich 69 n68
Hanslick, Eduard 176
Heckel, Emil 123 n146, 153
Heiland, Hans 16
Herwegh, Georg 20, 193, 194
Hofmann, Court Secretary 191
Hugo, Victor 32 n26, 181, 183, 184, 185

Jacoby, Johann 186

Klindworth, Karl 17, 191
von Kraft, Zdenko 157

Lachner, Franz 125
Laube, Heinrich 20, 157, 161, 162, 163
Levi, Hermann 192 n194
Lichtenberger, Henri 198 n199
Lingg, Hermann 186
Liszt, Franz 13, 16, 27, 36, 37, 41, 43 n46,
    45, 62 n53, 63, 64, 65 nn62 and 63, 66, 67,
    71, 72, 72 n75, 73 n77, 74, 75, 76, 89, 102,
    103, 119, 153, 157, 165, 172, 178 n184, 192,
    197
Ludewig, Doctor 173
Ludwig II, King of Bavaria 16, 18, 19, 25,
    26, 29, 35 n36, 38, 39, 40, 41, 42, 45, 46, 62,
    63, 66, 68, 69, 70, 71, 76, 78, 79, 80, 81, 82,
    83, 84, 85, 89, 90, 128, 131, 134, 144, 148,
    150, 151, 152, 156, 161 n165, 164, 171, 172,
    173, 174, 175 n181, 178, 189, 190, 191, 192,
    193, 194 n195, 195
Luther 20, 153, 154, 155, 173, 194, 202

Maier, Mathilde 35, 36, 37, 67, 69
Millenkovich-Morold, Max 15, 27, 35, 63, 63
    nn55–58, 153, 164, 165
Mrazeck, Franz 25, 29, 71, 76

217

Nietzsche, Friedrich 15, 37 n38, 179, 194

Offenbach, Jacques 181, 185

Paris 75, 91 n94, 118 n129
Penzing (Vienna) 32, 35
von Perfall, Intendant 172
Petzet, Detta and Michael 69 n68, 191 n192
von Pfistermeister, Franz 85
Plato 204
Pohl, Wagner's dog 25, 86, 121
Porges, Heinrich 75, 76, 157

Raabe, Peter 63 n55, 153
Ramayana, Indian national epic 33, 34
Renan, Joseph Ernest 203
Richter, Hans 172, 178, 189
Riemann, Pastor 73
Röckel, August 152
Rohde, Erwin 194
Rossini 20
Rothschild, Vienna banker 79 n85
Rubinstein, Josef 157, 192 n194, 197

Sachs, Hans 153
Schnorr von Carolsfeld, Ludwig 18, 20, 25,
  25 n17, 26, 30, 40, 42, 44, 62, 63, 67, 70,
  120, 121, 134–145, 146, 148, 192
– Malvina 26, 66 n66
Scholz, Hans 69 n69
Schopenhauer 104, 105, 148, 177, 201
Schott, publisher 35
Schuster, Anna 21
Schweninger, Ernst 17
Semper, Gottfried 16, 68, 69, 70, 71
– Manfred 69 n68
Spiegel, music teacher 189
Standhartner, Josef 75, 76, 79
Strauss, David 15, 20, 125, 126, 157, 194,
  195
Strobel, Gertrud 14, 21
– Otto 14, 18, 19 n14, 69 n68, 70 nn71 and
  72
Students' Association, German 73

Tausig, Karl 20, 192, 192 n194, 193
Thode, Daniela (v. von Bülow, Daniela)
Toscanini, Arturo 197
Tribschen 13, 19, 36, 62, 64 n58, 70, 88, 89,
  90, 91, 154, 164, 172

Vienna 25, 35, 75, 76, 77, 79, 167, 176

Wagner, Cosima passim to p. 91; 93, 146,
  150, 151, 152, 153, 154, 157, 164, 165, 166,
  170, 178, 179, 189 n189, 191, 194, 196, 197
– Eva 14, 15, 16, 17, 34, 36, 63, 64, 68, 74,
  81, 90, 91, 124, 164, 165, 170, 196, 197
– Isolde 26 n23, 26, 43, 74, 75, 76, 79, 88,
  170
– Minna 25, 35, 86 n92, 108
– Richard passim
  Works:
  Lohengrin 82, 173
  Mastersingers 13, 20, 70, 91, 150, 152,
    156, 161, 167, 176, 192
  Nibelung's Ring 20, 70, 150, 172, 173,
    176 n183, 179, 190, 191, 203
  Parsifal 18, 19, 20, 45, 46, 46–61, 62, 65,
    66, 78, 81, 192 n194, 195, 196, 197, 198
  Rhinegold 20, 172, 173, 174, 190
  Siegfried 20, 34 n35, 43 n44, 68, 69, 171,
    190, 191
  Tannhäuser 118 n129, 136, 137, 138, 142,
    197
  Tristan 26, 37, 40, 42, 43 n44, 62,
    134–145, 197
  Twilight of the Gods 176, 178, 189, 190,
    191, 192, 195 n197, 196
  Valkyrie 29 n25, 173, 174, 190
  Victors 46, 148, 198
– Siegfried 14 n5, 16, 17, 152 n155, 170
– Winifred 14, 21
– Wolfgang 20
Wesendonck, Mathilde 15, 16, 26 n19, 76,
  77, 78, 106, 107, 108, 114
– Otto 26 n19, 104, 110, 114, 115 n119
von Wesendonck, Karl 15, 26 n19
von Westernhagen, Curt 20 n16, 21, 35, 118
  n129, 128 n149, 146 n151, 148 n153, 158,
  158 n164, 176 n183, 179 n185, 203
Wiersbitzky, Margarete 21
Wild, Hans Walter 21
Wilhelm I, German Emperor 186, 187, 188,
  193
Wille, Eliza 13, 76, 77, 78
Wittgenstein, Carolyne, Princess 64 n60, 98
Wolkenstein, Marie, Countess 17
von Wolzogen, Hans 14 n3, 18, 157, 197

Zahlberg, violinist 33
Zahneisen, Dora 15, 16

218